Risk and Precaution

The rational approach to decision making fails to protect us from extraordinary risks, while inflexible application of the precautionary principle could inhibit innovation. How then are we to manage the risks, uncertainties, and "unknown unknowns" of the real world? In this book, Alan Randall unravels the key controversies surrounding the precautionary principle and develops a new framework that can be taken seriously in policy and management circles. Respecting the complexity of the real world, he defines a justifiable role for the precautionary principle in a risk management framework that integrates precaution with elements of the standard risk management model. This is explained using examples from medicine, pharmacy, synthetic chemicals, nanotechnology, the environment, and natural resources conservation. This carefully reasoned but highly accessible book will appeal to readers from a broad range of disciplines, including risk management and policy applied to health, technology, and the environment.

Alan Randall is a professor at the University of Sydney and professor emeritus at The Ohio State University, specializing in environmental economics and policy. His work has addressed environmental benefits and costs, regulatory issues, and conservation policy, and his concerns range from philosophical foundations to real-world implications. He is the author of *Making the Environment Count* (1999) and, with John C. Bergstrom, *Resource Economics* (Third edition, 2010).

Risk and Precaution

Alan Randall

The University of Sydney
and
The Ohio State University

CAMBRIDGE UNIVERSITY PRESS
Cambridge, New York, Melbourne, Madrid, Cape Town, Singapore,
São Paulo, Delhi, Dubai, Tokyo, Mexico City

Cambridge University Press
The Edinburgh Building, Cambridge CB2 8RU, UK

Published in the United States of America by Cambridge University Press, New York

www.cambridge.org
Information on this title: www.cambridge.org/9780521759199

First published 2011

Printed in the United Kingdom at the University Press, Cambridge

A catalogue record for this publication is available from the British Library

Library of Congress Cataloguing in Publication data
Randall, Alan, 1944–
  Risk and precaution / Alan Randall.
    p.   cm.
  Includes bibliographical references and index.
  ISBN 978-0-521-75919-9 (pbk.)
  1. Risk.   2. Risk management.   3. Precautionary principle.   I. Title.
  HB615.R364 2011
  338.5–dc22
  2010042532

ISBN 978-0-521-76615-9 Hardback
ISBN 978-0-521-75919-9 Paperback

Contents

v

10   Precaution for utilitarians?   172

11   A robust and defensible precautionary principle   184

Part IV   Precaution in action   193

12   Precaution: from principle to policy   195

13   Integrated risk management   217

Part V   Conclusion   241

14   A role for precaution in an integrated risk management framework 243

     References   251
     Index   257

Figures

Boxes

Authors cited

Acknowledgements

My interest in the limits of utilitarian welfare economics as a normative theory dates back at least as far as my work on a panel assembled by the Center for Philosophy and Public Policy at the University of Maryland, on the project that led to Bryan Norton's edited book *The Preservation of Species* (Princeton, 1986). There followed a project on the normative foundations of benefit–cost analysis and its uses in policy and management, sponsored by the National Science Foundation's program in Ethics and Values in Science in the late 1980s, and a series of book chapters and refereed articles in the 1990s, many of them with Michael Farmer, exploring the rationale for a conservation constraint on the domain of utilitarian principles for management of natural resources. One branch of this work placed the question in the more inclusive frame of sustainability, and led to a series of papers and publications, most recently Randall (2008).

This book began with a residency at the Rockefeller Study and Conference Center, Bellagio, Italy early in the spring of 2008. In that idyllic atmosphere, I was able to complete and submit a rudimentary book proposal, while enjoying rich interaction with a small but intellectually diverse group of scholars and artists. There followed a series of seminars on three continents that helped me develop and refine my argument, and an article (Randall 2009) that while standing alone served also as a detailed outline, in 15,000 words, for this book.

While all of the above-mentioned intellectual opportunities and interactions shaped this book in important ways, I would like to highlight the contributions of correspondence and/or discussions with Emery Castle, Michael Farmer, Henk Folmer, Mark Jablonowski, Neil Manson, Eric Naevdal, Ian Sheldon, and Tom Tietenberg. Colleagues and supervisors at Ohio State were supportive at all times throughout the writing process. Chris Harrison, Phil Good, and their associates at Cambridge have been unfailingly responsive and helpful. The support of my wife Beverley, the encouragement of our adult children Glenn and Nicole, and their spouses Michele and Brad and the joy that our grandchildren Isabel and Kendall bring to our lives, were all essential to the effort – without a strong family foundation, things would have been so much harder. I have kept my mother Margaret mostly undisturbed by the daily grind of completing this work, but I know she will be inordinately proud of the final product.

Acronyms

A	Asymmetric
AM	Adaptive management
BAU	Business-as-usual
BC	Benefit–cost (often an adjective)
BCA	Benefit–cost analysis
BLM	Bureau of Land Management
D	Disproportionate
DOI	Department of the Interior
E	Evidence
E(.)	Expected (.)
EPA	Environmental Protection Agency
ESA	Endangered Species Act
EU	Expected utility*
EU	European Union*
EV	Expected value
FDA	Food and Drug Administration
FS	Forest Service
GHG	Greenhouse gases
GM(O)	Genetically modified (organism)
MSY	Maximum sustainable yield
MTBE	Methyl tertiary-butyl ether
NGO	Non-governmental organization
NI	Novel intervention
NI_1	Novel intervention *ex ante*
NI_2	Novel intervention *ex post*
ORM	Ordinary risk management
OSY	Optimal sustainable yield
P	Prohibit
PBDE	Polybrominated diphenyl ether
PCB	Polychlorinated biphenol

PP	Precautionary principle
PRT	Pre-release test(ing)
PV	Present (i.e. discounted) value
QSR	Quarantine and stepwise release
R	Remedy
R	Release
SMS	Safe minimum standard of conservation
STEPS	System for Thalidomide Education and Prescribing Safety
STS	Screen(ing), pre-release test(ing), and post-release surveillance
T	Threat
T	Test
US(A)	United States (of America)
USDA	United States Department of Agriculture
WTP	Willingness to pay
WTA	Willingness to accept (compensation)

* Let context be your guide.

Part I

The precautionary principle – why so much fuss about such a simple idea?

1 Precaution as common sense: "Look before you leap"

What do thalidomide, asbestos, PCBs (polychlorinated biphenols), nuclear waste, depletion of international fisheries, and climate change have in common? They are serious public health and/or environmental problems with some common elements in their histories. In every case, activities undertaken for good reasons – to serve demands that were genuine, to reduce costs or keep them low, and in the process to raise standards of living – led eventually to enormous damage and expense, or the prospect thereof. What went wrong? After all, our societies were not born yesterday. They are aware of the risks posed by innovation, resource exploitation, and overstressing our environmental systems, and they maintain institutions to assess risks and regulate potentially harmful activities. Yet, these institutions failed quite clearly to prevent or minimize the potential harm.

In each of these cases, the standard approaches to risk management failed in several or all of the following ways: they did little to prevent the threat; were slow to diagnose it; tolerated far too much dispute about harm and cause before taking action; and acted only after the problem was obvious, widespread and built into the economy, society, and way of life, so that remedies were enormously expensive and relatively ineffective. Because remedies were implemented too late to forestall the damage or restore the *status quo ante*, they necessarily were focused more on remediation, mitigation, and adaptation.

Around 1960, many countries approved thalidomide for use in treating morning sickness in pregnant women, with (what turned out to be) inadequate pre-release screening and testing. In short order, about 10,000 children were born with serious birth defects (Box 8.3). The earliest indications that asbestos was harmful were noted at the beginning of the twentieth century, but it took most of the century before use of asbestos was banned in the USA and the European Union (Boxes 1.1 and 5.4). From the 1920s to the 1970s, PCBs were produced and used for a considerable variety of purposes. Known global PCB production was of the order of 1.5 million tons.

Despite evidence of toxicity dating to the 1930s, PCB manufacture and use continued with few restraints until the 1970s, when production was banned. Subsequent US expenditures on clean-up and remediation of PCB-damaged sites have exceeded $50 billion (Box 9.2), and the job is far from complete. Secure storage of nuclear waste remains an unsolved problem six decades after the first peaceful uses of nuclear technology (Box 9.10). Depletion of international fisheries continues, even though many countries have achieved some success in managing to sustain their national fisheries (Chapter 13). Although a scientific consensus has converged around a positive relationship between greenhouse gas (GHG) concentrations and climate change, global GHG emissions continue to accelerate and the major climate models predict a non-trivial likelihood of temperature rises sufficient to cause drastic damage (Weitzman 2009). While economists debate whether meaningful progress in limiting climate change can be achieved at reasonable expense, the fact is that concerted action on a global scale remains a distant prospect (Box 9.11).

In the cases of thalidomide, asbestos, PCBs, nuclear waste (and perhaps nanotechnology, although we don't seem yet to be hearing much public outcry), we sense a broad public impatience with the "charge ahead and, if necessary, clean-up the mess later" approach to risk management. In the cases of nuclear technologies, biotechnology, and perhaps nanotechnology, we observe a growing sense among the public that technology is developing the capacity for damage on a scale so vast that it is, for that reason alone, threatening. Depleted fisheries and climate change exemplify the difficulty of recognizing and acting to forestall the negative effects when familiar systems exposed to cumulative stress (e.g. unsustainable harvests or pollution loads), in the course of business-as-usual, experience drastic and damaging change.

Box 1.1 Murphy (2009) on asbestos

Proving cause and effect is a difficult undertaking. Consider the example of asbestos and mesothelioma. Asbestos was suspected of harming human health as far back as 1906. In 1911, studies of asbestos on rats suggested harm. In the 1930s and 1940s cancer cases were reported in workers involved in the manufacture of asbestos. Not until 1998–9 was there a complete ban on asbestos in the European Union and France. A Dutch study estimated that 34,000 lives could have been saved in the Netherlands alone if precautionary measures had been taken in the 1960s when it was deemed likely, but was still unproven, that asbestos caused mesothelioma (UNESCO 2005).

How different things would be, it might be reasoned, if we could get ahead of the game by pre-screening and testing new technologies for safety before they become dispersed throughout the environment and embedded in the economy. How different things would be, if the complex systems we depend upon were monitored systematically so we would be warned of potential overstress in time to take early and relatively inexpensive action to stabilize the systems.

Jablonowski (2007) has argued that the standard approaches to risk, where risk is identified *ex post* and assessment practices are based on the "safe until proven harmful" null hypothesis, can be expected to result in risk dilemmas – cases where the potential harm is horrific but so too is the cost of prevention or remedy (Box 9.12).

By the 1970s, these concerns began to crystallize in the form of the precautionary principle (PP) which emerged first among German environmentalists who urged a prominent role for the *Vorsorgeprinzip*, i.e. foresight principle (Raffensperger and Tichner 1999). The PP has been proposed as a guide for public policy in areas where there may be extraordinary risk, uncertainty, and gross ignorance about future consequences. It is fundamentally a claim that, when making multi-dimensional public decisions, acting to avoid and/or mitigate potential but uncertain harmful consequences should be accorded high priority. We already have theory and methods for decision making under risk, risk assessment, and risk management, but the whole PP movement is founded on the claim that something more, something stronger than customary risk management, is needed.

The idea of precaution

The concept of caution (noun: care and close attention to avoiding risks and hazards) is relevant at the level of individuals, firms, and public policy. Individuals may be comfortable playing the averages – technically, betting whenever the expected value (EV) of the bet is positive – when the risks are modest, i.e. the potential loss is small relative to the endowment and there will be repeated chances to play the game. Caution is something else. It is expressed by refusing positive EV bets when, for example, there is potential for a loss large enough to diminish one's future prospects – in the extreme, large enough to take one out of the game. One way in which individuals exhibit caution is by offering to purchase insurance at prices higher than the EV of potential losses if uninsured.

We might ask why insurance is available – are not firms cautious, too? If the game is stationary and well-specified, so that the possible outcomes, their probabilities, and the associated pay-offs are known, insurance providers have little reason for caution. The expected pay-out for an insurance contract is readily calculated, and an insurer who assembles a large pool of contracts with a representative group of individuals faces a very predictable aggregate pay-out, as "the law of large numbers" would predict. Under these conditions, cautious individuals rationally may be willing to pay more than the EV of potential losses to obtain coverage but, because individual risks are idiosyncratic (Chapter 3), the insurer faces very little risk so long as the game is unchanging.

When governments seek to protect individuals from some kinds of risks and hazards, an interesting question is how much protection should be provided. If we look at it from a national accounting perspective, the resources of government are large enough that it is an efficient self-insurer. Therefore, some economists reason, government should reduce hazards only to the point where the costs of further hazard reduction equal its EV at the margin. Yet, citizens commonly argue for a greater degree of protection than that. Individuals have reason to be cautious and some of them argue that government should be cautious on their behalf. In health, safety, and environmental regulation, this kind of caution is expressed most commonly by setting standards that include a margin of safety, such that modest exceedances of the standard present little risk to individuals (Chapter 10).

While well-specified games of chance have provided such a compelling analogy that the theory of decisions under risk is modeled upon them, real life tends to be not so orderly. The instinct for caution may well be stimulated when the magnitude of potential losses is unpredictable and their likelihood can only be guessed, and when the effectiveness and cost of preventive and remedial strategies are speculative. In such cases, caution may well apply to firms as well as individuals, and insurance might not be offered. Damage outcomes from climate change are poorly specified and we are not confident that we know their likelihoods, but that is not all. Many of the important climate risks may be systemic (Chapter 3) – e.g. coastal communities will suffer highly correlated losses if and when the sea-level rises. It follows that insuring against losses from climate change is a much tougher challenge. In the face of a poorly understood and systemic risk like climate change, individuals, firms, and governments may all exhibit caution.

Thus far, we have been discussing caution but not precaution. The prefix *pre-* means before, in advance, or preparatory. In the case of precaution, an interesting question is before what? The most common response, I think, is before we are sure about harm and cause, because early action provides opportunity, perhaps the only opportunity, to forestall harm. This reasoning puts great value on early warning of potential harm, and on acting upon such warning. There is another plausible response to the "before what?" question: before the agent causing the threat is widespread and embedded in business-as-usual practice. The cases of asbestos, PCBs, and nuclear waste demonstrate that the "charge ahead and, if necessary, clean-up the mess later" strategy can prove really expensive. Clearly *before* in this sense is relevant only when there is opportunity for precautionary intervention before the agent is widely dispersed and integrated into the way we live. In some cases, *before* in this sense is relevant, and in some cases it is not. Two kinds of situations, quite different from a precautionary perspective, can be distinguished on the basis of this second meaning of *before*.

Novel interventions

Novel interventions include new substances (e.g. synthetic chemicals), species that may be introduced to serve some particular purpose, and new technologies (e.g. biotechnology and nanotechnology) – anything that is novel in some important way and would be introduced into a system that has not been exposed to it previously. Novel interventions call for a go/no-go decision, and before that decision is made there is opportunity to study the intervention and, if it can be confined securely, to do some serious testing under controlled conditions, to learn about its properties and potential impacts on the system before it is released. Both kinds of *before* are relevant: we have the opportunity to regulate the intervention before we are sure that it presents a serious threat, and before it is released and dispersed widely. These are the cases that present the broadest menu of precautionary remedies, and perhaps the best prospects for cheap and effective hazard reduction. It follows that they are well adapted to "look before you leap" strategies – the discussion of the Hippocratic Oath (Chapter 3) applies to these cases.

Business-as-usual stresses

The systems upon which life and well-being depend have their limits (sometimes called carrying capacity) and, when overstressed (e.g. by unsustainable harvests or pollution loads) in the course of business-as-usual, may experience sudden and adverse regime shift. An obvious goal is to manage such systems sustainably, but many natural systems experience more variability than we anticipate, so that it is not always easy to read the signals. It seems often we are wrestling with fragmentary evidence and asking whether what we observe is a blip or a trend.

In these cases, the simple analogy is "be careful not to drive over the cliff," and the "rivet popper" discussion (Chapter 3) applies. The point of "be careful not to drive over the cliff" is that driving is a familiar business-as-usual activity but, without foresight and systematic gathering and interpretation of relevant information, we cannot be sure whether a cliff exists and whether the planned trip poses a danger of going over it. Managing for sustainability means alertness for evidence suggesting the system is at risk of regime shift, and willingness to act upon such evidence. Early warning tends to make action more likely to succeed and less expensive; but early warning is not always feasible and when the alarm comes late in the game, remedies may be drastic and highly disruptive of business-as-usual. Sometimes the cause of system overstress is simple (overfishing) and the remedy (suspension of harvest until the fishery recovers) may be locally disruptive, but is manageable in the larger scheme of things. In other cases, the causes are complex and remedies may require a whole suite of drastic changes in business-as-usual.

In cases of overstress from business-as-usual, we may be able to act before we are sure of causes and remedies, and there may be rewards for acting earlier rather than later, but there is no opportunity to act before the system is exposed to harm.

It is clear that novel interventions, before the go/no-go decision, provide the most fertile opportunities for precautionary intervention. But suppose we decide to charge ahead and, if necessary, clean-up the mess later. Then, the distinction between novel interventions and system overstress from business as usual disappears. Having forfeited the opportunity for pre-release caution, precaution can be expressed only by alertness to early warnings of damage and willingness to implement remedies before we can be sure of cause and effect. Asbestos, PCBs, and nuclear waste all fell into this category and, in the cases of asbestos and PCBs, early warnings made little impression, perhaps because taking them seriously would have been economically disruptive. In the end, of course, the procrastination bet was lost and remediation of asbestos and PCBs was undertaken at great cost.

Formalizing the PP

There are many definitions of the PP in the literature (Cooney 2004), but most of them can be grouped into three broad categories, on a weaker–stronger scale. The threads common to all three categories are the focus on uncertain consequences and precaution, which together imply not just aversion to demonstrated risk, but caution to forestall uncertain future harm. Below are examples of each category, with emphasis added to highlight key differences:

- Uncertainty about harmful consequences *does not justify failure to take precautionary action* (Bergen Declaration 1990).
- Plausible but uncertain harm *justifies precautionary intervention* (UNESCO 2005).
- Uncertain harm *requires intervention, and the burden of proof is shifted to the proponent of the proposed risky action* (Wingspread Statement).[1]

Adoption by governments and international bodies

Beginning in the 1980s, international conferences, agreements, and treaties endorsed precautionary measures (the Montreal Protocol on ozone-depleting substances, 1987; and the Framework Convention on Climate Change, 1992), the precautionary approach (the Rio Declaration on Environment and Development, 1992; the Cartagena Protocol on Biosafety, 2000; and the Stockholm Convention on Persistent Organic Pollutants. 2001), and the precautionary principle (the Third North Sea Conference, 1990; the [Maastricht] Treaty on European Union, 1992; and the UNESCO World Commission on the Ethics of Scientific Knowledge and Technology, 2005). Some commentators argue that choice of noun matters (Peel 2004) – to some, the precautionary approach signals more flexibility than the precautionary principle, especially in regard to social, economic, and political caveats. Furthermore, US negotiators, perhaps fearful of protectionism in international trade as well as excessive litigation at home, have insisted on precautionary "measures" or "approaches," rather than "principle" in multilateral environmental agreements (Shaw and Schwartz 2005).

Government entities including the European Union and Canada have committed to the PP as a guiding principle (European Commission 2000, Canadian Perspective … 2001). The US has been more circumspect about the PP (Wiener and Rogers 2002).

In US environmental matters, the endangered species laws remain one of the few applications of a systematic precautionary approach – threatened species are identified and monitored, and serious protections are provided for the critical habitats of those identified as endangered. Nevertheless, US endangered species laws often are criticized (even by PP proponents) for invoking remedies too late in the game, at which point drastic restrictions are required. In protection of the environment and public health and safety, the US approach typically is to wait until there is evidence of damage and then set a regulatory standard. Frequently the standard provides a margin of safety – which suggests an element of caution, but not *precaution*. In management of natural resources (e.g. fisheries), management for sustainability introduces an element of precaution, and restrictions on harvest often are invoked when evidence suggests a possible breach of the sustainability constraint.

The potential influence of the PP extends well beyond environmental and natural resources issues. Pharmaceutical products are tightly regulated by the Food and Drug Administration, which requires evidence of safety and effectiveness before approving drugs for general release. However, the US does not go as far as some other countries where patent law denies patentability for potentially harmful medical technologies (Kolitch 2006). There has been serious discussion of a possible role for the PP in clinical trials. The PP has been invoked in discussions addressing the security concerns of recent years. Bronitt (2008) appeals explicitly to the PP in justifying robust measures to deal with airplane incidents. Scholars have asked whether the PP justifies pre-emptive military strikes against rogue nations and/or those that may be sheltering terrorists (Wiener and Stern 2006), a matter of recurring debate in the blogosphere.

The case for precaution as commonsense

Proponents often claim that the PP is little more than ordinary commonsense: extraordinary risks call for extraordinary precaution (Raffensperger and Tichner 1999, Willis 2001, Murphy 2009). Rather than attempt to summarize the argument for precaution as commonsense, I think it best to reproduce in full with minimal editing a statement of this point of view by the Science and Environmental Health Network (SEHN 2000), addressed to a general (rather than scholarly or specialized) audience.

What is the precautionary principle?

A comprehensive definition of the precautionary principle was spelled out in a January 1998 meeting of scientists, lawyers, policy makers and environmentalists at Wingspread, headquarters of the Johnson Foundation in Racine, Wisconsin. The

Wingspread Statement on the Precautionary Principle summarizes the principle this way:

When an activity raises threats of harm to the environment or human health, precautionary measures should be taken even if some cause and effect relationships are not fully established scientifically.

Key elements of the principle include taking precaution in the face of scientific uncertainty; exploring alternatives to possibly harmful actions; placing the burden of proof on proponents of an activity rather than on victims or potential victims of the activity; and using democratic processes to carry out and enforce the principle – including the public right to informed consent.

Is there some special meaning for "precaution"?

It's the common sense idea behind many adages: "Be careful." "Better safe than sorry." "Look before you leap." "First do no harm."

What about "scientific uncertainty"? Why should we take action before science tells us what is harmful or what is causing harm?

Sometimes if we wait for proof it is too late. Scientific standards for demonstrating cause and effect are very high. For example, smoking was strongly suspected of causing lung cancer long before the link was demonstrated conclusively, that is, to the satisfaction of scientific standards of cause and effect. By then, many smokers had died of lung cancer. But many other people had already quit smoking because of the growing evidence that smoking was linked to lung cancer. These people were wisely exercising precaution despite some scientific uncertainty.

Often a problem – such as a cluster of cancer cases or global warming – is too large, its causes too diverse, or the effects too long term to be sorted out with scientific experiments that would prove cause and effect. It's hard to take these problems into the laboratory. Instead, we have to rely on observations, case studies, or predictions based on current knowledge.

According to the precautionary principle, when reasonable scientific evidence of any kind gives us good reason to believe that an activity, technology, or substance may be harmful, we should act to prevent harm. If we always wait for scientific certainty, people may suffer and die, and damage to the natural world may be irreversible.

Why do we need the precautionary principle now?

Many people believe that the effects of careless and harmful activities have accumulated over the years. They believe that humans and the rest of the natural world have a limited capacity to absorb and overcome this harm and that we must be much more careful than we have been in the past.

There are plenty of warning signs that suggest we should proceed with caution. Some are in human beings themselves – such as increased rates of learning disabilities, asthma, and certain types of cancer. Other warning signs are the dying-off of plant and animal species, the depletion of stratospheric ozone, and the likelihood of global warming. It is hard to pin these effects to clear or simple causes – just as it is difficult to predict exactly what many effects will be. But good sense and plenty of scientific evidence tell us we must take care, and that all our actions have consequences.

We have lots of environmental regulations. Aren't we already exercising precaution?

In some cases, to some extent, yes. When federal money is to be used in a major project, such as building a road on forested land or developing federal waste programs, the planners must produce an "environmental impact statement" to show how it will affect the surroundings. Then the public has a right to help determine whether the study has been thorough and all the alternatives considered. That is a precautionary action.

But most environmental regulations, such as the Clean Air Act, the Clean Water Act, and the Superfund Law, are aimed at cleaning up pollution and controlling the amount of it released into the environment. They regulate toxic substances as they are emitted rather than limiting their use or production in the first place.

These laws have served an important purpose: they have given us cleaner air, water, and land.

But they are based on the assumption that humans and ecosystems can absorb a certain amount of contamination without being harmed. We are now learning how difficult it is to know what levels of contamination, if any, are safe.

Many of our food and drug laws and practices are more precautionary. Before a drug is introduced into the marketplace, the manufacturer must demonstrate that it is safe and effective. Then people must be told about risks and side effects before they use it. But there are some major loopholes in our regulations and the way they are applied. If the precautionary principle were universally applied, many toxic substances, contaminants, and unsafe practices would not be produced or used in the first place. The precautionary principle concentrates on prevention rather than cure.

What are the loopholes in current regulations?

One is the use of "scientific certainty" as a standard, as discussed above. Often we assume that if something can't be proved scientifically, it isn't true. The lack of certainty is used to justify continuing to use a potentially harmful substance or technology.

Another is the use of "risk assessment" to determine whether a substance or practice should be regulated. One problem is that the range of risks considered is very narrow – usually death, and usually from cancer. Another is that those who will assume the risk are not informed or consulted. For example, people who live near a factory that emits a toxic substance are rarely told about the risks or asked whether they accept them.

A related, third loophole is "cost–benefit analysis" – determining whether the costs of a regulation are worth the benefits it will bring. Usually the short-term costs of regulation receive more consideration than the long-term costs of possible harm –and the public is left to deal with the damages. Also, many believe it is virtually impossible to quantify the costs of harm to a population or the benefits of a healthy environment. The effect of these loopholes is to give the benefit of the doubt to new and existing products and technologies and to all economic activities, even those that eventually prove harmful. Enterprises, projects, technologies, and substances are, in effect, "innocent until proven guilty." Meanwhile, people and the environment assume the risks and often become the victims.

How would the precautionary principle change all that without bringing the economy to a halt?

It would encourage the exploration of alternatives – better, safer, cheaper ways to do things – and the development of "cleaner" products and technologies. Sometimes simply slowing down in order to learn more about potential harm – or doing nothing – is the best alternative. The principle would serve as a "speed bump" in the development of technologies and enterprises.

It would shift the burden of proof from the public to proponents of a technology. The principle would ensure that the public knows about and has a say in the deployment of technologies that may be hazardous. Proponents would have to demonstrate through an open process that a technology was safe or necessary and that no better alternatives were available. The public would have a say in this determination.

Is this a new idea?

The precautionary principle was introduced in Europe in the 1980s and became the basis for the 1987 treaty that bans dumping of persistent toxic substances in the North Sea. It figures in the Convention on Biodiversity. A growing number of Swedish and German environmental laws are based on the precautionary principle. International conferences on persistent toxic substances and ozone depletion have been forums for the promotion and discussion of the precautionary principle.

Interpretations of the principle vary, but the Wingspread Statement is the first to define its major components and explain the rationale behind it.

Will the countries that adopt the precautionary principle become less competitive on the world marketplace?

The idea is to progress more carefully than we have done before. Some technologies may be brought onto the marketplace more slowly. Others may be stopped or phased out. On the other hand, there will be many incentives to create new technologies that will make it unnecessary to produce and use harmful substances and processes. These new technologies will bring economic benefits in the long run.

Countries on the forefront of stronger, more comprehensive environmental laws, such as Germany and Sweden, have developed new, cleaner technologies despite temporary higher costs. They are now able to export these technologies. Other countries risk being left behind, with outdated facilities and technologies that pollute to an extent that the people will soon recognize as intolerable. There are signs that this is already happening.

How can we possibly prevent all bad side effects from technological progress?

Hazards are a part of life. But it is important for people to press for less harmful alternatives, to exercise their rights to a clean, life-sustaining environment and, when they could be exposed to hazards, to know what those hazards are and to have a part in deciding whether to accept them.

How will the precautionary principle be implemented?

The precautionary principle should become the basis for reforming environmental laws and regulations and for creating new regulations. It is essentially an approach, a way of thinking. In coming years, precaution should be exercised, argued and promoted on many levels-in regulations, industrial practices, science, consumer choices, education, communities, and schools.

Nevertheless, PP is controversial

The SEHN statement in support and explication of the PP is persuasive and confident in style, but it is easy to see that it was not written in a vacuum. The authors seek not only to make the case for the PP as commonsense. It is clear that they are concerned also with rebutting the PP critics, and the SEHN statement would tip off the uninitiated that the PP had been criticized on several fronts. In fact, PP opponents addressing general audiences have raised a variety of objections, and here I highlight the most fundamental:

- The PP proponents' argument that delaying remedies until harm and cause are proven can cost lives is countered by opponents' claims that precautionary delay in implementing new technology (e.g. new drugs for serious diseases) can be deadly, too. This argument is a particular case of the more general complaint that just as there is risk in charging ahead there is risk in precautionary hesitation, and the PP ignores risk–risk trade-offs. In extreme renditions, it is argued that the PP is meaningless because risk–risk trade-offs render it mute.
- PP, implemented broadly, would undermine business-as-usual, and stifle innovation and economic growth (Bailey 1999, Guldberg 2003).[2] There is a variant of this argument directed explicitly to fears that science would be stifled (Harris and Holm 1999, 2002; Foster *et al.* 2000).
- The "PP is anti-innovation" argument is often combined with the claim that PP gives voice to the irrational fears of the noisy and untutored mob to produce the charge that broad implementation of the PP would induce a "paralysis of fear."

As Willis (2001) notes, in a rather comprehensive statement of the "PP as commonsense" position intended for a general audience:

But the precautionary principle has had a bad press of late … The backlash against it is well under way among some in the business world, particularly in the US, where it's lambasted as a brake on all kinds of legitimate activity and stigmatized as a Luddite blast against technology.

In Chapter 2, these criticisms will be developed in some detail, again using where appropriate the words of the critics with minimal editing. Then having established the extent of the controversy that surrounds the PP and the passion brought to the debate by some PP critics, the chapter closes with a brief statement of the objectives of this book. The aim is not only to settle at least some of the key PP controversies, but to sketch a framework for integrated risk management that systematically incorporates some key elements of precautionary thinking, and make the case that this integrated framework represents a considerable advance over risk management as we know it.

NOTES

1 Note that the Wingspread Statement, while widely circulated and influential, has no official status, being the product of a working group of prominent environmentalists, mostly from non-government organizations.

2 Some PP opponents have countered the PP with a Proactionary Principle (More 2005). Following a general statement, it offers ten component principles, beginning with: "People's freedom to innovate technologically is valuable to humanity. The burden of proof therefore belongs to those who propose restrictive measures."

2 Commonsense precaution or paralysis of fear?

In Chapter 1, we saw how failures of foresight and decisive action allowed the hazards of novel interventions (asbestos and PCBs) to go unattended until remedies were enormously costly and remediation remains a work in progress. Clearly, the "charge ahead and, if necessary, clean-up the mess later" strategy can go horribly awry. Similarly, failure to heed the warning signs and take quick action has allowed greenhouse gases to accumulate to the degree that non-trivial human-induced warming seems already inevitable. The concept of precaution was introduced, and we saw that the precautionary principle, PP, had been adopted in one form or another by various governments and international bodies. Proponents often present PP as ordinary commonsense: extraordinary risks call for extraordinary precaution.

Nevertheless, there is plenty of opposition to the PP, and the passion of some of that opposition matches or surpasses the passion of PP proponents. In this chapter, we highlight the criticisms raised most frequently, and with perhaps the most vehemence, in discussions aimed at general audiences – PP, taken seriously, would create a regulatory nightmare; it ignores risk–risk trade-offs; it would stifle innovation, threatening the foundations of modern prosperity; and it is anti-science, because it privileges the irrational fears of the mob. To the extent possible, these criticisms are presented in the words of the critics with minimal editing. A more complete array of criticisms found in the scholarly and specialist literature is considered in Chapter 6.

A regulatory nightmare

It seems obvious that serious precautionary policy would require a bureaucracy to implement it. For those who dislike bureaucracy on principle, that is enough to raise the alarm, but PP opponents tend to believe also that precaution would require an especially intrusive kind of bureaucracy. Bailey

(1999) combines distaste for bureaucracy with another common criticism of precaution – it could be invoked by unfounded fears and science would be sidelined, unable to prove that there is no possibility of harm:

Look before you leap.

Sounds reasonable, doesn't it? But how reasonable would it be to take such proverbial wisdom and turn it into a Federal Leaping Commission? The environmentalist movement is seeking to create the moral equivalent of just that. In effect, before you or anybody else can leap, you will not only have to look beforehand in the prescribed manner, you will have to prove that if you leap, you won't be hurt, nor will any other living thing be hurt, now and for all time. And if you can't prove all of that, the commission will refuse to grant you a leaping license.

Risk–risk trade-offs

As the Social Issues Research Center points out:

Everything in life involves a risk of some kind. Throughout our evolution and development we have sought to minimize and manage risk, but not to eliminate it. (SIRC undated)

The choices we face are seldom between risk and no risk, but between more and less risky options and among different sorts of risk. Often the risk–risk trade-off is explicit: a risky treatment might be proposed to deal with an affliction that imposes risk if left untreated. In other cases, the trade-off is more indirect and speculative, but nevertheless plausible: precaution that delays availability of new drugs until they have been tested and shown to be safe may cost lives that might have been saved had the drugs been made available sooner. In yet other cases, the appeal is to the human experience with modernity: while some novel innovations have caused serious harm, innovation has on the whole increased longevity and quality of life; so a turn to a more precautionary stance would likely risk doing more harm than good in aggregate. Guldberg (2003) argues that precaution is not the safe option:

The fact is that most scientific and technological developments raise possible 'threats of harm'. Despite often minimizing, or even eradicating, old risks, they expose us to new and often unpredictable risks. It seems clear that an excessive preoccupation with hypothetical novel risks will be detrimental to scientific and technological progress, and to society as a whole. Yet these tensions have not prevented the rapid development of the precautionary principle in recent decades, and its incorporation into various spheres of life …

Regardless of what many might believe, the precautionary principle is not the 'safe option'. It incurs the cost of 'false positives'. That means forgoing many social benefits – most of which tend to make our lives safer rather than less safe.

History has shown us that, while scientific and technological progress may often introduce new risks, its general trajectory has been to reduce many other, more serious, risks. Examples are plentiful: including the development of vaccinations, organ transplantation, blood transfusion, the chlorination of drinking water, the use of pesticides, and much more.

The precautionary principle will therefore not make us any safer. But we could pay a very heavy price for taking it on board, by missing out on future social benefits that are unimaginable to us today.

Offering another perspective on risk–risk trade-offs, Graham (2004) argues in favor of addressing known risks rather than the speculative risks that he assumes would be the focus of precautionary risk management:

(Under the PP) public health and the environment would be harmed as the energies of regulators and the regulated community would be diverted from known or plausible hazards to speculative and ill-founded ones.

Sunstein (2005), in a widely read book, argues that the failure of PP to take risk–risk trade-offs seriously renders it meaningless and self-defeating – it would forbid any and all risky alternatives, yet even the no-action alternative involves risk. In an article published in 2008, he asks us to consider the following cases:

- Genetic modification of food has become a widespread practice. The risks of that practice are not known with precision. Some people fear that genetic modification will result in serious ecological harm and large risks to human health; others believe that genetic modification will result in more nutritious food and significant improvements in human health.
- Many people fear nuclear power, on the ground that nuclear power plants create various health and safety risks, including some possibility of catastrophe. But if a nation does not rely on nuclear power, it might well rely instead on fossil fuels, and in particular on coal-fired power plants. Such plants create risks of their own, including risks associated with global warming. China, for example, has relied on nuclear energy, in a way that reduces greenhouse gases and a range of air pollution problems.
- There is a possible conflict between the protection of marine mammals and military exercises. The United States Navy, for example, engages in many such exercises, and it is possible that marine mammals will be threatened as a result. Military activities in the oceans might well cause significant harm; but a decision to suspend those activities, in cases involving potential harm, might also endanger military preparedness, or so the government contends.

In these cases, what kind of guidance does the Precautionary Principle provide? It is tempting to say, as is in fact standard, that the principle calls for strong controls. In all of these cases, there is a possibility of serious harms, and no authoritative scientific evidence demonstrates that the possibility is close to zero. Put to one side the question of whether the Precautionary Principle, understood to compel stringent regulation in these cases, is sensible. Let us ask a more fundamental question: is more stringent regulation really compelled by the Precautionary Principle?

The answer is that it is not. In some of these cases, it should be easy to see that in its own way, stringent regulation would actually run afoul of the Precautionary Principle. The simplest reason is that such regulation might well deprive society of significant benefits, and hence produce a large number of deaths that would otherwise not occur. In some cases, regulation eliminates the 'opportunity benefits' of a process or activity, and thus causes preventable deaths. If this is so, regulation is hardly precautionary. Consider the case of genetic modification of food. Many people object to genetic modification, with the thought that 'tampering with nature' can produce a range of adverse consequences for the environment and for human health. But many other people believe that … genetic modification holds out the promise of producing food that is both cheaper and healthier … The point is not that genetic modification will definitely have those benefits, or that the benefits of genetic modification outweigh the risks. The claim is only that if the Precautionary Principle is taken literally, it is offended by regulation as well as by nonregulation.

Regulation sometimes violates the Precautionary Principle because it would give rise to substitute risks, in the form of hazards that materialize, or are increased, as a result of regulation. Consider the case of DDT, often banned or regulated in the interest of reducing risks to birds and human beings. The problem with such bans is that in poor nations, they eliminate what appears to be the most effective way of combating malaria – and thus significantly undermine public health.

Or consider the 'drug lag,' produced whenever the government takes a highly precautionary approach to the introduction of new medicines and drugs into the market … The United States, by the way, is more precautionary about new medicines than are most European nations – but by failing to allow such medicines on the market, the United States fails to take precautions against the illnesses that could be reduced by speedier procedures …

We should now be able to see the sense in which the Precautionary Principle, taken for all that it is worth, is paralyzing: it stands as an obstacle to regulation and nonregulation, and to everything in between.

Before moving on, I must observe that Sunstein's argument is much more dependent on two closely related unstated assumptions – PP is invoked by any and all risks; and the typical risk problem involves equally balanced risks of action and inaction – than he lets on. If the PP is reserved for extraordinary risks, and if it is in fact quite common to encounter choices where a few of the alternatives involve extraordinary risk while the risks entailed in other alternatives are more run-of-the-mill, there may be a meaningful role for precaution. But that is getting ahead of the story!

Stifling innovation

In arguing that innovation has on the whole made us very much better off, so precaution is not the safe option, Guldberg (2003) prepares us for the argument that precaution would stifle innovation and forestall future advances in prosperity, longevity, and quality of life. There is a variant of this argument directed explicitly to fears that science would be stifled (Harris and Holm 1999, 2002; Foster *et al.* 2000). Graham (2004) makes the case:

There is no question that postulated hazards sometimes prove more serious and/or widespread than originally anticipated. Ralph Nader has previously argued that this is the norm in regulatory science, while the European Commission recently issued a report of case studies where hazards appear to have been underestimated. However, the dynamics of science are not so easily predicted. Sometimes claims of hazard prove to be exaggerated, and in fact there are cases of predictions of doom that have simply not materialized …

Students of risk science are aware that the number of alleged hazards far exceeds the number that are ever proven based on sound science. Consider the following scares: electric power lines and childhood leukemia, silicone breast implants and auto-immune disorders, cell phones and brain cancer, and disruption of the endocrine system of the body from multiple, low-dose exposures to industrial chemicals. In each of these cases, early studies that suggested danger were not replicated in subsequent studies performed by qualified scientists. Efforts at replication or verification were simply not successful. At the same time, when early studies are replicated by independent work, such as occurred with the acute mortality events following exposure to fine particles in the air, it is important for public health regulators to take this information seriously in their regulatory deliberations.

Given that the dynamics of science are not predictable, it is important to consider the dangers of excessive precaution. One of those is the threat to technological innovation. Imagine it is 1850 and the following version of the precautionary principle is adopted: No innovation shall be approved for use until it is proven safe, with the burden of proving safety placed on the technologist. Under this system, what would have happened to electricity, the internal combustion engine, plastics, pharmaceuticals, the Internet, the cell phone and so forth? By its very nature, technological innovation occurs through a process of trial-and-error and refinement, and this process could be disrupted by an inflexible version of the precautionary principle …

In summary, (one of the) major perils associated with an extreme approach to precaution is that technological innovation will be stifled, and we all recognize that innovation has played a major role in economic progress throughout the world.

PP privileges irrational fears

Sunstein (2005) argued also that the PP is foolish, being susceptible to unfounded public panic, whereas ordinary risk management (ORM) assigns authority in risk assessment to the scientific mainstream. He calls upon a substantial literature in experimental psychology to argue that the public deals badly with risk, predictably and repeatedly making choices that might be judged irrational. There is little disagreement with the evidence Sunstein marshals, but there are alternative views of implications of that evidence for a public role in policy toward risk (Chapters 6 and 8).

O'Neill (2007) focuses on the fear of what we *don't* know, arguing that when officials and scientists concede that they do not know enough to dismiss every possible danger, they feed a culture of fear:

The latest study, published yesterday by the UK Mobile Telecommunications and Health Research Programme, is the work of 28 teams of experts. With a budget of £8.8million, they spent the past six years exploring possible health impacts of mobile phone-use. Their conclusion? That there's no evidence that mobiles cause cancer. The experts said their findings were 'reassuring', showing no association between mobile phone-use and brain cancer and 'no evidence' of immediate or short-term harms to health from mobile phones. The six-year study also 'failed to substantiate' any of the wild claims that have been made about mobile phone masts causing increased cancer rates amongst the communities in which they are erected …

Phew. Except … the authors of the study decided to flag up what they *don't know* as well as what they do. Professor Lawrie Challis, chairman of the research program, said: 'We cannot rule out the possibility that cancer could appear in a few years' time, both because the epidemiological evidence we have is not strong enough to rule it out and, secondly, because most cancers cannot be detected until 10 years after whatever caused them.' So while the report was 'reassuring' on the safety of mobile phone-use now, 'we can't reassure people about the long-term use', said Challis … Surely health advice should focus on warning people of proven dangers, rather than pushing us to fantasize about hypothetical worst-case scenarios?

As well as talking up future unknowns, the research coordinators threw into the debate what we might call 'present unlikelies'. They said there was a 'very slight hint' of increased incidences of brain tumors among long-term users of mobiles, which is at 'the borderline of statistical significance'. That sounds to my admittedly unscientific mind like a roundabout way of saying there is possibly a statistically insignificant risk of harm to some users ...

The mobile is the ideal metaphor for today's culture of fear ... This fear of mobiles is likely to be doing more damage than mobiles themselves, certainly in the here and now. While we can be fairly sure that mobile phones are not damaging our health, the precautionary principle *is* harming society: it is slowing down new technological developments, stunting investment in newer and improved forms of communication, and spreading fear and queasiness amongst the population.[1]

The Social Issues Research Center takes the argument a couple of steps further: activist groups make cynical use of public susceptibility to irrational fears; and the PP is itself anti-science or, at least, is useful to those who seek to undermine science (SIRC undated):

In itself the precautionary principle sounds harmless enough. We all have the right to be protected against unscrupulous applications of late twentieth century scientific advances – especially those which threaten our environment and our lives. But the principle goes much further than seeking to protect us from known or suspected risks. It argues that we should also refrain from developments which have no demonstrable risks, or which have risks that are so small that they are outweighed, empirically, by the potential benefits that would result. In the most recent application of the doctrine it is proposed that innovation should be prevented even when there is just a perception of a risk among some unspecified people.

The precautionary principle is, however, a very useful one for consumer activists precisely because it prevents scientific debate. The burden of evidence and proof is taken away from those who make unjustified and often whimsical claims and placed on the scientific community which, because it proceeds logically and rationally, is often powerless to respond. This is what makes the principle so dangerous. It generates a quasi-religious bigotry, which history should have taught us to fear. Its inherent irrationality renders it unsustainable.

Some authors have combined the "PP stifles innovation" and the "PP privileges the irrational fears of the mob" arguments to produce the claim that PP undermines venturesome spirit:

Even if (eliminating all risk) were possible, it would undoubtedly be undesirable. A culture in which people do not take chances, where any form of progress or development is abandoned 'just to be on the safe side', is one with a very limited future. The very nature and structure of all human societies are what they are because individuals, in co-operation with each other, have taken their chances – seeking the rewards of well-judged risk-taking to the enervating constraints of safe options. (SIRC undated)

More (2005) has countered what he takes to be the pusillanimous spirit of the PP with a Proactionary Principle:

People's freedom to innovate technologically is highly valuable, even critical, to humanity. This implies a range of responsibilities for those considering whether and how to develop, deploy, or restrict new technologies. Assess risks and opportunities using an objective, open, and comprehensive, yet simple decision process based on science rather than collective emotional reactions. Account for the costs of restrictions and lost opportunities as fully as direct effects. Favor measures that are proportionate to the probability and magnitude of impacts, and that have the highest payoff relative to their costs. Give a high priority to people's freedom to learn, innovate, and advance.

The Proactionary Principle is elaborated with ten components spelled out immediately following the principle reproduced above, the first of which is:

Freedom to innovate: Our freedom to innovate technologically is valuable to humanity. The burden of proof therefore belongs to those who propose restrictive measures.

This completes the list of major objections to the PP raised by its opponents in the literature aimed at general audiences. For the most part, I have steered clear of assessing these objections and considering counter-arguments – that comes later, beginning in Chapter 6. By now, it should be clear that, while the PP may or may not be the benign and commonsensical defense against unreasonable risks that that its proponents claim it is, it arouses more than ordinary skepticism among its detractors. It taps directly into some of the deepest conflicts about worldview: just how large should government be, and how should we bound its proper domain; what limits should be placed on pursuit of economic growth and prosperity, in order to protect us against the concomitant risks; should precedence be accorded to entrepreneurial and venturesome spirit or to the instinct to regulate every harm real and imagined; and should a prominent role be reserved for the public in assessing and managing risks or should these tasks be delegated to mainstream scientists and decision professionals?

To this point, the goal has not been to resolve these controversies – whether viewed as meta-controversies about worldview or as controversies particular to risk and precaution – but simply to establish that the PP is controversial.

Those seeking to define a role for precaution in risk management have work to do in defending precaution, before they can proceed to constructing a framework that includes a meaningful role for precaution. But, before moving on, there are a couple of additional objections that deserve mention.

PP is susceptible to misuse in service of disreputable objectives

There is a strand of criticism to the effect that PP is susceptible to misuse in service of less than noble objectives, such as protectionism in international trade (D. Peterson 2006). Witness United States objections to European Union restrictions on importing genetically modified commodities (Matthee and Vermersch 2000) and beef raised with artificial hormones. Furthermore, in unsubtle application, PP-based objections to international food aid may invite certain disaster for the very poor as the "acceptable" cost of avoiding a more speculative risk (Turvey and Mojduszka, 2005).

PP is nothing special

Ironically, given the passionate objections that PP is meaningless, self-defeating, and inimical to venturesome spirit, there is also a line of critique arguing that the PP is nothing special – just good science, risk assessment, benefit–cost analysis, and so on (Farrow 2004). The problem, of course, is that such a PP would be redundant, given that we already include these tools in the standard approach to risk management. Gollier (2001) is a little more circumspect, but pursues this line of thought at least part way: what is good in the PP tradition – risk aversion, precautionary savings, and so on – is consistent with standard approaches to risk management. Those who take the PP seriously need to defend it on both flanks, i.e. to argue that it is neither a radical, dangerous, and incoherent new approach to regulating risks nor redundant given the standard approaches to risk management.

Objectives of this book

The primary objective for this book, at the outset, was to define and elaborate a PP that is meaningful and coherent, and offers a distinct contribution to the policy and management arsenal for dealing with threatened harmful prospects. If projects such as this succeed in bringing more conceptual clarity and coherence to the design and justification of the PP, they may lead eventually to more appropriate, consistent, and beneficial application in a world fraught with risk, uncertainty, and gross ignorance.

Having completed the manuscript, I now confess that a second objective occurred to me part-way through Chapter 9, and became increasingly important as I grappled with issues of implementation in Part IV: to sketch a substantively and procedurally coherent integrated risk management framework that incorporates precautionary elements as necessary and appropriate.

To accomplish these objectives, Part II develops the concepts of harm, chance, and threat, relates them to standard definitions of risk and uncertainty, introduces the more recent ideas of gross ignorance and "unknown unknowns," reviews the standard approach to assessing and managing risks (here called ordinary risk management, ORM), and identifies some problems that render ORM less than adequate for dealing with major risks. In particular, utilitarian decision theory deals unconvincingly with high-damage but unlikely prospects; and the reductive mode of ORM risk assessment, which fails to apprehend the non-linearity and unpredictability of complex systems, tends systematically to underestimate the extent of risk in the real world. These areas of incompleteness in ORM – especially in the treatment of poorly understood, perhaps unlikely, but potentially high damage threats – establish scope for a unique precautionary contribution to decision making and risk management.

Scope for precaution alone is not sufficient to justify a role for the PP in risk management. It is necessary also to address the criticisms of PP forthrightly, and define a PP that can be taken seriously. In Part III, the major objections to the PP in the scholarly and policy-oriented literatures are addressed. The case for taking the PP seriously can be made only for a PP that withstands or circumvents those PP criticisms that are substantive. To develop such a PP, a set of twelve challenges is identified (Box 6.3). To foreshadow my conclusion, such a PP can be specified, but it is a heavily circumscribed PP. It does, however, target the risk management problems where the weaknesses of ORM are most evident.

Commentators have suggested that the problems with many PP formulations are due to, or at least exacerbated by, rather weak connections between the elements of harm, uncertainty, and action (Manson 2002, Hughes 2006). Here, harm is defined as *threat* (i.e. chance of harm), which includes the kinds of uncertainty that are attributes of the real-world system; the uncertainty concept is *evidence*, which addresses the uncertainty attributable to our lack of knowledge; and action is captured by the concept of *remedy*. The circumstances that might invoke a legitimate precautionary response PP would be recognized as extraordinary – a scientifically credible scenario that generates a disproportionate and perhaps asymmetric threat – and therefore avoids at least two kinds of foolishness: the imperative to avoid all risks, and susceptibility to false alarms. Attention is paid to the concept of scientifically credible evidence in an era of persistent attempts to politicize science; and to the design of remedies, with particular attention to iterative remedies with sequential decision points, designed to create opportunities for learning and reassessment of threat and remedy.

To avoid redundancy given ORM, this PP is distinguished carefully from utilitarian precaution and from the quantity restrictions and regulatory safety margins that often serve as practical heuristics when ORM-based policies are implemented. Then, to complete Part III, a coherent PP is stated, and shown to provide satisfactory responses to the twelve challenges (Box 6.3).

Attention is paid to implementation issues in Part IV. Because a principle is not an implementation-ready rule, a framework is outlined for acting on principles in practical governance. The moral foundations of the PP are outlined, and a process for mediating clashes among principles is sketched – after all, the PP is just one principle among many that may be relevant to a particular risk problem.

A meaningful PP for real-world application must be both substantive and procedural. The insight that came to me midway through writing Chapter 9 concerns the central role of iterative and sequential precautionary processes in undertaking, revising, and refining threat assessments. It follows that we seldom can make a simple binary decision at the outset that a given threat is either disproportionate and therefore calls for precautionary remedies or not, in which case it should be assigned to ORM. Instead, in the paradigm case of novel interventions, we are best protected by processes that incorporate screening for risks and pre-release testing with release/not decisions after each step, followed by post-release surveillance. This way, more novel interventions are likely to be screened for threats, but many will be released after screening or just a few rounds of pre-release testing. The upshot is that what is needed is a truly integrated risk management framework, and such a framework is sketched in Chapter 13. Part IV ends with a review of risk management approaches actually implemented in several US and international contexts. It turns out that there are models in the USA and elsewhere of effective integrated risk management, despite the efforts of PP opponents to paint the PP as some sort of radical neo-Luddite foolishness. The goal going forward should be to improve the design and practice of integrated risk management, and to institutionalize its application to broad categories of potential serious threats.

NOTES

1   But Willis (2001) argues that the public proved to be well able to deal calmly with official and scientific acknowledgment that not all conceivable dangers of mobile phone use can be dismissed (Chapter 8).

Part II

Harm and chance – managing risk

3 Harm, risk, and threat

To lay some essential groundwork for an exposition and critique of standard risk management theory and practice, this chapter clarifies some key concepts, including harm, risk, and threat; introduces the ideas of insurable risk and systemic risk; distinguishes caution and precaution; and uses two stylized cases to introduce the two kinds of novel prospects that are candidates for precautionary response.

Caution is consistent with aversion to demonstrated risk. Precaution goes beyond caution in two ways: it is concerned to not just to avert harm in the here-and-now but to forestall future harm, and this vigilance applies not only to demonstrated harmful prospects but also to the chance of future harm. Precaution gets us into the business of forestalling prospects of future harm that are in some sense speculative.

Chance of harm

To begin thinking carefully about precaution, we need to bring some precision to the concept of chance of harm. The term, harm, has clear meaning.

Harm (noun): damage, impairment. Commonly, there is an additional shade of meaning – the damage or impairment can be attributed to some particular thing, circumstance, or event. We are much less likely to apply the concept of harm to some general, existential malaise.

Chance concerns possibilities that are indeterminate, unpredictable, and (in some renditions) unintended.

Chance (noun): something that happens unpredictably without discernible human intention or observable cause; something mediated by the fortuitous or incalculable element in existence, i.e. luck, contingency.

The term *risk* is used commonly to characterize situations involving an element of chance. Unfortunately, risk in everyday usage is an etymological mess. For *risk* (noun), we find meanings that include chance of harm or loss;

hazard; and statistical odds of a harmful event, or of damage exceeding some threshold. In common usage, risk jumbles the concepts of harm and chance, sometimes referring to one, sometimes to the other, and sometimes to the interaction of both. But clarity is important to the precautionary principle discussion.

Chance, because outcomes are generated by a random process

Scholars have not been unambiguously successful in bringing clarity to the concept of risk. The early-twentieth-century economist Frank Knight defined risk rigorously as a situation where more than one outcome is possible, and we can enumerate the outcomes and specify their probabilities. By this definition, a lottery where every ticket has an equal chance of winning a prize, and we know the number of tickets sold, the price of a ticket, and the amount of the prize(s) would qualify as a Knightian risk; and in fact we frequently encounter hypothetical and experimental lotteries of various kinds in conceptual and empirical research on risk. Conceptually, we can calculate the odds (i.e. the probability) of winning a prize in each category (if there is more than one category of prizes), and the expected value of buying a ticket (the sum of the various prizes each multiplied by its odds, minus the price of a ticket). Risk analysis and risk management (Chapter 4) begin with calculations of these kinds. Empirical research focuses on questions such as why people buy tickets when the expected value is negative (if it were not negative, lotteries would be ineffective as fund-raising devices), and whether people tend to exhibit consistency and rationality when asked to make a series of choices among different lotteries.

However, it seems a little odd to call the typical lottery a risk – my guess is that most people would call it a gamble rather than a risk. The typical lottery offers the unlikely prospect of a rich prize and the very much more likely prospect of losing the rather modest investment in a ticket. Most people, I expect, think of risk as the opposite situation: a modest gain is very likely (I proceed uneventfully to wherever I am going) but the trip entails a very small chance of great harm (I am involved in a serious accident on the way). The typical lottery, then, captures the element of chance but it does not capture the prospect of serious hazard that, I think, most people associate with the idea of risk.

There is a more serious objection to the Knightian definition of risk. We seldom if ever know as much as Knight suggests – in the "lotteries" of real life, we cannot enumerate precisely the complete set of possible outcomes, and we cannot assign deterministic probabilities to each. More typically we can at best list broad categories of potential outcomes and assign probability ranges to each.

Chance, because we do not understand the system that generates outcomes

Knight defined uncertainty as a situation in which we can enumerate the possible outcomes but cannot assign probabilities to them. The implication is that, facing uncertainty, we cannot make the sorts of calculations that an informed person could make about a lottery. Under uncertainty it is impossible to calculate expected values, and it is not so clear what patterns of choices would count as consistent and rational. In real-life uncertainties, it seems likely that we know less about the possible outcomes than Knight suggested, but perhaps more about the probabilities (perhaps we can think about ranges of probabilities, or maybe we can characterize some of the potential outcomes as more likely than others).

Lindley (2006) firmly places uncertainty in the realm of our knowing – uncertainty is a matter of not knowing, of not having full information:

There are some things that you know to be true, and others that you know to be false; yet, despite this extensive knowledge that you have, there remain many things whose truth or falsity is not known to you. We say that you are uncertain about them. You are uncertain, to varying degrees, about everything in the future; much of the past is hidden from you; and there is a lot of the present about which you do not have full information. Uncertainty is everywhere and you cannot escape from it.

Not knowing, of course, has several meanings. One cannot read far into the technical literature on risk management without encountering the idea that, with the passage of time (and perhaps some purposeful investment in research), new information will resolve at least some of the uncertainty. I interpret that idea as pertaining to society as a whole, or at least to its decision makers. The resolution of uncertainty at this level involves not just getting to know but convincing others, experts, and eventually the informed public.

Yet Lindley emphasizes the personal aspect – my uncertainty reveals something about me and the state of my knowledge. The indie rock band Modest Mouse takes personal uncertainty one step further – to them, uncertainty is (perhaps among other things) a state of mind, a deeply unsettling feeling that tilts toward apathy and perhaps fatalism rather than purposeful pro-activity:

We were certainly uncertain, at least I'm pretty sure I am.[1] ("Missed the Boat"©
2007)

If the reader is concerned that uncertainty seems a little mushy – it is manifested at the personal and emotional levels, but even in its most objective
third-party-verifiable sense it denies the sorts of calculations that are fea-
tured in risk analysis or, at best, substitutes rough approximations for rigorous calculations – what follows will only heighten that concern.

Scholars have begun to extend the analysis to cases that drop the Knightian
assumption that we can enumerate the outcomes. So, we have the relatively
recent concepts of gross ignorance, unknown unknowns, and surprises.
Henry and Henry (2002) have defined *gross ignorance* as a situation in which
the outcome set is undefined.

Donald Rumsfeld can be credited with bringing the term *unknown
unknowns* into ordinary discourse (apparently it had some currency inside
the Pentagon before he brought it out of the closet): "… but there are also
unknown unknowns, the ones we don't know we don't know" (Secretary
Rumsfeld, US Department of Defense briefing, February 12, 2002). The term,
unknown unknown, refers to circumstances or outcomes that were not conceived *ex ante* by observers (or planners). The meaning of the term becomes
clearer when it is contrasted with the known unknown, i.e. circumstances or
outcomes that are believed to be possible, but it is unknown whether or not
they will be realized.

In this context, the term surprises has acquired a technical meaning: *surprises* are defined as realized events that were not in the *ex ante* outcome set.[2]

These concepts – gross ignorance, unknown unknowns, and surprises –
extend Knight's categorization of risk and uncertainty, providing a language
for addressing cases where we cannot enumerate the possible outcomes. But
why can't we? One obvious answer is that we do not know enough – we have
inadequate knowledge of the system that generates outcomes. But there is
another answer that deserves serious consideration: the system itself is inherently less predictable than we think.

Chance, because the system itself is complex and/or non-stationary

Knight's concepts of risk and uncertainty, and the risk analyses that spring
from them, assume something quite crucial but perhaps not immediately
obvious: that the underlying system that generates outcomes is itself stationary. That is, Knightian risk and/or uncertainty derive from our ignorance (we

do not know everything we need to know about the system), not from the properties of the system itself. To Knight the system may be inscrutable to us, but at least it is regular and stationary, in the Newtonian tradition. It throws off signals that may look random to us, but that is only because its inner workings have not yet been revealed to us. Yet intuition suggests a world that may be less regular than we would like to imagine, and contemporary chaos theory and complexity theory are questioning the stationarity assumption in fundamental ways.

Complex systems theory offers insights that point toward a much richer account of complex systems (e.g. ecosystems, climate systems, even the system of global finance[3]). In complexity theory (Chapter 5) concepts such as regime shifts, flip-flops, and resilience replace the older Newtonian concepts of reductionism (the system may be understood by understanding its pieces) and equilibration (systems have a tendency to return to equilibrium following disturbance). Resilience is the complex systems property that replaces equilibrium, and it promises much less predictability. Resilience – the tendency of the system, following perturbations, to return toward its prior trajectory and/or to tolerate disturbances while retaining its structure and function – is not unlimited. Exogenous disturbances of sufficient magnitude may induce regime shifts that change the system in unpredictable ways (Folke *et al.* 2004). Resilience may be undermined by sudden anthropogenic shocks that precipitate regime shifts, or by sustained anthropogenic pressures (e.g. harvest, or effluent inflows) that reduce resilience and increase vulnerability to regime shifts (Holling 2001, Folke *et al.* 2004).

All of this suggests that gross ignorance, unknown unknowns, and the possibility of surprises play a greater part in determining system outcomes than the older Newtonian model would accommodate. Not only have we expanded the concept of *chance* to include Knightian risk (we can specify the possible outcomes and their probabilities) and uncertainty (we can specify the possible outcomes but not their probabilities), but also gross ignorance (the outcome set is unbounded), unknown unknowns (circumstances, possibilities, or outcomes that were not conceived in advance), and surprises (outcomes that were not in the *ex ante* opportunity set); we have also provided reasons to take seriously the prospect of unknown unknowns and surprises.

Threat – the "chance of harm" concept

To avoid difficulties inherent in the concepts of risk and uncertainty, I propose to encapsulate the concept of chance of harm in the term threat.

Threat (noun): an indication of impending harm; a signal correlated with contingent future harm.

Threat has an obvious advantage over risk: its meaning is clear and consistent. It captures the notions of harm and the chance thereof, without straitjacketing the discussion into outmoded frameworks of risk and uncertainty and archaic models of the systems that generate opportunities and threats.

Box 3.1 Risk – language conventions for this book

The common usage of risk is muddled: in an ordinary dictionary, we find meanings for risk (noun), that include: chance of harm or loss; hazard; and statistical odds of a harmful event, or of damage exceeding some threshold. For risk (verb), we find: expose someone or something to danger; incur the chance of harm. For risky, we find: dangerous; perilous; hazardous. In common usage, risk jumbles the concepts of harm and chance, sometimes referring to one, sometimes to the other, and sometimes to the interaction of both.

Knightian risk, however, has a precise meaning: a situation where more than one outcome is possible, and we can enumerate the outcomes and specify their probabilities.

For the remainder of this book, I will use *risk, risky, risk-taking*, etc. in the colloquial manner; and I will use other words when I seek to be rigorous. When I want to refer to the specific concept that Frank Knight called "risk," I will use *Knightian risk*.

Individual and collective threats

Let us return for the moment to Knightian risk. Why is automobile insurance offered? Insurers do not know when your car or mine will be involved in a collision, but they have good information about how many cars in aggregate will be involved in collisions and what will be the cost of the average claim against insurers. Insurance companies can offer automobile insurance at actuarially sound prices that cover risk exposure and transactions costs. There is a "law of large numbers" that works for the insurance companies, because they have deep pockets and they can write large numbers of policies whose average performance is predictable. Why do individuals buy this insurance at prices that are not "fair" (i.e. that are higher than the expected value of individual loss)? Because they do not have deep pockets and they cannot count on large numbers of trials. For individuals, "in the long-run there may be no long-run," i.e. one bad collision may be financially devastating to an uninsured individual. In this and many other relevant cases, the law of large numbers does not work for individuals. It is rational for individuals to transfer their risk to the insurance companies, even when asked to pay more than the expected value of their losses. Specialists refer to the risk of automobiles being involved in collisions as idiosyncratic risk.

With idiosyncratic risk, individuals may take precautions while insurers simply manage risk. Individuals know some things about collisions in the abstract or from experience, but they cannot predict their particular collisions in number (zero is possible and would be preferred), timing, and severity. In this circumstance there is a precautionary element to the purchase of insurance, and other precautions – maintaining the safety systems on the vehicle, using seat belts, driving carefully, and carrying a first-aid kit – often are implemented. For the insurers, things are quite predictable, at least in the short to medium run. Their insured pool will suffer a predictable number of collisions, and they will pay claims of predictable aggregate value. They do have opportunities for risk management. They can use pricing policies to attract and maintain a pool of relatively safe drivers, and they can lobby government for safer roads and higher standards of automobile safety. Government, too, has risk management opportunities – in addition to road improvements and higher safety standards for vehicles, it can regulate traffic and promote driver awareness.

Insuring against losses from climate change is a much tougher challenge. Climate change is more in the nature of *systemic risk* – e.g. coastal communities will suffer highly correlated losses if and when the sea-level rises. With systemic risk, the law of large numbers is much weaker and "in the long-run there may be no long-run" not just for individuals but for insurers, too. That is, insurance companies may not get the benefit of a long sequence of draws from a known and stable distribution. The recent financial crisis provides another example of systemic risk – were mortgage-holders able to protect themselves from the risk that under-qualified borrowers would default by assembling large pools of under-qualified borrowers? No, the law of large numbers cannot compensate for deterioration in the quality of the insured pool.

Standard techniques of risk management are designed for idiosyncratic risks, and are at risk of failure when the risks become systemic. The logic of complex systems theory, which downplays equilibrating systems and recognizes non-trivial possibilities of drastic regime-shift, suggests that we should take systemic risk more seriously than we customarily do. Thus, systemic risk challenges society, its institutions (including insurers), and its governments to consider precautionary strategies – with systemic risk, precaution is not just for individuals. One could argue for precautionary policies in the more encompassing case of collective threats, which include (in addition to truly systemic risks) threats where individuals cannot choose their own level of exposure.

Novel threats

The idea of systemic risk suggests novelty. Competent insurers would be wary of contracting to bear known systemic risk. Much more likely, they may find themselves exposed to systemic risk if the system (the regime) shifts in important ways, as happened in the global financial crisis and is threatened by the prospect of serious global warning. It seems that novel outcomes could emerge in two distinct ways. An exogenous force could be unleashed in the system, which reacts in unexpected ways; or a complex system exposed to cumulative stress under business as usual (e.g. unsustainable harvests or pollution loads) may experience drastic regime-shift. The literature on the precautionary principle addresses both cases – novel interventions and systemic over-stress – but not always systematically; in fact, it is not always made clear which case is being addressed.

Using stylized cases to start thinking about threats and precaution

Here I propose to start thinking about the idea of chance of harm and our response to it, by working through a couple of simple stylized scenarios.

1. Threats from novel interventions – the Hippocratic Oath

Consider the well-known Hippocratic Oath, attributed to Galen who was influenced by Hippocrates' earlier work: "Above all, do no harm." Clearly it is intended to apply to medical practice and typically, I think, to the handling of individual patients (although it also provides some insights and guidance about the kinds of treatments that should be authorized for general use). It posits a potential intervention for the good of the patient, and commands that the physician, who may be unable to assure that the treatment will do good, at least assure that it will do no harm. What can this possibly mean?

If taken literally, many commonplace and effective treatments, even an incision, would be impermissible – they cannot promise no pain, no weakness during the recovery period, and no risk of infection or worse. The point is that interventions are seldom literally harmless, even if any potential harm were overshadowed by the potential good.

Perhaps it means do no harm in the net: it is up to the physician, before intervening, to determine that harm from intervention will be less than harm from letting the patient's affliction take its (perhaps grisly) course. This would recognize that the conscientious physician must often choose the lesser of the harms. Today's reader is likely to recognize this as a *benefit–cost* criterion; before intervening, make sure that the benefits of intervention will exceed the costs.

But there is risk in intervention and risk in letting the patient's condition take its course. Perhaps the admonition means that the physician should determine that the expected value of harm from intervention will be less than the expected value of harm from letting things take their course. That is, perhaps an *expected value* criterion is being proposed.

Perhaps there is a role for explicit risk aversion: interventions should do better than minimize harm on average. That could be accommodated within a utilitarian framework by an *expected utility* criterion: the expected utility of intervention should be greater than the expected utility from letting the affliction take its course.

Perhaps the Hippocratic Oath calls for an asymmetric calculus: the physician should determine that harm (or perhaps expected harm) from intervention will be disproportionately less than the (expected) harm from letting the affliction take its course. One could imagine several reasons for such a requirement:

- Perhaps there is a special duty on the intervener to get things right.[4]
- Perhaps we would not want to increase the totality of risks in our lives and, because familiar risks are built into our society and economy and therefore more disruptive to remove (a path-dependence argument), we should impose high barriers to accepting novel risks.
- Perhaps we believe it is basically unfair if people who trust their government get blind-sided by an authorized treatment (or, for that matter, a regulated food supply) that harms them, even if on average the treatment helps and the food nourishes.
- Or perhaps the motivation lies in the novelty of the treatment. If the intervention is truly novel, it may raise plausible possibilities of harm

disproportionately greater than the likely harm from letting things take their course.

Finally, perhaps "do no harm" is nothing more than an admonition, before intervening, to pause and consider the potential for unintended consequences?

This brief look at the implications of the Hippocratic Oath has served several purposes. It has highlighted the risk–risk and harm–harm nature of many decisions about potential interventions – there is a chance of harm from intervention, and also from letting things take their course. It has identified the benefit–cost, expected value, and expected utility approaches that are common in risk management; and it has opened the door to two approaches that are outside the usual range of risk management – a stronger stand that calls for asymmetric treatment of uncertain but potential disproportionate harm, and a weaker stand that calls only for sensitivity regarding possible unintended consequences.

The Hippocratic Oath discussion here has been framed in terms of one of the two kinds of novelty that might motivate precautionary measures: the case of an intervention, novel either in general or in the case of the particular patient, that carries along with the hope of benefits a chance of harm.

2. Threats from overstressing systems in the course of business as usual – the rivet popper

Consider the Ehrlichs' (1981) rivet-popper. While your plane is idling on the runway prior to take-off you notice someone removing and collecting rivets from the wings. Alarmed, you ask what is going on, and you are told that the rivet-popper has been operating at this airport for a while now because scrap metal is selling well; and nothing bad has happened to any of the planes despite the rivets popped thus far.[5] The intuition seems clear that the removal of rivets is a cumulative stress which, if continued long enough, will eventually bring-down a plane. Surely it makes sense to demand that the rivet-popper stop immediately.

However, there is a cost to quitting the popping, and perhaps some risk management involved on that side of the equation because the price of scrap metal, and the economic consequences of stopping, may be volatile. This is a standard criticism of precautionary thinking – there is risk on both sides of the equation, and precautionary measures (motivated – it might be claimed – by fear of the unknown, rather than demonstrated risk) would waste economic opportunity and stunt growth. But surely the threat to the plane is at least a candidate for classification as disproportionate relative to the threat to the economy from stopping the rivet-popping.

The rivet-popper example advances the precautionary principle discussion in several ways. It addresses the second kind of novelty that might motivate precautionary measures – the case of a business-as-usual pattern of exploitation (or pollution) that might overstress natural and/or economic systems, potentially resulting in a novel and threatening outcome (regime shift). It moves the discussion in the direction of collective threats (if the wings fail, all aboard the plane face danger). And the threat from damage to the plane is *prima facie* disproportionately greater than the threat to the economy from stopping the harvest of rivets. Let the plane serve as a metaphor for a major ecosystem, or for the planet Earth itself, and we have imagined a realistic and disproportionate policy-relevant threat of the collective kind.

Looking ahead

This chapter has clarified the idea of threats, and shown that novel threats can arise in two quite different ways: an exogenous force unleashed in the system may cause it to react in unexpected ways; or a complex system exposed to cumulative stress under business-as-usual (e.g. unsustainable harvests or pollution loads) may experience drastic regime-shift. With this as background, the standard approach to risk management will be sketched in Chapter 4 and critiqued in Chapter 5. Then in Part III we undertake the hard work of defining and justifying a meaningful and coherent precautionary principle that makes a distinct contribution, beyond standard risk management, to the policy and management toolkit for dealing with threatened harmful prospects.

NOTES

1 One of the things I like about this passage is that the song-writers' uncertainty pertains even to tense – or maybe I give them too much credit: the switch to present tense may be just an artifact of the imperative to rhyme.
2 This may be at some variance with common usage, where realized events that *ex ante* were recognized as possible but thought to be very unlikely might be called surprises.
3 See May *et al.* 2008.
4 This seems sensible enough, but there are some special problems with the idea of an intervention. Attempts to ground ethical requirements in the distinctions between acts

and omissions, and between doing something and allowing it to happen, have proven problematic.

5 The rivet-popper example is controversial among ecologists, if interpreted as a parable about redundancy in ecosystems. Its use here is more straightforward – it is simply a metaphor for stressing a system cumulatively, when we do not know how much stress it can bear.

4 Ordinary risk management: risk management as we know it

A rather standardized approach to assessing and managing risks has evolved, and I propose to call it ordinary risk management (ORM). One might ask, do I mean the management of ordinary risks or the ordinary approach to managing risks. In fact, I would accept both interpretations – ORM encapsulates the particular approach to risk management that has come to be accepted as ordinary and, whatever its virtues more generally, ORM is at its best when applied to the management of ordinary risks.

Applying ORM to particular risk situations involves characterizing the hazards and their likelihood, making decisions about what actions to take to avert the hazards or mitigate the harm, and implementing those actions; that is, it involves risk assessment, decisions under risk, and risk management.

Risk assessment

Risk assessment for ORM typically defines risk as the probability of a specific hazard occurring. For example, the risk of aircraft accidents can be expressed as the number of accidents (or the number of casualties, or deaths) per million flights (or billion flight-miles). Risk can be expressed in many ways, so long as it addresses the likelihood of a specified hazard. One can use the methods of science, mathematics, engineering, and statistics in order to characterize and estimate risks. The intent is to measure or estimate risk objectively, so that different people can take the same data and come up with a similar assessment of the risk.

According to the website Airsafe.com, the risk assessment for a particular issue forms the foundation for making a decision about future actions. That decision may be to perform additional analyses, to perform activities that reduce the risk, or to do nothing at all (www.airsafe.com/risk/basics.htm). The US Environmental Protection Agency uses risk assessment to characterize the nature and magnitude of health risks to humans (e.g. residents, workers, recreational visitors) and ecological receptors (e.g. birds, fish, wildlife) from chemical contaminants and other stressors that may be present in the environment (www.epa.gov/riskassessment/basicinformation. htm#arisk). In what follows immediately below, I draw liberally on these two websites (Airsafe.com and Epa.gov) in order to convey not only the substance but the flavor of ORM as viewed by its practitioners.

Airsafe.com describes the objectives and procedures of risk assessment, and the approaches to estimating risk, with admirable clarity and brevity:

The basic goals of risk assessment include the following:
- identify potentially hazardous situations;
- apply appropriate methods to estimate the likelihood that a hazard occurs, and the uncertainty in that estimate;
- provide alternative solutions to reduce the risk;
- estimate the effectiveness of those solutions;
- provide information to base a risk management decision;
- estimate the uncertainty associated with the analysis.

Epa.gov advises beginning the risk assessment with a planning and scoping stage where the purpose and scope of a risk assessment is decided, and then continuing with a series of steps very much like Airsafe.com's four-step procedure for assessing risk:

1. Hazard identification.
2. Evaluate relationships between exposure to a risk and adverse effects.
3. Exposure assessment – evaluate the conditions that lead to exposure to a risk.
4. Risk characterization – describe nature of adverse effects, their likelihood, and the strength of the evidence behind these characterizations (often done by using probability and statistics).

Epa.gov notes that risk (from chemical contamination of the environment) depends on the following factors:
- How much of a chemical is present in an environmental medium (e.g., soil, water, air).
- How much contact (exposure) a person or ecological receptor has with the contaminated environmental medium.
- The inherent toxicity of the chemical.

Risk can be estimated in several ways (Airsafe.com):
- with historical data.
- by modeling.
- by breaking down the system into known subsystems using techniques such as event trees or fault trees.

- by analogy with similar situations.
- by comparison with similar activities.
- by using a combination of methods.

Risk assessment involves a model of the system that generates the hazard, the application of appropriate data, and calculation of the imputed risks. The process of analyzing the potential losses from a given hazard typically combines solid data about the situation, conceptual and perhaps empirical knowledge about the underlying process, and expert judgment to augment the information that is incomplete and/or well understood.

Developing a risk assessment is often an iterative process, which involves researchers identifying and filling data gaps in order to develop a more refined assessment of the risk. This in turn may influence the need for risk assessors and risk managers to refine the scope of the risk assessment further triggering the need for more data or new assumptions. (Epa.gov)

Appropriately, Epa.gov emphasizes the uncertainty and ignorance that characterize at least some aspects of the resulting risk estimates.

For this reason, a key part of all good risk assessments is a fair and open presentation of the uncertainties in the calculations and a characterization of how reliable (or how unreliable) the resulting risk estimates really are.

Rosenzweig and Kochems (2005), propose that two qualitative categories of risk, thinkable and unthinkable, be distinguished. While the case they were addressing (risk of attack by terrorists) invites thinking about the unthinkable, these categories are useful in any inquiry that aims to consider catastrophic possibilities. To them, thinkable risks are bounded spatially and temporally, whereas unthinkable risks have horrific impacts spread over time and space. There are implications for risk management, according to Rosenzweig and Kochems: the goal is to prevent unthinkable risks even at great cost, whereas for thinkable risks the priority is to advance speedy recovery while eliminating obvious points of vulnerability. Without this kind of prioritization, the tendency is to build long lists of worst-case vulnerabilities, which are unhelpful in making risk management decisions.

What prompts a risk assessment?

We do not undertake a risk assessment for every action or business-as-usual practice that entails a prima facie chance of harm. Instead, it seems that most activities most of the time proceed routinely without any formal *ex ante* assessment of the risks involved. The cases where *ex ante* risk assessment is routine fall in two categories: those for which risk assessment is required by law and/or regulations, and those where organizations (e.g. firms and agencies) have established risk assessment as a routine practice. Beyond those cases, risk assessment occurs on a rather *ad hoc* basis after the alarm has been raised for specific cases and situations.

It is interesting also to ask what exactly we mean by *ex ante* in this context. For novel interventions, *ex ante* may well mean what we would expect it to mean – before the intervention is undertaken. But in other cases, including novel interventions after the fact and overstress from business-as-usual, *ex ante* may mean little more than before we decide what action to take. We become aware of these latter kinds of threats long after they have become built into our environment and economy, when reports of damage start accumulating and some observers start to make connections with what turns out to be the causal agent. Typically, controversy precedes consensus about the extent and the cause of the damage, and debate may become impassioned as some people see the emerging awareness of the threat as threatening their livelihoods. At that point, formal risk assessment is likely to precede legislative and/or regulatory action, or non-mandatory action by involved firms and organizations, to address the threat.

Rational decision making under risk and uncertainty

The standard economic theory of decision-making under risk and uncertainty is well developed. It draws upon the Knightian concepts of risk and uncertainty, the statistical notion of probability as relative frequency, and the standard apparatus of welfare economics: preference-based valuation at the individual level, a rather narrow view of rationality as logical coherence, and in most cases a simple utilitarian aggregation of individual gains and losses. The foundation is benefit–cost analysis (BCA), the formal assessment of the prospective benefits and costs of possible actions under consideration, so this exposition will start with BCA. Then, I will sketch the various amendments to standard BCA that have been introduced to address risk and uncertainty.

Benefit–cost analysis. From beginnings in the eighteenth and nineteenth centuries – Adam Smith's discussion of public works, Jules Dupuit's suggestion that we might think of the benefit of building a bridge as the sum of the users' willingness to pay, and Vilfredo Pareto's notion that public action is

Box 4.1 Definitions of key terms

Benefit. Benefits are the value of goods and services received. To get these goods and services, people are willing to pay as much but no more than the benefits. It follows that willingness to pay (WTP) is a measure of benefits.

Cost. Costs are the value of goods and services given up or foregone. To induce people to give up these goods and services voluntarily, they would need to be given acceptable compensation. It follows that willingness to accept compensation (WTA) is a measure of costs.

Present Value (PV) and discounting. To induce commitment of capital now in expectation of benefits later, the acceptable net benefit must be at least as great as the amount of interest that could be earned by simply banking the money. In BCA, it is standard practice to systematically account for the value of capital committed over time by discounting the future costs and benefits by the rate of interest, which reduces them to present value.

justified if it benefits at least one person at the expense of none. The foundations of modern BCA were established when Nicholas Kaldor and John Hicks proposed independently in the early 1940s that Pareto's demanding test might be relaxed: if the gainers from a proposed action could hypothetically compensate the losers, the action would be considered to have passed a BC test. This opened the door for constructing the BC test as the unweighted aggregate of individual benefits and costs, where individuals are the judges of the costs and benefits they (expect to) experience.

By the 1970s the theory of welfare-change measurement (basically, utilitarian accounting consistent with modern microeconomic theory) was well established as the foundation of modern BCA. WTP for gains (see Box 4.1) and WTA for losses have been recognized as the ideal measures of value in BCA; market prices, demand, and supply are also acceptable insofar as they reflect WTP and WTA accurately. BCA often requires effort to infer accurate values for public works (which may be priced and rationed inefficiently) and environmental goods and services (which often go unpriced), and specialized techniques have been developed for this purpose.

Despite some persistent criticisms of the application of BCA (especially, to environmental issues), BCA based on the above conceptual framework can provide a plausible account of the potential net gain or loss from a proposed public project. It evaluates proposed actions by providing a reasonably good accounting of their prospective contribution to the satisfaction of human preferences. It follows that positive net benefits are at least correlated with the good of society (Hubin 1994). So, it makes sense to take benefits and costs seriously in public life. Not surprisingly, BCA provides the soundest guidance in those cases that are relatively straightforward. But BCA may be insufficiently alert to the value of unique and fragile environmental entities; and it might be based on simplistic models of natural systems that lead it to understate the potential for regime shift due to overstressing the system.

BCA to evaluate a proposed project compares two states of the world, "with project" and "without project." Long-lived projects will generate modi-fied flows of goods and services for many years, but these goods and services have opportunity costs: in the absence of the project, there will also be flows of goods and services. The goal of BCA is to project the streams of goods and services for both the "with project" and "without project" states and compare their present values. The practice of conducting a BCA can be summarized in five succinct statements:

1. An existing environment[1] can be viewed as an asset, producing services that people value.
2. A proposed project or program is a proposal to modify that environment at some cost, changing the services it produces.
3. BCA compares (a) the value of the "with project" environment, minus the costs of transforming the environment into that state, with (b) the value of the "without project" environment. If (a) exceeds (b), the project will pass the BC filter.
4. The process of comparing these values requires:
     (i)   valid models of the systems involved (natural, human-made, social, and economic) and their complex interactions, capable of predict-ing accurately the flows of goods and services under "with project" and "without project" conditions as well as the goods and services required to transform the environment into the "with project" state;
     (ii) conceptually valid and empirically accurate valuations of those flows of goods and services; and
     (iii) present-value calculations using an appropriate rate of discount rep-resenting the social opportunity cost of capital.
5. A proposal will pass the BC filter if, and only if, those who prefer the "with project" environment are willing to pay enough to buy it (or, equivalently, its time-stream of services) from those who prefer the "without project" environment, and pay for the conversion costs. The actual purchase, which would fully compensate those who prefer the "without project" environ-ment, is not required for the BC test.

Benefit–cost analysis in the presence of risk and uncertainty. Performing BCAs of old projects can provide a useful reality check. But most BCAs are addressed to proposed projects. It follows that the task is to evaluate and compare alternative futures. However, prediction is very difficult, especially when it concerns the future.[2] To this point, we have been discussing BCA without addressing the challenge of prediction – implicitly, we have been assuming a deterministic world in which all relevant relationships are known without error. But in the real world two kinds of error are perhaps the norm: error in the statistical sense, where there are random elements in the system; and error in the sense of mistakes, i.e. due to deficiencies in our knowledge we mischaracterize key quantities and relationships, with the result that our estimates of the flows of goods and services and their values are biased. Random error is consistent with the Knightian concept of risk; Knightian uncertainty, as I interpret it, is a state in which there is random error but we have little confidence in our measures of it; and mistakes might come from biased estimates. Mistakes also may arise from gross ignorance, in which case they would be manifested in surprises.

The simplest adaptation of BCA to a risky world is to substitute *expected values* (in the sense of mathematical expectations) for deterministic values. For a normal distribution, the expected value is the mean, which is equal to the median and the mode – the mean value is also the value of the mid-ranked observation when observations are arrayed from lowest to highest, and the most frequently observed value. For non-normal distributions, mean, median, and mode will diverge.

Use of expected values in BCA invokes the "law of large numbers" – the expected value tends to approach the sample mean as sample size grows large. It implies risk neutrality, in that it assumes indifference between a gamble with given expected value and a certain outcome of the same magnitude (technically, it treats the expected value as certainty equivalent). Risk neutrality is appropriate for a deep-pockets entity assured of a large number of draws from a known and stationary distribution (the automobile insurance company, in Chapter 3), but it may not be appropriate for individuals who operate without any such assurance, or for large entities facing systemic risks, as might arise from unknown and perhaps non-stationary distributions. In those cases it seems more appropriate to assume risk aversion.

The certainty equivalence of expected value is clearly a special case. The more general case assumes certainty equivalence of *expected utility*, i.e. the individual will be indifferent between a certain payment and a lottery that yields equal utility. The expected utility formulation recognizes that preferences pertain to risk (i.e. outcomes and their probabilities are evaluated together in utility terms). Risk-averse and risk-loving preferences are admissible, but risk aversion is thought to be more common and of greater relevance for policy.

A risk-averse decision maker who wants to buy some given item at a future time but is uncertain about its availability may be willing to pay to secure certainty of supply, that is, willing to pay for an option to purchase the item at a specified price at a future date. In still more complicated decision problems, where there is uncertainty about the future wanting as well as the availability, the decision maker might be willing to pay something (a little less, we might expect) for the option. The uncertainty about own demand and future availability would both play into the amount of *ex ante* WTP.

An analyst seeking to incorporate risk aversion into a BCA of some uncertain prospect may have a choice of methods. She could estimate benefits and costs in expected value terms, and then mathematically impose an assumed degree of risk aversion. Alternatively, she could inquire about *ex ante* WTP for the relevant prospects that are uncertain – the WTP data obtained would take the form of an *option price*, i.e. the expected value of *ex post* WTP adjusted for an *option value*, positive or negative, reflecting the impact of risk attitudes on *ex ante* WTP for the uncertain prospect. Option value can be positive or negative, even in the case of risk aversion, because uncertainty cuts both ways: demand and supply are both uncertain.

Extended BCA. The idea of extended BCA is to obtain a more complete accounting of benefits and costs, especially in the cases involving rare and perhaps fragile environmental resources, by systematically including options values, and passive use values where they are relevant. Passive use value arises in the case where there is genuine WTP to secure the continued existence of some rare but valued entity, without any intent or expectation of actively using it, e.g. by visiting it. The concept of total economic value is the sum of use and passive use values including any option values. A BCA based on total economic values would in principle provide a complete accounting of benefits and costs under Knightian risk and/or uncertainty. It would not provide a complete accounting in cases where outcome sets were unbounded (gross ignorance), unknown unknowns persisted, and surprises were possible.

Real options. Arrow and Fisher (1974) and Henry (1974) offered a different perspective on option value as the value of the opportunity to defer a decision given that new information resolving (some of) the uncertainty may emerge in the interim. Real options thinking (Dixit and Pindyck 1994, Pindyck 2007) emphasizes that any sunk cost or stranded investment introduces irreversibility, so that there is always value in delaying commitments, i.e. keeping options open. Real options theory generalizes the value of keeping options

Box 4.2 Real options – a simple global warming example

Suppose the cost of reducing GHG now is C, and the pay-off from so doing is stochastic with values W(T) if it turns out T years from now that harm from global warming, GW, is real and is reduced by GHG reduction, and 0 if not. We may conceptualize the act of GHG reduction as purchasing a real option O_1 with pay-offs (0,W(T)). The possible outcomes are spend C in either state, and gain W(T) if the option is exercised (i.e. harm from GW is real and is reduced by GHG reduction). The value of O_1, V_1, is $-C + e^{-rT}E[\max(0,W(T))]$, i.e. $-C$ + the present value of expected utility from the (0,W(T)) lottery. It would be optimal to buy O_1, that is, reduce GHG, at prices up to V_1.

However, GHG reduction incurs sunk costs, so there would be a real option O_2 to delay it until we learn more about GW, the harm it causes, and how to mitigate both. Possible outcomes are save C in either state, lose W(T) if GW is harmful and unmitigated. O_2 is worth $V_2 = C - e^{-rT}E[\max(0,-W(T))]$. It would be optimal to buy O_2, that is, delay GHG reduction until we know more, at prices up to V_2.

Both options protect us against a potential irreversible loss: O_1 against the loss of W(T) should the harm from GW turn out to be real and avoidable; and O_2 against the loss of C should GW turn out to be an empty threat or unavoidable. Would we buy both options? $V_1 + V_2 = 0$, i.e., $V_2 = - V_1$. We would not simultaneously hold both options.

open – the value of waiting, including the value of any learning that may occur while we wait – and adapts the theory and methods of valuing financial options to the real options case. As with the earlier option value concept, uncertainty may cut both ways. In environmental regulation, uncertainty may induce earlier and more intense intervention, or later and less intense intervention – it all depends on the balance of uncertainties associated with damage and intervention (Kolstad 1996). In a simple global warming example (Box 4.2), we can imagine a real option to prevent uncertain harm from global warming by reducing greenhouse gas (GHG) accumulations and a real option to defer that expenditure in case it turns out that global warming is less harmful than expected or GHG reduction is ineffective in reducing damage. Starting with a clean slate and the same set of prior expectations, these options are exact antonyms – the value of the second option is equal to minus the value of the first. Obviously, the real option that should be purchased is the one with positive *ex ante* value.

ORM decision making under risk and uncertainty – a bottom line. In the end, ORM is committed to a weighing of the prospective benefits and costs of threat avoidance and/or mitigation. Weighing is at the heart of all these approaches – in this context, the expected utility approaches open the door for explicit risk aversion; the extended benefit–cost approaches expand the menu of ways to weigh; and the real options approach brings environmental risk analysis under a general theory of asset valuation under risk. ORM approaches meet their limits when the threat is catastrophic – we are not confident we know enough to predict catastrophes reliably, and decision frameworks that depend on the law of large numbers are unconvincing when applied to potential catastrophes.

Risk management tools – an economist's perspective

Although developments in risk management tools continue apace, the toolkit still may be organized into Ehrlich and Becker's (1972) classic categories of market insurance, self-insurance, and self-protection. Individuals who do not have deep pockets and cannot count on large numbers of trials may be able to purchase market insurance, thereby transferring risks to deep-pockets insurance companies that can write large numbers of policies whose average performance is predictable.[3] Not only that, the insurers themselves may buy re-insurance to protect themselves against unexpectedly large losses. Self-insurance is mostly a matter of diversifying one's risk exposure and setting aside resources sufficient to survive losses should bad outcomes eventuate – being rich offers serviceable protection from many threats.

Self-protection involves actions and investments that help avoid bad outcomes and/or mitigate those that may eventuate – self-protection strategies may be complex and sophisticated, but they may also be as simple as repairing the roof on a warm dry day because a storm may come eventually.

Most people and most organizations use all three categories of risk management tools, each in its appropriate context, and often in combination. I buy automobile insurance not just because the law in my state requires it, but also because the outcome set a road-user faces includes very large liability claims. I self-insure against auto repairs, as opposed to buying the extended warranty, because it is hard to imagine an auto repair charge big enough to threaten my financial reserves. In both of these cases, I add a layer of self-protection by wearing seat-belts, maintaining safety equipment, and trying to drive safely, and by performing routine auto maintenance diligently.

Economists would counsel individuals and firms to optimize across all three categories of risk management tools, acquiring the right amount and the right mix of risk management. Their policy advice addresses a broader range of issues, including design of insurance contracts with adequate incentives to induce the insured to contribute optimally to risk management (for example, there are things that individuals can do by way of self-insurance and self-protection to manage some particular risks more efficiently than the market insurers, and disincentives for individuals to do those things that should be avoided), and policy choice to manage catastrophic risk.

Risk management

In business management and public administration, risk management is understood as a set of procedures for implementing insurance, self-insurance and, especially, self-protection in the particular context of the firm or agency.

The US EPA offers the following examples of risk management problems in the context of environmental stressors (epa.gov): deciding how much of a hazardous substance a company may discharge into a river; deciding which substances may be stored at a hazardous-waste disposal facility; deciding to what extent a hazardous-waste site must be cleaned up; setting permit levels for discharge, storage, or transport; establishing national ambient air quality standards; and determining allowable levels of contamination in drinking water.

The Agency completes a risk assessment to determine potential health or ecological risks. Risk management is the suite of actions then taken based on consideration of that and other information, as follows:

- Scientific factors provide the basis for the risk assessment, including information drawn from toxicology, chemistry, epidemiology, ecology, and statistics – to name a few.
- Economic factors inform the manager on the cost of risks and the benefits of reducing them, the costs of risk mitigation or remediation options, and the distributional effects.
- Laws and legal decisions are factors that define the basis for the Agency's risk assessments, management decisions, and, in some instances, the schedule, level, or methods for risk reduction.
- Social factors, such as income level, ethnic background, community values, land use, zoning, availability of healthcare, lifestyle, and psychological condition of the affected populations, may affect the susceptibility of an individual or a definable group to risks from a particular stressor.

- Technological factors include the feasibility, impacts, and range of risk management options.
- Political factors are based on the interactions among branches of the Federal government, with other Federal, state, and local government entities, and even with foreign governments; these may range from practices defined by Agency policy and political administrations through inquiries from members of Congress, special interest groups, or concerned citizens.
- Public values reflect the broad attitudes of society about environmental risks and risk management.

Airsafe.com provides a complementary perspective:

The process of combining a risk assessment with decisions on how to address that risk is called risk management. Risk management is part of a larger decision process that considers the technical and social aspects of the risk situation. Risk assessments are performed primarily for the purpose of providing information and insight to those who make decisions about how that risk should be managed. Judgment and values enter into risk assessment in the context of what techniques one should use to objectively describe and evaluate risk. Judgment and values enter into risk management in the context of what is the most effective and socially acceptable solution.

The combined risk assessment and risk management process can be described as a six-step process (Airsafe.com). The first three steps are associated with risk assessment and the last three with risk management:

1. Formulate problem in a broad context. Do this by answering questions like: what is the problem, what are its various facets and dimensions, who must manage the problem, and who are the stakeholders? Establish relationships among the various components of the overall problem, and take stakeholder input seriously in problem identification and characterization.
2. Perform the risk analysis. Evaluate the risk in order to determine the hazard, the likelihood of the hazard occurring, and any uncertainties in the estimate.
3. Define the options. Determine what can be done about the risk issue and the ways that it could be done. Determine potential consequences, costs, and benefits.
4. Make sound decisions. Determine the best solutions and how they could be implemented in ways that are feasible, cost effective, and socially acceptable.
5. Implement decisions. Take the actions that are necessary to implement the decisions made, and make mid-course corrections as indicated by lessons learned along the way.

6. Evaluate actions taken. Evaluate the effectiveness and appropriateness of the risk management actions taken. If deficiencies are discovered, revisit the whole six-step process beginning at the step where the first serious failure occurred.

Conclusion

Ordinary risk management attempts to combine risk assessment, decisions under risk, and risk management into a coherent process that can be implemented routinely when hazards are suspected. Typically, risk assessment is based on simple models (usually reductionist, typically Newtonian, and often linear) of the system under threat, and utilitarian decision criteria are applied to determine the course of action to manage the threat.

It is important to make myself clear – ORM is a pretty good process for managing run-of-the-mill risks. At this point in our inquiry an appropriate working hypothesis is that ORM – as it is now, and as it continues to evolve with further use – is an appropriate default approach to risk management. The question that motivates this book, however, is whether something more, something explicitly precautionary, is needed for the extraordinary risks, threats, and hazards that we encounter.

NOTES

1 Here, I am using the term "environment" broadly to suggest a sub-system that may be disturbed by a proposed project. Some proposed projects are in fact focused on natural environments and/or ecosystems, but I do not mean to restrict the present discussion to those cases.

2 This aphorism is often attributed to Yogi Berra, the legendary baseball manager and dispenser of folk wisdom, but the great physicist Niels Bohr said it first.

3 Freeman and Kunreuther (2003), in the context of considering the potential for market insurance against global disaster, provide a useful review of the principles of insurance. The discussion of idiosyncratic and systemic risk (Chapter 3) is helpful in this context.

5   Problems with ordinary risk management

Ordinary risk management typically applies utilitarian decision criteria to simple models (reductionist, often linear) of the system. It is best adapted to cases where the outcome set is well defined, probabilities can be estimated accurately, and the law of large numbers is in effect (as when the decision maker is assured of many draws from a stable distribution, or can transfer the risk to an insurer who has such assurance). In this chapter, we look a little deeper into the nature of the hard cases, considering some limitations of utilitarian decision theory (issues of irreversibility, and unlikely but catastrophic events), and challenges to ORM models of the way the world works that are raised by the emerging understanding of complex systems. Complexity theory warns us that uncertainty, gross ignorance, and unknown unknowns are greater problems, and surprises are more likely, than we might have thought. That is, we are more likely than we might have thought to encounter the kinds of cases that stretch ORM beyond its limits.

Challenges to utilitarian decision theory

Utilitarian decision theory is committed to a weighing of the prospective benefits and costs of the various risky alternatives. There is no question that modern extended benefit–cost analysis has facilitated a more sophisticated weighing. The idea of extended BCA is to obtain a more complete accounting of benefits and costs, especially in the cases involving rare and perhaps fragile environmental resources, by systematically estimating total economic value, including options values, and passive use values where they are relevant. Expected utility approaches open the door for explicit risk aversion, and the explicit consideration of option values is aimed at accounting for the effect of present decisions on future options and the value of delaying decisions when we expect to learn more as time passes. The question addressed in this section is whether ORM is up to the tasks of dealing coherently with "irreversibility" and unlikely but catastrophic events.

Extended benefit–cost analysis and real options theory: the problem of irreversibility

Irreversibility as paving paradise. Consideration of option value in extended benefit–cost analysis was motivated by the idea of irreversibility (Krutilla 1967, Weisbrod 1964). The essential reality captured by irreversibility is that some kinds of decisions are harder to reverse than others. For some actions there is, for all practical purposes, no going back. In the environmental arena, many of these cases involve converting highly evolved complex natural systems into simpler, more generic resources: for example, natural river basins into flat-water reservoirs, and prairie ecosystems into monocultural farmland. Conversion changes relatively low entropy states into states with much higher entropy, and restoration, if it is possible, takes a lot of time and effort. In the 1960s, there was growing disenchantment among the public as the age of large-scale water resources projects was winding down, and Weisbrod and Krutilla were beginning to articulate a formal rationale for questioning the continuing conversion of the unique into the generic, in the name of economic progress.

Their point was that decisions to take these kinds of actions should be made with due consideration for the options that might be foreclosed – "you can't go if it ain't still there." Joni Mitchell ("Big Yellow Taxi" ©1970) made the concept unforgettable for my generation: "They paved paradise and put up a parking lot." The intuition of Krutilla and Weisbrod seemed obvious and compelling – one would be willing to pay something extra to secure the opportunity for future use of a resource under threat. In technical terms, the risk-aversion option price (WTP for the option of future use) would exceed expected use value, so that option value would be positive.

In the summer of 1969, when I was a graduate student at Oregon State University, John Krutilla was visiting and raised the idea of option value with the resource economics seminar. One of my cohort, Derek Byerlee, had a background in decisions under uncertainty and volunteered to do a little work that might add some rigor to the concept. After a few days, he came in with an analysis that showed that uncertainty would tend not to raise but to reduce willingness to pay to secure supply. Byerlee had analyzed the case of a consumer with uncertain demand – one who was unsure whether she would want to use the resource when the time came (Byerlee 1971). For an uncertain demander, the value of making sure that it is still there is diminished by the possibility that she might no longer wish to use the resource. At the time, Krutilla seemed to think this was rather missing the point, but in due course formulations appeared in the literature addressing uncertainty in both supply and demand.[1] With risk aversion, WTP is increased (relative to expected use value) by uncertainty as to future availability, but it is decreased by uncertainty about future demand.

Irreversibility as committing too soon. Arrow and Fisher (1974) and Henry (1974) offered another concept of option value that came to be known as quasi-option value, to distinguish it from the Weisbrod-Krutilla kind. Quasi-option value is the value of the opportunity to defer a decision given that new information resolving (some of) the uncertainty may emerge in the interim. Quasi-option value still hinges on the "paving paradise" kind of irreversibility – committing too soon would hardly matter if it were easy to undo an action once regret set in – but the analytics are different. The analysis posits alternatives in period 1 that are asymmetric in terms of reversibility: the choice of A_1 (paradise, in the first period) permits either A_2 or B_2 (paradise or a parking lot, in the second period), but the choice of B_1 permits only B_2. If we expected new information relevant to the choice between A and B to emerge at the beginning of period 2, that expectation would add value to the A_1 alternative because it keeps next-period options open whereas B_1 does not. Of course, the relative reversibility of A does not clinch the case for A_1. If B is overwhelmingly the more rewarding choice for period 1, the opportunity cost of choosing A_1 may well exceed the quasi-option value.

Irreversibility as sunk costs. Real options theory (Dixit and Pindyck 1994, Pindyck 2007) generalizes the value of keeping options open – the value of waiting, including the value of any learning that may occur while we wait – and adapts the theory and methods of valuing financial options to the real options case. As Pindyck (2007) emphasizes, one implication of real options theory is that any sunk cost or stranded investment introduces irreversibility. Note that, as with the earlier option value concept, uncertainty may cut both ways. In a real options analysis of environmental regulation, Kolstad (1996) showed that uncertainty may tilt the economist's prescription toward earlier and more intense intervention, or later and less intense intervention – it all depends on the balance of uncertainties associated with damage and intervention.

Irreversibility as entropy. The real options concept of irreversibility as sunk costs parallels the thermodynamic concept of entropy – ubiquitous entropy suggests that sunk costs and irreversibility, too, are ubiquitous (Manson 2007). In the end, the real options concept of irreversibility highlights the temporal dimension of opportunity costs – if I do A there will be some costs sunk and some non-salvageable resources stranded if I then switch to B, and vice-versa (Box 4.2). Irreversibility in real options theory is continuous – it is just a cost, and some costs are greater than others. This solves an obvious problem with the concept of irreversibility – it dichotomizes what is surely a continuum. Few if any decisions can be reversed costlessly, but few would be infinitely costly to reverse. In solving that problem, it raises another – how to frame the issue that motivated the whole irreversibility enterprise: some alternatives are very different than others in the extent to which they foreclose future options, and that fact should influence today's decisions. Ubiquitous irreversibility, much of it relatively trivial, is rhetorically unhelpful. One could define categories of irreversibility – including strong irreversibility, which would apply to decisions that could be reversed only at insurmountable cost – but that hardly helps scholars struggling to capture what, if anything, is special about the strong irreversibility that worried Krutilla and Weisbrod.

Irreversibility as path dependence. One implication of real options theory is that any sunk cost or stranded investment introduces irreversibility (Pindyck 2007). As Manson (2007) has noted, sunk costs seem to be one kind of entropy, which is itself ubiquitous. Just as time marches on, irreversibility is ubiquitous and much of it is trivial. Breakfast may have disappointed me, but there is no meaningful sense in which I can do it over. This is clearly a case of irreversibility, but it is most likely inconsequential – breakfast would have had to be more than ordinarily disappointing, to put my life on a meaningfully different trajectory. More likely, the disappointing breakfast soon gets lost in the hurly-burly of life.

For a polar case of strong irreversibility, consider evolution. Permit me the metaphor of evolution as a motion-picture saga. If we could rewind the evolutionary movie and watch it again as mere observers, there is no reason to think it would turn out anything like the one we are watching now. There is simply nothing reversible or repeatable about evolution. Nevertheless, our decisions and actions matter to evolutionary processes and outcomes. We are unable to direct evolution to any particular outcome, but we can limit its potential (and we have been doing some of that) by allowing the extinction of some species, the destruction of some complex ecosystems, and the simplification of the gene pool as native cultivars and heritage varieties disappear. Each time we meddle, consciously and unconsciously, with evolutionary potential, we move evolution to a different path.

The breakfast example makes the point that the irreversibility that matters is the kind that would move the system to a meaningfully different trajectory.

As a result of a consequential decision to do A instead of B, the system travels a different path and ends up at a different place. Any subsequent attempt to move from the A path to the B path will fall short in meaningful ways – without an exogenous input of resources, the system may not be able to attain the B path, and even with the boost of exogenous resources it cannot make up the lost time.

Just when it seemed that economists grappling with irreversibility have hit a wall, the notion of path dependence holds some promise. We will leave the issue of irreversibility here for a moment but return a little later, after we have surveyed and considered some additional challenges to extended BCA and some recent developments in the understanding of complex systems. Perhaps new and emerging ways of modeling how the world works may yield insights that add relevance to the path dependence idea.

High damage but unlikely events – utilitarianism and infinite prospects

It has long been known that rational decision theories have difficulty dealing with infinite prospects. Pascal's wager – an argument that it is rational to believe in God because the promised reward is infinite; belief therefore dominates other options even if the probability that God exists is very small – has been criticized from many perspectives (for example, perhaps there are many gods, which would introduce the possibility of negative reward for believing in one of the wrong ones), but even on its own terms it seems not entirely convincing. The mathematics – the product of an infinite prospect and a tiny probability is infinite – supports the argument but, for many of us, intuition does not.

The St. Petersburg paradox (Bernoulli 1738) reinforces the point. Players are invited to pay a fixed fee to enter a game in which a fair coin is tossed repeatedly until a tail first appears, ending the game. The pot starts at $1 and is doubled every time a head appears. The expected value of this bet is infinite (because there is a tiny chance that a tail will never appear). Yet, most people are willing to pay very much less (typically less than $20) to enter the game. Various explanations have been offered. For example, players would surely discount the possibility of an infinite payoff in the real world – the "bank" does not have infinite resources. Economists have settled on Bernoulli's preferred explanation: players value not the amount of the pay-off but its utility, and utility is finite because increasing pay-offs deliver diminishing marginal utility. Finite utility would lead to finite WTP to play. Nevertheless, this explanation seems scarcely adequate to explain why willingness to pay for a bet with very high expected value is so low.

Behavioral economics, which has advanced dramatically since Kahneman and Tversky's seminal contribution (1979) showing that the choices made by people facing risk deviate in systematic ways from the predictions of standard economic theory, offers a variety of insights into the weaknesses of rational decision theory as a predictor of human response. However, in the case of the St. Petersburg paradox, we do not really need to call on behavioral insights. Despite the infinite expected value of the bet with infinite resources, its value is really quite modest if the bank has limited resources, or if the player has limited patience. Simulations (www.mathematik.com/Petersburg/Petersburg.html) have generated results such as the following:

- If the bank's losses are capped at $1 million, the expected value of the bet is only about $11. If the cap is $1 billion, the expected value is not quite $16.
- Consider repeated games. To achieve an expected value of $10 per bet, one would need to play about one million games; for an EV of $20 per bet, one would need to play about one trillion games.

The commonsense intuition – that most of the time the game will produce small pay-offs, and that very high pay-offs will be very rare – seems enough to explain the observed modest WTP to play.[2]

Most of the perils we face threaten less than infinite damage, but similar difficulties arise in the more common circumstance that we are asked to make sense of problems involving possible damage that is very large and imprecisely estimated. It only makes matters worse that the likelihood of such damage is itself imprecisely known even if intuition suggests it is small.

Chichilnisky (2000) has produced a proof that the expected utility approach is insensitive to unlikely but potentially catastrophic events. Her argument proceeds as follows. By convention expected utility (EU) analysis is implemented with bounded utility functions (to avoid the St. Petersburg paradox). With bounded utility, lotteries are EU-ranked independently of the utilities of states whose probabilities are lower than some threshold, the value of which depends on the particular lotteries being compared. The practical implication she draws is that coherent public decision making requires that the desire to avoid unlikely but catastrophic outcomes needs expression above and beyond that which it gets in expected utility calculations.

Limits of the law of large numbers – emerging systemic risk

In Chapter 3, I drew attention to the distinction between idiosyncratic risk and systemic risk. To automobile insurers, the risk of claims is idiosyncratic – they cannot predict who among their pool of insured drivers will be involved in a collision on what day but, if their insured pool is large enough, they have reliable predictions of their aggregate risk exposure. The "law of large numbers" works for the insurance companies, because they have deep pockets and they can write large numbers of policies whose performance on average is predictable. Drivers buy insurance, even at prices higher than their expected losses, because they do not have deep pockets and they cannot count on large numbers of trials. Claims that would be devastating to individuals are conceivable, so they draw little comfort from the law of large numbers.

Idiosyncratic risk, the ideal kind from the perspective of insurers, can be undermined in several ways. Adverse selection (offering sub-prime mortgages attracts less-qualified borrowers) and moral hazard (solvent borrowers who realize that their loan balance exceeds their equity may choose to withhold payments even at the risk of foreclosure) may undermine the insurers' (in this case, mortgage-holders') risk projections. Yet these problems are manageable in many cases – strategies are available and effective for minimizing adverse selection and moral hazard – even though they do not appear to have been used effectively in the recent mortgage meltdown.

A much greater challenge to idiosyncratic risk arises from circumstances that change the system that generates the outcome distribution. The law of large numbers protects insurers who can be confident that they are taking many draws from a known and stable distribution. But they are at risk when the distribution and its underlying system change in unanticipated ways. Automobile insurers have been much more comfortable in recent years than property insurers with large pools of Florida policy-holders. Real estate development there has become even more concentrated in coastal areas, and it seems that hurricanes are becoming more frequent and hurricane losses more severe. The system seems to be changing, and the aggregate risk exposure to property insurers in Florida is growing. To them, their idiosyncratic risk has acquired a systemic element.

Because insurers can lay off much of their risk with re-insurers, things would not be so disturbing if increasing hurricane exposure in Florida was idiosyncratic at the global level – re-insurance of Florida policies may become more expensive, but it would still be available. But suppose increasing hurricane exposure in Florida is a symptom of global warming, so that coastal communities worldwide can expect to suffer highly correlated losses if and when the sea-level rises. Then, the risk would be systemic at a global level, a serious challenge for re-insurers as well as insurers.

Standard techniques of risk management are designed for idiosyncratic risks, and are at risk of failure when the risks become systemic. Because competent insurers would be wary of contracting to bear known systemic risk, they would presumably accumulate a portfolio of systemic risks only if they were unaware of so doing. This suggests novelty, as might arise from unstable outcome distributions influenced by unexpected shifts in the underlying systems, or from the impact of unpredicted exogenous forces.

ORM risk assessment models are typically reductionist, linear, and Newtonian. *Reductionist* models deduce the nature of complex things from the interaction of elemental components with defined properties. Models that assume *linear* change impose a sequence of events that affect each other in their order of appearance. *Newtonian* models conceive of the universe as governed by rational and understandable laws, laying the groundwork for what is now called modernism in science (both the natural and social sciences). Regularity and stability are properties often attributed to Newtonian systems, as in Newton's celestial mechanics which is often cited as the inspiration for the equilibrating systems that are the foundation of neoclassical economics. Stable systems tend to return toward their initial position when disturbed. Equilibrating systems have a self-correcting tendency: the disturbance caused by an exogenous shock tends to be dissipated over several rounds of adjustment. A new equilibrium may emerge, but it will be closer to the initial equilibrium than the first-round effect would suggest, and the new equilibrium will be stable in the absence of further exogenous shocks.

A worldview conditioned by reductionist, linear, and Newtonian models will tend to think of order, regularity, and predictability as normal, and will tend to not to take seriously phenomena that would seem to challenge this view of normality. For example, most economists of my acquaintance are skeptical about the possibility of "bubbles," asset prices that rise far higher than can be sustained only to crash back to earth, despite having lived through the "tech bubble" that burst in 2000–1 and the "housing bubble" that burst in 2007–8.[3] We might expect people with a tendency to discount surprises to be surprised a lot. Our risk models might systematically understate our risk exposure.

New models of how the world works – complexity and path dependence

From today's perspective, the classic (Knightian) definitions of risk and uncertainty tend to assume we know more than we usually do. Risk is defined as a situation in which we can enumerate the possible outcomes and we know their probabilities, yet it is likely at best that the magnitudes of outcomes and their probabilities are estimates. Under classical uncertainty, the probabilities are unknown (practically speaking, we cannot estimate the probabilities with confidence), but we can still enumerate the possible outcomes. Note that all of this assumes we are dealing with a system that, while imperfectly understood, is stationary – the real-world process that generates outcomes and probabilities is unchanging. Yet intuition tells us to be concerned about actions and events that might shock the outcome set and its probability distribution, and to take seriously the possibility of surprises, defined here as realized events that were not in the *ex ante* outcome set. Recent literature takes seriously the concept of gross ignorance (Henry and Henry 2002) and Rumsfeld's unknown unknowns, "the ones we don't know we don't know" (US Department of Defense briefing, February 12, 2002). However, the exposition to this point offers only intuition to support the idea that surprises are perhaps more normal than is usually thought; and the sources cited immediately above are not natural scientists. Henry and Henry are economists and Rumsfeld was a politically appointed senior administrator; rather than natural scientists, these are just intelligent people struggling to make sense of the world around them.

New models of how the world works are emerging, and it is time to ask whether they help us to a more serviceable understanding of risk.

Complex systems

If we think of mechanistic (Newtonian) systems as simple, that would imply that complex systems depart from mechanistic properties in some important ways. Complex systems may be defined as those that exhibit one or more properties or behaviors not obvious from the properties of the individual parts. Some of the complex systems properties that may generate non-obvious outcomes include: reciprocal dependence among components some of which themselves are complex, sub-systems operating on quite different spatial and temporal scales, and non-linear and perhaps discontinuous linkages between components. As a result, system activity is typically non-linear and complex systems may exhibit emergent behavior including self-organization. Complex systems may change in ways that cannot be described by a single rule or a single level of explanation, and outcomes may include features whose emergence cannot be predicted from their current specifications.

Box 5.1 Features of complex systems

Complex systems may have the following features:

System boundaries may be difficult to determine. It can be difficult to determine the boundaries of a complex system. The decision is ultimately made by the observer.

Complex systems may be open. Complex systems are usually open systems – that is, they exist in a thermodynamic gradient and dissipate energy. In other words, complex systems are frequently far from energetic equilibrium; but despite this flux, there may be pattern stability.

Complex systems may have a memory. The history of a complex system may be important. Because complex systems are dynamical systems they change over time, and prior states may have an influence on present states. More formally, complex systems often exhibit hysteresis.

Complex systems may be nested. The components of a complex system may themselves be complex systems. For example, an economy is made up of organizations, which are made up of people, which are made up of cells – all of which are complex systems.

Dynamic networks of multiple scales with interconnectivity. As well as coupling rules, the dynamic network of a complex system is important. Small-world or scale-free networks which have many local interactions and a smaller number of inter-area connections are often employed. Natural complex systems often exhibit such topologies. In the human cortex for example, we see dense local connectivity and a few very long axon projections between regions inside the cortex and to other brain regions.

Emergent phenomena may be produced. Complex systems may exhibit behaviors that are emergent, which is to say that while the results may be deterministic, they may have properties that can only be studied at a higher level. For example, the termites in a mound have physiology, biochemistry, and biological development that are understandable at one level of analysis, but their social behavior and mound building is a property that emerges from the collection of termites and needs to be analyzed at a different level.

Relationships are non-linear. In practical terms, this means a small perturbation may cause a large effect, a proportional effect, or even no effect at all. In linear systems, effect is *always* directly proportional to cause.

Relationships contain feedback loops. Both negative (damping) and positive (amplifying) feedback are often found in complex systems. The effects of an element's behavior change the element itself in some way.

Complex adaptive systems

Complex adaptive systems are complex systems that have the capacity to change and learn from experience. Examples of complex adaptive systems include the biosphere and the ecosystem, the brain, the immune system, the cell, social insect colonies, the corporation, the stock market, the economy,

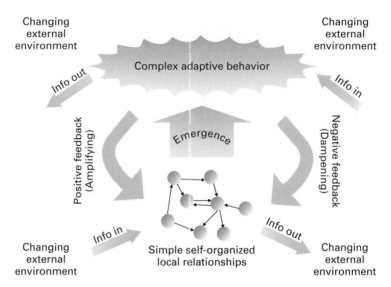

Figure 5.1   Complex adaptive behavior (source: *Wikimedia Commons*)

and human social group-based endeavors such as political parties or artistic communities.

Complex adaptive systems have the properties of self-organization, non-linearity, increasingly unpredictable development, and emergence.

Self-organization. Change occurs naturally and automatically in systems in order to increase efficiency and effectiveness, as long as the systems are complex enough as defined above. This change is accomplished by the elements that make up the system when they respond to feedback from the environment the system inhabits.

Elements that survive negative environmental feedback will automatically re-settle themselves, or reorganize themselves and their interactions in order to better accomplish the system's survival. Success assures their continued existence by also protecting or reinforcing the structures of which the elements are a part.

Such responsiveness occurs even when the elements and system are non-organic, unintelligent, and unconscious as long as the system is complex as described above.

Non-linearity. When change occurs in complex systems it occurs in a non-linear fashion. In linear change there is a sequence of events that affect each other in their order of appearance, and the net effect can be predicted from the properties of the stimuli. In non-linear systems, everything in the sequence has the possibility of affecting everything else before and after it. The end result may be non-proportional to the original input.

Hysteresis. Nonlinear systems often have the property of memory in the sense that prior states affect later states. Such a system is said to exhibit path-dependence, or "rate-independent memory" (Mielke and Roubicek 2003).

In a deterministic system with no dynamics or hysteresis, it is possible to predict the system's output at an instant in time, given only its input at that instant in time. In a system with hysteresis, this is not possible; there is no way to predict the output without knowing the system's current state, and there is no way to know the system's state without looking at the history of the input. This means that it is necessary to know the path that the input followed before it reached its current value.

Increasingly unpredictable development. Suppose we knew a lot about the current state of a complex adaptive system, and its history. It may be fairly easy to identify a range of possibilities for the next stage of system development. But the range of possibilities increases dramatically as we try to predict stage after stage of development. So, the task becomes exponentially more difficult as we try to predict stages of development further into the future, even though the development from stage to stage has logical explanation in retrospect.

Emergence. The unpredictability inherent in the natural evolution of complex systems can yield results that are strictly unpredictable based on knowledge of the original conditions. This process is called emergence. Emergent properties are logical results, in that they have logical explanations despite their lack of predictability.

Note that there is no inconsistency between increasingly unpredictable development and emergence on the one hand, and self-organization on the other – one definition of emergence is: the arising of novel and coherent structures, patterns, and properties during the process of self-organization in complex systems. In the case of strong emergence, the system develops qualities not directly traceable to the system's components, but rather to how those components interact; these new qualities are irreducible to the system's constituent parts (Laughlin 2005).

Resilience – stability and instability in complex systems

The concept of regime is central to complex systems theory. We may think of regimes as characteristic states of systems, in the sense that a regime is not just any state, but a state that has a degree of stability. Imagine the array of possible states of the system as a landscape consisting of valleys each separated from the neighboring valley by a separatrix (e.g. a divide, in the geographical sense). Then, each valley can be considered a "domain of attraction"; when the system is in a domain of attraction it will tend to move to a fixed interior point (the lowest place in the valley). The state and conditions that lead the system to tend toward that particular fixed point is called the regime.

Small ephemeral perturbations will move the system away from the fixed point, but it will tend to return. Small but persistent changes in conditions might move the fixed point to somewhere else in the domain of attraction. But we can also imagine a one-time shock, or an accumulation of stresses, sufficient to propel the system across the separatrix into a different domain of attraction. Such an event is called a *regime shift*.

Within a domain of attraction the system tends (other things equal) to move to a fixed interior point. A system is said to have the property of *stability* to the extent that, when shocked, it tends to return to the fixed interior point. The separatrix is an impediment that can be overcome only with the help of stimuli exceeding some threshold (an economist would describe such processes and system trajectories as lumpy). Stimuli may arise from external sources (e.g. humans invest resources purposefully, or stress the system thoughtlessly), or endogenous system processes. If the impediments separating the particular domain of attraction from others are so great that the system will tolerate substantial disturbance without undergoing regime shift, the system is said to be *resilient*. If the separatrix is easily overcome, modest stimuli (perhaps endogenous) may induce the system to *flip-flop*, i.e. shift from one regime to another and back again, perhaps repeatedly.

Coupled human and natural systems. Coupled human and natural systems are complex adaptive systems of particular relevance to the subjects of risk and risk management. Climate systems, weather systems, hydrological systems, and ecosystems are examples of key systems that interact with each other and with human systems to generate the outcome sets that characterize risk, uncertainty, gross ignorance, and unknown unknowns.

Research on coupled human and natural systems is showing that these systems may exhibit resilience in the sense that they tend, following perturbations, to return toward their prior trajectory and/or to tolerate disturbances while retaining their structure and function. However, resilience is not unlimited – exogenous disturbances of sufficient magnitude may induce regime shifts that change the system in unpredictable ways (Folke *et al.* 2004). Under some conditions, small changes in exogenous forces may cause the system to flip-flop between regimes, but in other cases, there are substantial impediments to returning to something like the old regime. If the system is stochastic and incompletely understood, and we are unable to monitor all of the disturbing stimuli it encounters and all of the ways it responds to them, we may be surprised by seemingly spontaneous regime shifts. Resilience may be undermined by sudden anthropogenic shocks that precipitate regime shifts, or by sustained anthropogenic pressure (e.g. harvest, or effluent inflows) that reduces resilience and increases vulnerability to regime shifts (Holling 2001, Folke *et al.* 2004).

Regime shifts and surprises. Surprises are defined as realized outcomes that were not in the *ex ante* outcome set. Our cursory review of the current understanding of complex systems has identified several concepts – increasingly unpredictable development, emergence, and regime shifts – suggesting that the capacity to generate surprises may be a feature of complex systems. To call these properties and outcomes surprises is not to abandon logic, or even the idea of causation. They may be surprises, but they are nevertheless logical results of complex systems processes in that they have logical explanation despite their lack of predictability.

To what extent are surprises inherent features of complex systems, and to what extent are they one measure of the state of human knowledge and comprehension (if we were not so clueless, we would not be surprised; or maybe not surprised so often)? One way to think about this is to work through some hypothetical cases.

Imagine a system that is all-knowing and fully-endogenized. Everything that matters to the system is a fully articulated component of the system, and the system is all-knowing about its own history, status, and functioning. It follows that there are no relevant exogenous shocks, and the system can map its own outcome set. Such a system cannot surprise itself, and it cannot be surprised – in this sense, complexity alone is not sufficient to generate surprises. Nevertheless, depending on our comprehension of how the system works and our ability to monitor key indicators of its history and status, it may well surprise us.

Suppose the system is all-knowing but not fully-endogenized (i.e. it can be disturbed by external shocks). It follows that it cannot be all-predicting because it cannot predict the exogenous shocks that may impact it. Such a system can be surprised. We, too, can be surprised if the exogenous shock was a surprise to us, and we will be surprised by the system's response to the extent that our comprehension of the system and/or our ability to monitor key indicators is incomplete. What if the shock is anthropogenic? We can be surprised if we are unaware of what we are doing, and/or we don't fully comprehend and effectively monitor the complex system we are doing it to.

Can regime shifts and flop-backs be surprises to us? Yes, if the system flips or flops to a state not considered possible or not taken seriously *ex ante*. Furthermore, if the *ex ante* outcome set was limited to states in the baseline domain of attraction, any flip or flop would be a surprise.

We might even ask whether regime shifts and flop-backs are always surprises to us. Bussiere and Fratzscher (2008) emphasize the crucial role of early warning in risk management, and encourage enhanced research and investment in early warning systems. In this context, does complex systems modeling allow us to predict some regime switches?[4] Or does it identify some observable variables that we can monitor in order to predict some regime switches? Brock and Carpenter (2006) provide evidence that, in the case of large lake ecosystems, sudden increases in the variance of certain variables that can be monitored relatively easily provide early warnings of potential regime shift. This optimistic finding is tempered by the observation of Brock *et al.* (2008) that the prospects of early warning are much less favorable for some other types of complex ecosystems.

All of this suggests that surprises are mostly about us – the limits to what we can monitor reliably, our models of reality, and perhaps even how our minds work. If this is right, surprises are the realization of outcomes that run the gamut from prospects we were unable to imagine to those we simply did not take seriously – either way, we did not assign these prospects non-zero likelihood *ex ante*. Yet complex systems theory and research findings in the emerging field of coupled human and natural systems suggest that surprises are more likely (perhaps much more likely) than ORM risk assessment typically recognizes. Furthermore, surprises are the tip of the iceberg – any substantial and harmful *ex post* outcome that was not taken seriously because it seemed very unlikely *ex ante* is a failure for risk management.

Path dependence and learning

Irreversibility as path dependence with consequences. A rather trivial concept of path-dependence can be found in comparative-static welfare economics (to readers unfamiliar with welfare economics this may seem an arcane example, but it should be possible to get the point without understanding the technicalities). If a multipart policy is introduced stepwise, under certain conditions the calculated welfare effect of the policy depends on the order of things changed; but the difference typically is fairly small, and the result repeatable. This kind of path dependence is regarded as pathological and can be avoided by using welfare change measures that are not susceptible. It is not a property of the policy or of the world – it is attributable to the welfare-measurement framework itself. This example helps us define a minimal concept of path dependence in complex systems. First, the path dependence is a property of the system itself – whether it be (some portion of) the real world or a model thereof – not merely the techniques we use to study it. Furthermore, different paths take us to different places in the real world, or to different outcomes in the system we are modeling. Path-dependence is necessarily consequential in that sense – the place we end up depends on the path we took.

This minimal concept of path dependence solves the problem of ubiquitous and often trivial irreversibility that is raised by the sunk costs and entropy notions of irreversibility. In the example used earlier in this chapter, breakfast may have disappointed me, but there is no meaningful sense in which I can do it over – in the sunk costs and entropy senses, my breakfast experience is irreversible. Yet breakfast would need to have been more than ordinarily disappointing to set in motion processes that would lead me to meaningfully different life-outcomes. The typical disappointing breakfast is irreversible but inconsequential; it does not reach the threshold of path dependence. However, for sunk costs, stranded investments, and entropic degradation that reach such a threshold, path dependence does in fact set in – the system travels a different path and arrives at a different destination.

Evolution served earlier to exemplify a polar case of path-dependence – if we could rewind the evolutionary movie, there is no reason to think it would turn out anything like the one we are watching now. There is nothing reversible or repeatable about evolution.

In the dynamic economics of technology and investment, path-dependence recognizes that first movers have advantages – they may foreclose opportunities for competitors – and the place where the world ends up may be substantively different as a result. It is a reasonable conjecture that we would be computing in fundamentally different ways today if Microsoft had not become the dominant player in software in the early 1980s, which suggests that our lifestyles, economy, and society would be quite different. It might be reasonable to place the impact of Microsoft somewhere in the middle, on the path-dependence scale: surely consequential and irreversible in that sense, and maybe (I am not sure) as unrepeatable as evolution.

So, path dependence will serve as the concept to capture the realities that motivated the original conceptions of irreversibility as paving paradise and as premature commitment. Those irreversibility concepts are unsatisfactory because, among other things, their binary rhetoric (reversible/irreversible) is unconvincing. Path dependence may exhibit discontinuities, threshold effects, etc. because there are always impediments to switching from one path to another, and in some cases the impediments are large. Nevertheless, the path dependence concept allows a wide range of costs of reversion, from small to insurmountable. However, unlike the sunk costs / stranded investments /

entropy concepts of irreversibility, it avoids triviality by insisting on a consequentiality threshold – a stimulus is said to activate path-dependence in a system only when subsequent outcomes are meaningfully affected.

Complexity, path dependence and learning – the roads taken and not taken. Complexity theory informs a concept of path dependence that seems more serviceable for our purposes here.[5] At every step, it matters where the system has been and where it is now, because that determines the opportunities for further regime shifts and the impediments that must be overcome if a shift is to occur. As the steps add up, it becomes evident that the system is on a particular path but, because the system may respond in lumpy rather than smooth fashion and has some endogenous capacity to surprise us, the implications of our path are revealed to us only as we travel along it and even then only grudgingly. This is not a claim that we learn only passively by some sort of osmosis. To the contrary, we learn about where we have been via systematic empirical research, we project trends into the future, and we pursue at least two avenues of forward-looking research.

Box 5.2 Real options and path dependence

In Box 4.2, we compared a real option O_1 to prevent uncertain harm from global warming by reducing greenhouse gas (GHG) accumulations and a real option O_2 to defer that expenditure in case it turns out that global warming is less harmful than expected or GHG reduction is ineffective in reducing damage. Starting with a clean slate and the same set of prior expectations, these options are perfect antonyms, and the value of the second option is equal to minus the value of the first.

However, the antonym status of O_1 and O_2 is perhaps an artifact of the 2-period model used, wherein both options are evaluated *ex ante* in period 1 using the same set of expectations. If time is continuous, costs and pay-offs are time-dependent, and decisions could be made at any time from the set of opportunities available at that time, we might expect path-dependence to emerge. At any given time, the choice of one option precludes choosing the others available. As time goes on and decisions taken add up, a particular path emerges from a complex path-tree (for want of a better term) of possibilities. The implications of the path we take are revealed only as we travel along it, which implies that the path we choose would influence – in addition to the costs we sink and the investments we strand – the things we learn, the technologies we acquire, the stream of costs and benefits we experience, and the opportunities we face at every point in time. From any point on any path, the set of opportunities going forward will be conditioned on the sequence of choices made earlier. Then O_1 and O_2 will not be discrete options but emerging paths, which destroys any notion that they can be exact antonyms with the value of one equal to the negative of the value of the other.

A *reductive program of systematic research* remains relevant despite its limitations in a complex systems environment. Such a program is capable of yielding new and useful knowledge, often of a *ceteris paribus* kind (in the simplest case, the effect of *x* on *y* other things equal). Justifications for reductive approaches to research are of two kinds. First, the pragmatic justification – reductive research is what works – invokes the many successes of reductive approaches to bolster the argument that reality is just so complex, and generates so much noise and distracting signals, that the obvious path to progress involves abstraction, simplification, and controlled experimentation.

The principled justification for reductive approaches claims more and is thus more exposed to criticism. The logical positivists of the early twentieth century asserted that all complex propositions are derived logically from elemental propositions, a proposition that itself is uncontroversial if it means (1) that starting with a complex proposition it is possible to show its logical connection to a set of simple priors, but is much more assailable if taken to mean (2) that given a set of simple priors it is possible logically to map the outcome set. Complexity theory endorses the first of these meanings but explicitly denies the second in the case of complex systems – for example, it posits that emergent properties are logical results despite their unpredictability, and the system develops properties that are irreducible to the system's constituent parts (see p. 67, above). The second meaning, taken seriously, would lead us to expect more predictability than complex systems can provide, and to discount too much the possibility of surprises.

Let us grant the pragmatic argument that the demonstrated successes of reductive approaches argue against abandoning them. There remains the issue of unintended consequences: research-based interventions in natural and/or systems frequently induce unintended consequences for good or ill. Complexity theory helps us comprehend how unintended consequences can emerge; not only that, complexity theory warns us to expect unintended consequences.[6]

A program of complex systems research. Complex systems research usually begins with *modeling*, to better understand the system under study and in the process to probe the properties of complex systems more generally. A typical objective of a modeling exercise addressed to coupled natural and human systems is to model the dynamics and connectivity of sub-systems of different spatial, temporal, and organizational scales. Modeling foci include the dynamics of uncertainty, the resilience of coupled systems, and their vulnerability to environmental change and human-generated stresses. Modeling results can be calibrated and validated to some degree (it seems that validation is always a matter of degree) by monitoring key indicator variables characterizing the natural and human systems under study, to judge the validity of predictions from the model and adjusting the model as indicated. For practical purposes, the modeling exercise generates useful information if it helps us understand the resilience and vulnerability of the system and, especially, if it identifies variables that indicate increasing susceptibility to regime shift (Brock and Carpenter 2006).

Ideally, modeling results will support a program of *monitoring* key indicator variables capable of identifying system stressors and vulnerability; and policy and management can be adjusted to avoid unintended consequences of human-generated stresses.

Given a complex system model that has been validated, *simulation* experiments – shocking the model purposefully, to learn how it reacts – can be conducted to explore system response and identify vulnerabilities. It is also possible to *experiment* with the system itself, by "poking it with a stick" so to speak, i.e. stimulating and/or stressing it purposefully to learn at least a little about how it may respond. Obviously, caution is advisable when experimenting with complex systems in the real world. A serviceable approach might involve "baby steps" experimentation and careful monitoring of outcomes.

In principle, we can often gain information and understanding via purposeful *cross-sectional comparative research*. By examining the experiences of others who face different circumstances and/or have undertaken different strategies, we may be able to reveal relationships between circumstances, actions, and outcomes, perhaps even causes and effects – and indeed much research effort goes into attempting exactly that. However, this approach may be of more limited usefulness in the case of complex systems. Once on a given path, we cannot experience the paths not taken,[7] so we are much less effective at learning directly about those paths; in short, the path we take shapes our knowledge and our opportunities for learning going forward. The cross-sectional approach remains feasible when the complex systems involved are of modest size and scope, so that people and organizations operating in different systems can be found and studied readily. But opportunities for a cross-sectional approach are limited when dealing with large-scale systems, and entirely absent in the case of global systems.

Novelty and management in complex systems

Novel interventions and outcomes

In Chapter 3 we saw that novelty plays an important role in the case for precaution. ORM may well be adequate for addressing chance of harm arising because outcomes are generated by a random process. However, chance of harm can also arise because we do not understand the system that generates outcomes, and because the system itself is non-stationary, and ORM is challenged seriously in these cases. In these cases, surprises (outcomes that were not in the *ex ante* outcome set) may be experienced. At this point, the question is: in what ways does complexity increase the likelihood of novelty and surprises?

Two sources of novel outcomes were distinguished (Chapter 3): a novel intervention may be introduced into the system, which reacts in unexpected ways leading to novel outcomes; or a complex system exposed to cumulative stress under business-as-usual (e.g. unsustainable harvests or pollution loads) may experience drastic regime-shift. In the case of novel interventions, complexity is not a necessary condition for novel outcomes – PCBs and MTBE turned out to be persistent toxics in simple and complex systems – but intuition suggests much richer outcome sets in complex systems. In the case of novel outcomes from cumulative stresses of familiar kinds, complexity increases the chance of novel and threatening outcomes (regime shifts), perhaps with little warning – in the worst case, unpredicted system collapse.

Managing complex systems

If we seek to manage complex systems in some way – possible goals include adjusting the system to improve its performance as we see it, preventing threatened regime shifts, returning to a prior regime, promoting a shift to a regime we think would be more desirable, and promoting system resilience – we would need to expend resources and energy, that is, encounter costs. The costs of intervention may be small or enormous, threshold phenomena may induce discontinuities in costs, and system response to intervention may be unpredictable – it all depends on system properties, and it is unlikely that we know as much as we need to know about them.

The possible avenues for learning discussed above – reductive research, complex systems modeling, monitoring, simulation, experimentation, and cross-sectional comparative research – may improve our knowledge and ability to predict outcomes. Nevertheless, it is likely that the limits to what can be learned and what can be predicted will remain fairly close at hand. Rather than manipulating a system we fully comprehend, we are often reduced to poking it with a stick, watching how it responds, and trying to figure out what to do next. This, in caricature, is the idea behind *adaptive management* (Box 5.3), but that concept is introduced here with serious purpose because it provides a richer perspective on the process of learning as we manage. Ideally, adaptive management is a structured iterative process that aims to

Box 5.3 Adaptive management

Period 1	Period 2	Period 3	Period 4	Thereafter
Plan Implement Monitor Adjust				
	Plan Implement Monitor Adjust			
		Plan Implement Monitor Adjust		
			Plan Implement Monitor Adjust	
				Plan Etc, …

reduce uncertainty over time by managing in modest incremental steps and monitoring of system outcomes carefully.

Adaptive management seems more like groping in the dark – groping intelligently, and systematically monitoring the outcomes, but groping nevertheless – than scientific risk management. Complexity challenges the very concept of scientific risk management, which assumes more predictability than complex systems can promise.

Complexity and high damage but unlikely events – taking big risks seriously

If utilitarian decision criteria and simplistic models of how the world works characterize ORM thinking, both have been questioned seriously. As we saw earlier, Chichilnisky (2000) has shown that, given an expected utility approach, the standard assumption of bounded utility induces an under-appreciation of catastrophic possibilities.

Recently, Weitzman (2009) has provided a telling example of how simplistic thinking about how the world works supports under-statement of the potential for catastrophe: the ORM focus on most likely outcomes reflects bell-curve thinking – the normal statistical distribution focuses attention on central tendency – whereas a proper appreciation of the statistical distributions we actually face would focus attention on catastrophic possibilities that are not only possible but non-trivially likely. Examining the predictions of warming from the leading climate models (Figure 5.2), he observes that,

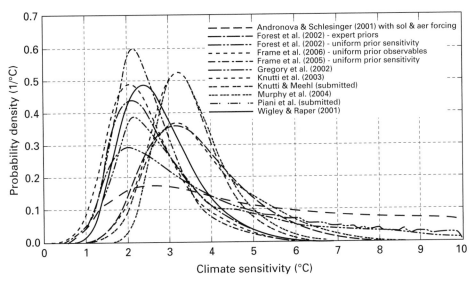

Figure 5.2   Predicted probability distributions for global temperate increase (Meinshausen 2006)

while policy analysts focus on the most likely warming scenarios, most of the models generate warming probability distributions strongly skewed toward the high end of the temperature-change range. The models suggest non-trivial probabilities (around 5–7 percent) of catastrophic warming (say, a 7°C increase in global temperatures): the obvious implication is that risk assessment and management should pay much more attention to improving estimates toward the tail of the distribution.

At one level, this is a purely statistical argument: the distribution of outcomes is skewed toward the high-damage end (i.e. it is fat-tailed), so catastrophic warming should be treated as a serious possibility, rather than submerged by a focus on much less harmful "most likely" scenarios. But Weitzman argues that the fat tail is no mere statistical quirk, but a logical outcome for complex systems composed of many stochastic variables and sub-systems: cascading probabilities in complex systems generate the fat tails. He offers a "dismal theorem" showing that exposure to catastrophic risks can be potentially unlimited.

Roe and Baker (2007) provide a foundation for Weitzman's conjecture that fat tails are an inevitable outcome for complex systems. They show that the feedback mechanisms in the climate system generate systematically skewed distributions of temperature increases, and that the "breadth of the distribution and, in particular, the probability of large temperature increases are relatively insensitive to decreases in uncertainties associated with the underlying climate processes" (p. 629).

Weitzman sums up his argument with an aphorism: when the potential harm is large, there is no justification for risk assessment practices that implicitly treat low and imprecise probabilities as precisely zero. This accords with Parfit's (1984, 1988) conclusion from an ethical perspective that there is no defensible reason for ignoring small chances of disastrous outcomes.

Weitzman's aphorism captures the reader's attention, but it sells his argument short. The argument is not just that there is no justification for ignoring the bad tail of the outcome distribution when the bad possible outcome is catastrophic, but that conventional thinking (mis)informed by the bell curve vastly underestimates the probability of catastrophic outcomes.

Earlier, it was noted that the decision criteria typical of ORM do not address coherently the possibility of surprises. The discussion immediately above suggests that the reductionist and often linear models that undergird typical ORM risk assessments are likely to understate seriously the likelihood and magnitude of surprises.

Implications

This chapter has addressed two fundamental challenges to ordinary risk management: (1) ORM decision criteria, while well enough adapted to chance of harm arising from known random processes, are ill-adapted to chance of harm from surprises arising because we do not understand the system that generates outcomes, and because the system itself is non-stationary; and (2) the new and emerging understanding of complex systems increases, perhaps dramatically, the perceived likelihood of surprises.

Complex systems research challenges scientific risk analysis, which is reductionist and often linear in logic and assumption. Risk analysis attempts to calculate the mathematical likelihood that a new technology or substance will cause harm to the public or the environment. We might expect this sort of analysis to systematically underestimate the chance of surprises in complex systems (May *et al.* 2008) – and in practice, too often, harm has occurred long before the science catches up (Murphy 2009, and Box 5.4).

The bottom line is that high damage but relatively unlikely events offer a serious challenge to ORM with its commitment to weighing, one way or another, the costs and benefits of threat avoidance and mitigation (Jablonowski 2005). Weitzman (2009) argues that when the potential harm is large there is no justification for risk assessment practices that implicitly treat low and imprecise probabilities as precisely zero. Parfit (1984, 1988) points

Box 5.4 Asbestos: harm, evidence, and political will – a case study in playing catch-up

Scientific risk analysis has not been very effective at predicting effects within complex systems. The risk analysis model that has long been used in the USA attempts to calculate the mathematical likelihood that any new technology or substance will cause harm to the public or the environment. The trouble is that it has not been very effective in predicting effects within complex systems. Too often, harm is widespread long before the science catches up (Murphy 2009).

Near the end of the nineteenth century, the use of asbestos increased dramatically as a result of the industrial revolution. Asbestos was used in the manufacture of more than 3,000 products including textiles, building materials, insulation and brake linings. Asbestos was used even for filtering water. As far back as 1906, asbestos was suspected of harming human health. In 1911, studies of asbestos on rats suggested harm. In the 1930s and 1940s cancer cases were reported in asbestos workers. Despite the evidence of severe health risks related to exposure to asbestos dating to much earlier times, the use of products containing asbestos continued to grow in the USA until the mid-1970s, when the US Environmental Protection Agency and Occupational Safety and Health Administration began to regulate asbestos. Not until 1999 was there a complete ban on asbestos in the European Union. Unfortunately, legislation cannot undo the damage that was done to those who worked in asbestos-related jobs for a full century before it was banned.

The history of asbestos use in Britain is similar. By 1900, the first health effects were documented in Britain and, not long after, asbestos-related deaths became commonplace. Yet it took a whole century to deal with the problem – it wasn't until 1999 that the British government finally imposed a total ban on new uses. Remediation of existing asbestos in buildings proceeds with deliberate speed. Around 3,500 people a year still die from asbestos-related disease in Britain.

For years, governments and corporations alike denied the risk of asbestos, paralyzed in the face of mounting evidence and of pressure to act (Willis 2001).

out that there is no ethically defensible reason for ignoring small chances of disastrous outcomes. Yet ORM seems unable to offer consistent and coherent responses to these challenges.

Conceding that ORM does a reasonably good job of handling the kinds of risk problems to which it is well adapted, there remains a need to supplement it with approaches that can be invoked in the case of high damage but unlikely events. This conclusion suggests that there is scope in risk management for something along the lines of the precautionary principle. However, the PP has attracted controversy and a variety of specific criticisms. In the end, the case can be made only for a PP that withstands or circumvents those PP criticisms that are substantive. It is my task in Part III to define and justify such a PP.

NOTES

1 Meier and Randall (1991) provide a review and interpretation of that literature.
2 But Robert Martin (http://plato.stanford.edu/entries/paradox-stpetersburg/) finds a way both to accept this practical conclusion and defend classical decision theory: "Classical unrestricted theory … tells us that no amount is too great to pay as an ideally rationally acceptable entrance fee, and this may be right. What is reasonable for real agents, limited in time, patience, bankroll, and imaginative capacity to do, given the constraints of the real casino, the real economy, and the real earth, is another matter, one that the theoretical core of classical decision theory can be forgiven for not specifying."
3 My standard commentary on the financial crisis as it was unwinding in the autumn of 2008 began with: My daughter, a relatively junior attorney at one of the big downtown law firms, called me at work a few weeks back, and said "All this talk of financial crisis has me worried, Dad. What do you think?" I replied "Don't ask me. I'm an economist – I'm committed to the theory that this can't possibly be happening!"
4 In Chapter 9, we consider a question that is interesting in this context: under what knowledge conditions is a regime switch in simulation output reason enough for taking possible regime switches seriously *ex ante*?
5 Narain *et al.* (2007), offer an economic account of irreversibility as benefits nonseparable in time, which seems compatible with path dependence as the term is used here.
6 This raises difficult questions of responsibility. Ignorance is the usual excuse offered *ex post* for unintended harmful consequences. Yet complexity theory provides warning enough, it seems, at least to be alert for unintended harm and to take steps to minimize it. Worse, when harm arises from foolhardiness – that is, betting against harmful outcomes known to be possible – the "unintended consequences" excuse seems thoroughly vacuous.
7 Robert Frost (1920) captures the notion:
  Two roads diverged in a yellow wood, And sorry I could not travel both
  …
  Oh, I kept the first for another day!
  Yet knowing how way leads on to way, I doubted if I should ever come back.

Part III

Defining and justifying a coherent precautionary principle

6   A defensible precautionary principle must withstand these challenges

Ordinary risk management was developed from formal analysis of games of chance (lotteries, card games, etc.) where the outcome set can be defined precisely. Possible outcomes can be enumerated and their probabilities calculated precisely. Because ORM was modeled on the "games of chance" paradigm, the ideal application of ORM is to games of chance. In Part II, we saw that ORM does a reasonably good job of handling the kinds of risk problems to which it is well-adapted, i.e. idiosyncratic risks in stationary systems where the outcome set is stable and well known.

ORM typically applies utilitarian decision criteria to simple Newtonian models of the real world. However, simple Newtonian models are often misleading, attributing more stability and predictability to the real world than is justified. The potential for high damage but unlikely events is greater than is commonly understood. We are beginning to understand that complex systems may not be stationary in the sense that stationarity is attributed to Newtonian systems (or simple games of chance), which suggests that complex systems have the capacity to generate surprises (outcomes that were not in the *ex ante* outcome set) and unknown unknowns. Furthermore, utilitarian decision criteria are better adapted to manageable risks – where possible outcomes can be specified, probabilities are knowable, and risks are idiosyncratic – than to surprises, unknown unknowns, and systemic risks. All of this suggests scope in risk management for something along the lines of the precautionary principle, perhaps to supplement ORM in those cases that stretch it beyond its limits.

However, the PP has attracted controversy and a considerable variety of specific criticisms. In the end, the weaknesses of ORM do not provide sufficient reason to justify a role for the PP in risk management. The case can be made only for a PP that withstands or circumvents those PP criticisms that are substantive and potentially damaging. It is my task in Part III to define and justify such a PP. To get started, in this chapter I consider a select set of sweeping objections to the PP. To be considered here, an objection must be targeted at the PP in general (not just particular PP specifications or applications), it must have acquired some prominence in the scholarly literature, and it must have passed an informal filter for seriousness (either I concede that it is serious or I observe others in the literature taking it seriously). The set of such objections addressed here may not be comprehensive. However, to the extent that most of the major objections are captured, it could be conjectured that a PP capable of dealing effectively with these objections, one way or another, might *prima facie* be taken seriously.

PP is meaningless, self-defeating, and incoherent

I begin by considering a set of criticisms claiming that the PP is meaningless, self-defeating, and incoherent. Claims of this kind would be devastating, should they be in some sense validated.

PP is meaningless and self-defeating

In his widely noticed book *Laws of Fear*, Sunstein (2005) defines his task as to critique an extreme version of the PP, effectively "avoid all risk," because (he claims) more moderate and circumscribed versions are mere platitudes providing no practical guidance. Thus, moderate versions of PP may be uncontroversial, but only at the price of being uninteresting. It is correct that the injunction to avoid all risk is self-defeating, because there is risk in every conceivable course of action including the no-action alternative. The problem is that no serious PP proponent defines PP as an injunction to avoid all risk. Serious PP proposals (e.g. UNESCO 2005) are focused on risks that pass some test of seriousness.[1] In this critique, Sunstein is simply playing tennis with the net down – critiquing a version of PP that serious PP supporters would be unwilling to propose or defend. More moderate and nuanced versions of PP are "uninteresting" only if real life, real problems, and real solutions are uninteresting.

While the "meaningless and self-defeating" criticism attacks a straw-man version of PP, it highlights the polar extreme case of a concern that has been expressed by many commentators: risk–risk trade-offs, where some kinds of risks may be exacerbated in the attempt to manage other kinds (Box 6.1 and Hansen *et al.* 2008), are not taken seriously enough in many PP formulations. *Prima facie*, this concern should be given due consideration. ORM risk

Box 6.1 Risk–risk trade-offs – a pesticides example

Gray and Hammitt (2000) identified eight categories of countervailing risks that could potentially be exacerbated by a ban on use of organo-phosphate/carbamate (OP/C) pesticides.

Target Risk	Countervailing Risk
Neurotoxicity from chronic consumer exposure to OP/C insecticides	Cancer risk from substitute pesticides
	Neurotoxicity from substitute pesticides
	Other toxicity effects from substitute pesticides
	Cancer and other toxic effects from higher levels of natural pesticides in foods
	Negative impact on economy → decreased nutrient intake
	Negative impact on economy → adverse health effects
	Decreased farm income → adverse health effects on farm families
Acute toxicity to farm-workers applying OP/C insecticides	Acute toxicity to farm-workers applying substitute insecticides

assessment done right includes a thorough accounting of risk–risk trade-offs and seeks to estimate net change in risk induced by alternative actions. A PP that seeks to inform ORM and constrain its domain should take risk–risk trade-offs seriously, too.

Bottom line: Taking risk–risk trade-offs seriously suggests that a serious PP should be specified carefully so as to direct it toward risks that are in some sense unusually serious. Furthermore, procedures for implementing PP should include provisions for mitigating risk–risk trade-offs (Chapter 9).

PP is logically incoherent

M. Peterson (2006) claims to provide informal and formal proofs that the PP is logically incoherent. Incoherence of PP is taken to mean that PP would recommend some actions that are less-preferred than alternative feasible actions. That kind of incoherence, of course, is contextual; it depends on what we are assumed to know and to value. Peterson defines PP as a class of criteria that are lexicographic in the probability of fatal outcomes (i.e. probability of fatal outcomes is the only consideration in choosing among alternative actions and, of course, lower probabilities are preferred).[2] He assumes that people can enumerate the complete set of possible outcomes and can evaluate them in terms of preference; we know the probability of each possible outcome; our preferences are complete, asymmetric (if x is preferred to y, it cannot be true that y is also preferred to x), and transitive; and we can rationally trade off the probability and value of outcomes including fatal and non-fatal outcomes (that is, there is some increase in the probability of a bad but non-fatal outcome that we would judge as compensating exactly for a given decrease in the probability of a fatal outcome, and vice-versa). With these definitions and assumptions, Peterson shows that PP is incoherent, because decisions using criteria along the lines of ORM would lead to actions that we would prefer to actions recommended by PP.

Of course, given Peterson's set-up we should not be surprised at his result. He assumed conditions ideal for ORM: a complete enumeration of the outcomes with each possible outcome assigned a known probability; and rational preferences that are complete over fatal and non-fatal outcomes and their probabilities, such that trade-offs between outcome values and probabilities can be specified. It is not that these conditions just happen to be ideal for ORM; rather, ORM decision rules were derived formally from exactly these kinds of conditions.

So, what Peterson actually showed is that a person applying rationality axioms and facing ideal conditions familiar to economists would choose ORM rather than a precautionary restraint. This is reasoning of impregnable circularity, since ORM is exactly what one gets when one derives optimal decision rules from economic rationality assumptions and ideal conditions. Barrieu and Sinclair-Desgagné (2003) also noted the inconsistency of PP and the expected utility framework for decision making under risk and uncertainty.

Bottom line: If the virtues of ORM are conceded, as is the underlying premise of Part II, the scope for a meaningful PP is concentrated on the class of cases where conditions ideal for ORM are absent.

PP is redundant

At the opposite pole to claims that PP is meaningless, self-defeating, and incoherent are claims that PP is redundant given that we have ORM.

PP is just one piece of ORM done right

This claim usually takes the form of an argument that the ORM theory of decision making under risk and uncertainty, the hallmarks of which are utilitarian decision rules and rationality assumptions, allows for risk aversion and corner solutions (Gollier *et al.* 2000, Gollier and Treich 2003). A corner solution is a case where it is optimal to impose a quantity restriction (perhaps, but by no means necessarily, at the zero level) on risky undertakings. If ORM admits strong risk aversion, and is open to quantity restrictions that may go so far as to prohibit certain actions thought to be "too risky," then some might argue that the whole PP controversy is moot. Gollier (2001) and Farrow (2004) take the argument a step further, by arguing that ORM in practice encourages additional pragmatic safeguards in high-risk situations.

However, even if ORM is open in principle to strong risk aversion and prohibitions of actions thought too risky, one might expect continued controversy about the legitimacy of strong risk aversion and prohibitory decisions in the ORM framework. After all, strong risk aversion and prohibitory restrictions have at best the status of special cases in the ORM framework.

People who want to see precautionary policies invoked systematically for some class of very risky actions may be uncomfortable assigning these sorts of decisions to a fundamentally utilitarian decision framework, where everything is a matter of preference and nothing is a matter of principle. ORM may admit caution, or even precaution, but it does not guarantee it.

Bottom line: If PP were just one piece of ORM, and in that role satisfied all reasonable demands for precaution, it would be redundant in a world where ORM was well developed and implemented comprehensively. So, to avoid redundancy, an important desideratum in the following chapters is that the PP framework outlined be distinguishable from ORM both logically and practically. In Chapter 10, I address in more detail the distinction between utilitarian precaution and principled precaution.

PP privileges our worst fears and anxieties rather than engaging our hard-earned rationality

This class of objections to PP highlights again the contest between utilitarian rationality and principled precaution, but does so in ways that seek to elevate utilitarian rationality while assigning principled precaution to the domain of fear, panic, superstition, and anti-science and anti-progress motivations. Not surprisingly, one strand of this critique pits the experts with their commitment to rationality against the ordinary public, which is assumed to be susceptible to irrational fears and cynical manipulation by interested parties.

Sunstein (2005) argues that PP is inherently responsive to panics, even the unfounded ones, and too attentive to the ordinary public, which is given to irrational fears and susceptible to manipulation by various interest groups. In contrast, he argues, ORM is the province of experts who can be trusted to insist on scientific evidence and respond rationally to it.

This complaint raises at least two distinct issues, and I propose to separate them in the following way. The first is an argument addressed to evidentiary standards: because PP endorses precautionary intervention in response to uncertain harm, the evidentiary standards for triggering a precautionary action are (claimed to be) too low. The second issue concerns the role of the ordinary public in risk policy and management: because (it is claimed) research has shown that the ordinary public tends toward irrational response to uncertainty and PP is responsive to claims of uncertain harm, it empowers the "nervous Nellies" among the public and the interest groups that seek to manipulate their fears.

1. PP is foolish because it can be invoked by unfounded panic

I take this as an argument that the evidentiary standards for invoking PP are too low: PP threatens the general well-being (it might be claimed) because it would endorse drastic and disruptive action to avoid harm that is uncertain and, in the extreme, speculative (Sunstein 2005). ORM is mostly about dealing with demonstrated harm. However, every version of PP tackles head-on the issue of what action might be justified by uncertain harm:

- Uncertainty about harmful consequences *does not justify failure to take precautionary action* (Bergen Declaration 1990).
- Plausible but uncertain harm *justifies precautionary intervention* (UNESCO 2005).
- Uncertain harm *requires precautionary intervention, and the burden of proof is assigned to the proponent of the proposed risky action* (Wingspread Statement 1998).

The distinctions among these versions of PP (here paraphrased, with emphasis added to highlight differences, and arrayed from weaker to stronger) pale in comparison with the difference between PP and ORM. All versions treat precautionary intervention as a serious option, and all would endorse its application in response to uncertain harmful consequences.

PP justifies pre-emptive action and lowers the evidentiary requirement for action, yet it should not be assumed that there are no limits to how low the evidentiary requirements may fall. It would be hard to defend a PP with inadequate defenses against drastic remedies provoked by unfounded panic. A coherent defense of PP must address the issues of how great should be the potential harm, and how much (and what kinds of) evidence of potential harm is enough, to justify precautionary intervention.

Bottom line: An essential piece of the task ahead is to address the issue of knowledge and the relationship between evidence and remedy – what can be said about the kinds of evidence that would justify invoking more or less drastic precautionary interventions, and can approaches and procedures be designed that would make precaution less intrusive? Chapters 8 and 9 include extensive discussion of evidentiary issues in the context of PP.

2. PP tilts decision authority away from the experts and toward ordinary people who are susceptible to various cognitive biases and group effects that systematically distort their assessments of risk

I take this as an argument mostly about people and their capacity to arrive at the right answers to difficult questions involving scientific uncertainty about probability and magnitude of potential harm. It concerns what we believe about the capacity of ordinary people to deal coherently with incomplete and perhaps contradictory evidence about threat of harm. The opposing positions are conventionally framed as:

(i) Ordinary people have demonstrated behavioral tendencies to decide and act irrationally in the face of risk. They are prone to panic and susceptible to manipulation by special interests. At the level of policy and institutional response, rational response to threatened harm requires specialized study, learning, information, and discipline, and is therefore the province of experts.

(ii) Given access to information and the discussion in the media, and opportunity to talk among themselves, people have a way of figuring things out and coming to reasonable conclusions, even about matters of risk and potential harm. The process might be messy, and perhaps no individual gets it right, but individual errors tend to cancel out and people in aggregate tend to get risk roughly right.

In support of the first position, Sunstein (2005) marshals a substantial body of psychological research on risk perception and decisions under risk (Kahan *et al*. 2006, Kahneman *et al*. 1991). He cites several sources of systematic mis-assessment of risk among ordinary people:

- The availability heuristic – the kinds of examples that stick in people's minds (often extreme examples) unduly influence assessments of risk.
- The salience of new versus familiar risks – people tend to overstate new risks relative to familiar risks that may be much more dangerous.[3]
- Neglect of (or insensitivity to) probabilities – in assessing new and scary threats, people tend to be inattentive to changes in the probability of harm.
- Loss aversion – people are more distressed by a loss from the *status quo* than they are pleased by the same-sized gain.
- Endowment effect – individuals value things in their possession more than they valued the same things before they acquired them.
- The role of affect – emotional response to the nature of the threatened harm is a strong predictor of how people evaluate risks.
- Group polarization – when individuals engage in deliberations over risks and how to abate them, they typically end up accepting a more extreme version of the views with which they began (Sunstein 2005, p. 98).

If this were all there is to say on the subject, it would amount to a strong case against taking the risk assessments of ordinary people seriously. Then, the case for Sunstein's parentalist position – because ordinary people get risk systematically and seriously wrong we have little choice but to place our trust in expert risk assessment and management – would seem unassailable.

Rather than defend the second position (that people in aggregate tend to get risk roughly right) directly, Kahan *et al*. combine it with a third consideration: research has shown that culture is cognitively prior to fact – i.e. worldview tends to shape what propositions people believe about the consequences of actions – and mutually inconsistent views of particular risks are often manifestations of different worldviews. They argue that this emerging understanding rather completely undermines Sunstein's argument against taking ordinary people's assessments of risk seriously. But Kahan *et al*. are much less sure about the normative implications of their own position:

… it is not clear that incorporating cultural cognition into the science of risk perception reduces the complexity of reconciling rational risk regulation with democratic decision making … If risk disputes are really disputes over the good life, then the challenge that risk regulation poses for democracy is less how to reconcile public sensibilities with science than how to accommodate diverse visions of the good within a popular system of regulation. (Kahan *et al.* p. 1073)

As Kahan *et al.* make clear, resolution of this controversy (especially the kind of resolution that they propose) would not by itself resolve the issue of what role in risk assessment and risk management should be reserved for the ordinary public.

Bottom line (a): A two-pronged approach seems appropriate. In what follows, I pay serious attention to the relationships between scientific evidence and pre-cautionary remedies (Chapters 8 and 9), and to procedures for informing ordinary people and consulting them in decision making (Chapters 12 and 13).

An implication often claimed for the two main arguments addressed in this section – the evidentiary standards for triggering a precautionary action are too low; PP attends too closely to the fears of a public that that gets risk seriously wrong; and interest groups play cynically upon these human frailties in order to influence policy outcomes (Wexler 2006) – is that PP would undermine business-as-usual, and stifle innovation and economic growth (Bailey 1999, Guldberg 2003). There is a variant of this argument directed explicitly to fears that science would be stifled (Harris and Holm 1999, 2002; Foster *et al.* 2000). It is clearly important to conceptualize and design precautionary remedies that are calibrated to provide precaution without stifling innovation. Such remedies can be outlined in principle, and examples can be found of regulatory institutions with just that kind of mission, e.g. the (US) Food and Drug Administration. The FDA serves as a stylized case for study (Chapter 9) – how it operates, whether and how it could work better, would expedited approval of new drugs with more systematic follow-up of users work better, and for what sorts of cases? What does a closer look at the FDA imply for precaution, more generally?

Bottom line (b): In what follows, I pay serious attention to the conceptualization and design of precautionary remedies that are calibrated to provide precaution without erecting undue impediments to innovation (Chapters 9, 12, and 13).

PP is best understood as a well-intentioned but non-binding endorsement of precaution

Commentators who are convinced that PP is incoherent if taken literally may nevertheless resonate to the good intentions that underlie the injunction to precaution.

PP is best understood as a kind of soft norm

A soft norm is little more than a statement of a widely-honored value, at best a non-binding normative standard – in this case, an appeal to precaution in the face of possible adverse consequences.

Mandel and Gathii (2006) are convinced, but not entirely so, by Sunstein's (2005) dichotomy: the strong PP is meaningless but weaker versions are mere platitudes. Nevertheless, they concede perhaps too much. The amendment they offer attempts to shore up the weaker versions of PP by raising their status from platitudes to soft norms. The practical import of PP as a soft norm would be to provide opportunity and process for bringing health and environmental risks to public attention, without predetermining any particular resolution of the issue at hand. As a soft norm, PP would help direct the use of decision-maker discretion in situations where it applies (p. 1073).

Such a soft norm would have a status perhaps akin to that of the so-called Hippocratic Oath. "Above all, do no harm" expresses an important caveat (be alert to the harm that treatment itself may cause), but cannot be taken literally in a world where well-intentioned, prudent, and effective intervention may nevertheless be intrusive and risky, and the recovery slow and painful.

However, as we conclude in Chapter 3, reasonable attempts to provide the Hippocratic Oath with clearer normative import can be successful, but the result depends on what additional considerations are brought to bear. Depending on additional normative input, the following decision criteria may result: the benefit–cost, expected value, and expected utility approaches that are common in risk management, and two approaches outside the usual range of risk management: a stronger stand that calls for asymmetric treatment of uncertain but potential disproportionate harm, and a weaker stand that calls only for sensitivity regarding possible unintended consequences. The point is that, while the Hippocratic Oath does not in itself yield clear guidance given the complexities of the real world, it can serve as a building block for a coherent decision framework.

One could argue that a soft norm undergirds the call to precaution, perhaps something like "do not take actions that pose unreasonable risks to society." This is not a bad place to start – there is social and political virtue in being clear about the things we value, and it makes sense to value avoidance of unreasonably risky undertakings – but a serious PP must offer more than just a soft norm. The real work of fleshing out a PP framework follows from commitment to a precautionary norm, and involves relating appropriate remedies to the nature of the threat and the evidence of potential harm, all in the context of social commitments to an array of complementary, competing, and conflicting principles and values.

Bottom line: Soft norms should not be trivialized – there is social and political virtue in being clear about the things we value – but a serious PP must offer more than just a soft norm. The agenda for Chapters 7–10 is to conceptualize and flesh-out a precautionary *principle* that avoids Sunstein's charge of meaninglessness but offers more, substantively and procedurally, than a soft norm.

The PP debate is just a quarrel about who bears the burden of proof

Following earlier versions of PP that focused mostly on establishing the legitimacy of intervention to prevent uncertain harm (e.g. the Bergen Declaration 1990), the Wingspread Statement (1998) raised the ante by adding that the proponent of a risky action bears the burden of proving that it is safe. Perhaps because it is so easy to caricature the PP debate as a stand-off between PP supporters demanding proof that proposed actions are safe and opponents demanding proof that they are harmful, some commentators have treated the assignment of the burden of proof as the heart of the issue.

The PP debate is just a quarrel about who owns the null hypothesis

Parson (2000) relates the burden-of-proof issue to the language and conventions of hypothesis testing, where two kinds of errors are possible: a true hypothesis might be rejected, and we might fail to reject a false hypothesis. Scientific tests are usually constructed as tests of a null hypothesis, typically that the treatment has no effect. There is a reason why this hypothesis is labeled the "null." The motivation for most projects is the researcher's hope and expectation that the null will be rejected leaving the alternative hypothesis – that the treatment has the predicted effect – as the tentatively accepted empirical finding.

Empirical knowledge is thought to be advanced, and the research project is considered a success, on those occasions when the null hypothesis is rejected. Yet, by convention, it takes overwhelming empirical evidence to reject the null hypothesis. We are so accustomed to the norm of requiring high levels of confidence (typically at least 95 percent) for rejecting null hypotheses that it is easy to lose sight of the motivation for such standards. These norms have become established in empirical science because they seem to erect about the right-sized barrier against accepting empirical propositions into the body of tentative scientific knowledge. The guiding intuition is that the right-sized barrier should be high because it seems much more harmful to science to accept an erroneous proposition than to reject an unproven claim that might be true. That any wiggle-room at all is acceptable (in the ordinary case, no more than 5 percent chance of falsely rejecting the null hypothesis) is a concession to the randomness thought to be an unavoidable characteristic of empirical evidence.

For many other uses we make of empirical knowledge, we simply do not hold evidence to a norm of 95 percent confidence. The norms relating to confidence in knowledge for action are quite different to those for accepting empirical propositions into the body of scientific knowledge. Individuals and organizations take a wide variety of actions – including many actions that commit our time and resources – with less than 95 percent confidence that the outcome will be as predicted. On the other hand, there are contexts where we customarily demand much greater security of expectations. Ninety-five percent confidence that the plane will not crash during my flight, or the bridge will not collapse while I'm crossing it, is just not good enough. Furthermore, the risks we are willing to accept are context dependent. If our default prospects are grim, as may be the case for someone with a debilitating disease that frequently is fatal, we may willingly submit to harsh and intrusive treatments that have only modest chances of success. On the other hand, we expect the risks of serious harm from ordinary cosmetics or pain pills used according to directions to be vanishingly small.

So, the standards pertaining to knowledge for action are quite different from those for rejecting a null hypothesis in empirical science. The domain of PP is the set of cases where harmful outcomes are plausible but uncertain, and PP is proposed to provide a framework for decision about the course of action in those cases. The issue of "proof" relevant to PP is about knowledge for action. Context matters a lot, in the knowledge for action case; and context includes the likelihood of a harmful outcome from the proposed action, the magnitude of potential harm, and the nature of the default outcome which may also be uncertain and potentially harmful, as well as the uncertainty or ignorance attached to our estimates of these likelihoods and magnitudes. There is another facet of context that matters to this discussion. In the precautionary context we are dealing with plausible but uncertain threats of future harm, where plausibility must be established, along with likelihood and magnitude of threatened harm. Yet it seems we do not have settled norms of "proof" for plausibility.

We might expect a coherent *precautionary* principle to set an evidentiary standard higher than merely "crying wolf" but lower than is appropriate for admitting empirical findings to the scientific knowledge base. Then the null hypothesis (and its implicit assignment of burden of proof) will be *ipso facto* less important. There will be work to do on both sides of the argument – establishing that (the thing or act) is potentially harmful, and making the case for its safety. Who "owns" the null hypothesis – or, equivalently, is the conjecture of harm or no harm treated as the null hypothesis? – matters a lot when the burden of proof is strongly asymmetric, e.g. it requires at least 95 percent confidence to reject the null. But it matters much less when the burden of proof is more nearly symmetric; in that case, there will be serious work to do both to establish a plausible threat and to make a case for the safety of the proposed action.

The preceding discussion has been about the importance of whether the "harm" or the "no harm" hypothesis bears the burden of proof. I have argued that the context of the precautionary principle is different in many ways from that of scientific hypothesis testing, and these differences are such as to make the assignment of burden of proof less central in the PP case. There is another piece to Parson's critique: that the PP debate is *just* a quarrel about who owns the null hypothesis; i.e. that there is nothing else at issue. To the contrary, I would argue that there are many other considerations at issue, including the most important of all: whether the fundamental policy stance to threats of harm should be precautionary, or whether it should be mostly about waiting until harm is established, preventing further harm, and mopping-up the damage that has happened already.

It might be argued that these questions – how the burden of proof should be assigned, and whether the fundamental policy stance should be precautionary or reactive – are merely two sides of the same coin. That is, it might be argued, precaution implies that safety bears the burden of proof whereas reactive protection is activated by proof of harm. However, the mapping between policy stance and burden of proof is by no means so rigid. True, in the US the Food and Drug Administration takes a precautionary stance and requires proof of safety before approving new drugs for general use, while the Environmental Protection Agency relies most often on post-release control of pollutants activated only after harm has been established; but the mapping does not have to go that way. Sequential filters for harm – pre-release testing in research facilities and post-release follow-up in the field – could be devised and each of the filters could be set in various degrees on a fineness–coarseness scale (Box 6.2). Intuitively, the filter should be finer (i.e. the

Box 6.2 Stylized strategies for protection from harm – combining pre- and post-release filters

	Pre-release		Post-release		
Case	Null Hypothesis	Filter	Null Hypothesis	Filter	Protection
1	harmful	strong	harmful	strong	strong
2	harmful	strong	safe	weak	intermediate
3	safe	weak	harmful	strong	intermediate
4	safe	weak	safe	weak	weak

required confidence in "no harm" greater) where the magnitude of the potential damage is greater; and it seems there would be some trade-off between fineness of the filters in the pre- and post-release stages, and perhaps an optimal sequence to achieve some desired level of public safety. The idea of pre-release filters can be expanded to a sequential and iterative pre-release testing framework that encourages learning and adaptation to information revealed. All of this suggests a much more nuanced view of precautionary and reactive approaches to protection from harm than "it is just a debate about who owns the null hypothesis."

Bottom line: The task ahead is to develop standards of evidence – typically higher than merely "crying wolf" but lower than are applied for empirical scientific propositions – for things and acts that plausibly could harm us. These standards of evidence are likely to be contextual, paying attention to the likelihood and magnitude of potential harm, broadly defined, with and without precautionary intervention. Strategies involving a sequence of pre- and post-release filters, and iterative approaches that encourage learning, should be taken seriously.

PP is not a complete and coherent stand-alone decision rule

Several related criticisms of the PP focus on its perceived incompleteness as a decision rule, and its lack of readiness for routine implementation. I do not disagree – PP is incomplete as a decision rule, and it is not road-ready for implementation in the real world; but I do not see these concerns as valid criticisms of PP.

To see why, let us start at the beginning: what reasonably can, and cannot, be expected of a principle that informs policy and management; and how do principles differ from laws and rules? To begin, consider principles in moral reasoning. Principles are general statements of normative moral positions for a class of concerns. Examples familiar to economists include "change that benefits some while harming none is morally desirable" and "each person's autonomy is morally valued." They can be formulated from moral intuitions and are, in that sense, logically prior to complete moral systems.[4] Yet, the absence of a complete and dominant moral theory (Williams 1985) provides good reason for taking moral principles seriously. As we might expect, some principles are so compelling that they are recognized by many competing moral systems.[5] To call a moral statement a principle does not grant it lexical priority over other principles – in complicated (that is, interesting) exercises in applied ethics, important principles will come into conflict and resolution requires a weighing of the principles involved and the facts of the case. Yet, a principle is much more than a preference – we feel a serious moral loss when we have to compromise a principle in a particular case. Finally, agreed principles provide not policies but a frame for policy resolution that anticipates and accounts for competing and conflicting principles.

Principle has a similar meaning in law. A legal principle is not a complete theory of normative law, but must be interpreted in ways that anticipate and account for competing and conflicting principles. To call a statement a legal principle does not grant it lexical priority over other legal principles. Agreed principles cannot be implemented directly – a principle provides a powerful argument in a particular direction, but does not determine a specific outcome (Cooney 2004) – but must be operationalized in laws, rules, guidelines, etc.

If the precautionary principle is viewed as a principle, then it succeeds if it serves as a principle that guides law and policy, in the sense that it embodies a considerable moral intuition to be consulted along with other pertinent principles and values when the issues it addresses come into play. A valid frame for resolving policy issues must anticipate and account for competing and conflicting principles and must be operationalized in laws, rules, and guidelines, which can then be interpreted and applied to particular cases.

Now, we are prepared to consider some specific criticisms that have been directed at PP.

PP contains no normative content

M. Peterson (2007) claimed that the PP lacks normative content. His specific charge is that it cannot guide action and decision because it is not structured and used as a stand-alone rule that tells us what to do and what not to do for each possible input of information. Here, Peterson is simply demanding too much. The PP is positioned as a principle, a general statement of a serious normative position for a class of concerns. It has normative content relevant for action and decision, but it alone cannot and should not tell us exactly what do to in every specific case. A stand-alone rule that passes Peterson's test of completeness simply would not be a principle.

There are about twenty different formulations of the PP in circulation, so how can it be taken seriously in real-world (law and) policy (Sandin 1999)?

First, can a principle that has been expressed in a considerable variety of formulations be taken seriously as a principle? The answer, I think, goes something like this. All of the PP formulations embody a common soft norm, perhaps something like "do not take actions that pose unreasonable risks to society." They begin to differ from each other when their authors try to build a more complete PP framework relating appropriate remedies to the nature of the threat and the evidence of potential harm, all in the context of social commitments to an array of complementary, competing, and conflicting principles and values. That discussion is an essential part of the process of bringing principles into practice, and its existence provides no argument against taking PP seriously. Second, the complaint that the PP cannot be taken seriously in law and policy ignores the distinction between a principle and a road-ready rule. The on-going discourse about how the PP might apply to real-world policy and management is an essential part of the process of developing rules, policies, and practices that are informed by principles.

Similarly, discussion of the PP in the context of international trade seems mostly to proceed in legalistic terms (D. Peterson 2006). Such discussion by its nature seeks enforceable interpretations, and is uncomfortable with competing definitions, and inconsistencies (either internal or with other widely-honored values). However, the precautionary *principle* cannot be expected to provide alone the clear, coherent, and enforceable laws demanded by critics in the trade literature. At best, it is just one of the touchstones for the on-going process of developing trade laws and interpretations that respect precaution in the face of certain kinds of threats *and* a broad slate of legitimate trade concerns.

The PP conflicts with other important values that good law and policy would surely respect, and it fails to provide clear instructions for resolving these conflicts (Lofstedt *et al.* 2002)

Again, what reasonably can be expected of a principle? A principle captures a serious moral intuition, but enunciating a principle neither claims nor establishes its lexical priority over other principles. In complicated exercises in law and policy, important principles will come into conflict, and the frame for resolving those conflicts requires and directs a weighing of the principles involved, the values at stake, and the facts of the case.

The Sandin and Lofstedt *et al.* critiques and M. Peterson's (2007) claim that PP is devoid of normative content all share a common misconception. Critiques of the PP as incomplete, inconsistent with other considerable principles and values, and altogether not a good stand-alone decision rule simply misunderstand the nature and role of principles in moral and legal discourse.

Bottom line: In addition to formulating a coherent PP the task ahead requires thinking seriously about how to frame the PP within the context of competing, complementary, and conflicting principles and values.

Scope for PP – the tasks ahead

Some environmentalists have defined the PP as invoked by any and all actions that risk harm to nature (Raffensperger and Tichner 1999). At the opposite extreme, some economists (e.g. Farrow 2004) have defined it as (merely) introducing explicit risk aversion into the standard expected welfare maximization calculus. Neither extreme makes sense. Sunstein (2005), among others, has emphasized the foolishness of a PP that is invoked by any and all risks. On the other hand, a PP that goes no further than ORM is not merely redundant; it fails to grapple seriously with the well-recognized weaknesses of ORM in dealing with the problem of unlikely but potentially devastating possibilities.

This review of some sweeping objections to the PP has clarified the task ahead – to explore the possibility of developing a coherent framework for a PP that can be taken seriously. The goal is to outline and defend a meaningful PP that is neither foolish nor redundant. To justify a role for the PP in risk

Box 6.3 The tasks ahead

1. Conceptualize and flesh-out a precautionary *principle* (PP) that avoids the charge of meaninglessness, by directing it toward risks that are in some sense unusually serious.
2. Concentrate the search for a meaningful PP on the class of cases where conditions ideal for ordinary risk management (ORM) are absent.
3. Specify a PP that is more than a soft norm, in that it systematically relates appropriate remedies to the nature of the threat and the evidence of potential harm.
4. To avoid redundancy, specify a PP framework that is distinguishable from ORM both logically and practically.
5. Develop standards of evidence – typically higher than merely "crying wolf" but lower than are applied to empirical scientific propositions – for things and acts that plausibly could harm us.
6. Elucidate the relationships between scientific evidence and precautionary remedies, addressing the kinds of evidence that would justify invoking more or less drastic precautionary interventions.
7. Include provisions for mitigating risk–risk trade-offs.
8. Explore the design of approaches and procedures to minimize the intrusiveness and disruptiveness of precaution, while providing adequate protection from threats of harm.
9. Conceptualize and design precautionary remedies that are calibrated to provide precaution without erecting undue impediments to innovation.
10. Consider strategies involving a sequence of pre- and post-release filters, and iterative approaches that encourage learning and adaptation, and develop them in promising cases.
11. Think seriously about how to frame the PP within the context of competing, complementary, and conflicting principles and values.
12. Develop procedures for informing ordinary people, and consulting them in decision making.

management, it is not enough to show that there is scope in risk management for something along the lines of the PP. The PP has attracted controversy and a variety of specific criticisms. So, the criticisms raised against the PP must be examined and evaluated forthrightly. In the end, the case can be made only for a PP that withstands or circumvents those PP criticisms that are substantive. To foreshadow my conclusion, such a PP can be specified, but it is a heavily circumscribed PP. It does, however, target the risk management problems where the weaknesses of ORM are most evident. A PP that passes these tests would be able, in carefully specified circumstances, to justify remedies beyond those justified by expected welfare considerations.

To specify the task ahead a little more completely, the *bottom line* statements generated in this chapter have been assembled in Box 6.3, edited down to simple declarative statements, and re-ordered. The remainder of this book is addressed to completing these twelve tasks.

NOTES

1   Not only that, serious PP proposals are moderated by various provisions addressed to the domain of application, the kinds of actions that are acceptable in pursuit of precautionary objectives, protection of vulnerable groups from undue burdens, and in some cases, cost-effectiveness.

2   Peterson's critique seems addressed to a PP for individuals facing life or death decisions, whereas I argue (Chapter 8) that PP is better adapted to collective threats where individual exposure is in considerable degree involuntary.

3   It is not entirely clear to me that the salience of new risks should count as evidence of irrationality. It may make sense, in principle, to erase the slate and optimize over all relevant risks new and familiar, in the end choosing the preferred portfolio of risks from the feasible set. Yet, in practice, our risk portfolio is path-dependent. We work on managing the familiar risks, alert to the economic disruption that might be entailed in suddenly and drastically reducing existing risks that are woven into the economic fabric. When new prospects arise, we may be reluctant to embrace the new risks involved because we (perhaps correctly) assess the choice before us as simply adding a new risk to our portfolio rather than reducing net risk by trading a new risk for a greater but familiar old risk.

4   Often, efforts to work out practical responses to ethical challenges (e.g. environmental ethics) take legal or political form before they are understood as works of normative ethics.

5   Groups and individuals often disagree about moral theories, but may nonetheless accept a surprisingly large body of common principles. Thus, they may be able to achieve substantial social agreement about actions, even though their theories are incompatible. Taylor (1989) emphasizes the search for principles capturing and generalizing prior moral intuitions that transcend and precede moral theories – principles that (he argues) routinely go under-valued in standard moral epistemology, but are forced to the front by value pluralism.

7 Toward a precautionary principle framework: evidence, threat, and remedy

The objective of this chapter is to outline an approach to a potentially meaningful and coherent precautionary principle. Such a PP must make a distinct contribution beyond ordinary risk management to the policy and management toolkit for dealing with threatened harmful prospects, and it must survive the criticisms discussed in Chapter 6. Several commentators (Gardiner 2006, Mandel and Gathii 2006) have identified one part of the task – to strengthen the weak versions of the PP without succumbing to the criticisms that have wounded overly strong PPs. I would set the goal higher than Mandel and Gathii did, to specify a coherent PP that has more structure and force than a soft norm, but stop short of an imperative to avoid all risks.

Most formulations of PP mention something about potential for harm, something about uncertainty of harm, and something about the action appropriate to these circumstances (Bergen Declaration 1990, Wingspread Statement 1998, UNESCO 2005). The differences among them revolve around exactly what is said about harm, uncertainty, and action. Commentators have argued that the problems with these formulations are due to, or at least exacerbated by, rather weak connections between these three elements – harm, uncertainty, and action (Manson 2002, Hughes 2006). The framework offered in this and the next several chapters is intended to define a PP that explicitly relates harm, uncertainty, and action; and does it in ways that:

- structure the PP framework;
- take damage conditions, knowledge conditions, and remedies, and the relationships among them seriously; and
- do this in ways that define a coherent PP and its domain of application.

Harm. Given the uncertainty that premises most versions of the PP, I have argued that the relevant damage concept is **threat**, defined as chance of harm (Chapter 3).

To begin, consider *harm*: what can be said about the nature of the harm that might justify invoking a precautionary remedy? We can start by saying

Box 7.1 Threat – the "chance of harm" concept

Threat. The damage concepts in play in the literature include harm (which has clear meaning: damage, impairment) and risk which, unfortunately, is an etymological mess. The classical Knightian definition of risk is clear: a situation in which possible outcomes can be enumerated and their probabilities are known. But things are not so clear in common usage, where acceptable meanings for risk include: a chance of something going wrong; a hazard; and the statistical odds of danger. In common usage, risk jumbles the concepts of harm and chance, yet clarity is important to the PP discussion.

While *Knightian risk* has conceptual clarity, it captures only a small piece of the relevant range of chanciness. Uncertainty, gross ignorance, and unknown unknowns are much riskier (colloquially speaking) than Knightian risk (Chapter 3).

For these reasons, the damage concept used here is *threat*, defined as a chance of harm, an indication of impending harm, or a signal correlated with future harm.

something about the magnitude of harm – to avoid any implied imperative to avoid all risks, it seems intuitively obvious that the PP should be focused on situations where the potential harm is great. *Prima facie*, ordinary harm is manageable with ORM.

Many authors have suggested that the case for the PP requires (or at least is strengthened by) a claim that the potential harm is irreversible. Given the problems raised by the concept of irreversibility (irreversibility is hardly the binary concept – reversible/irreversible – that the term suggests; and there are several interpretations of irreversibility in the literature, most of them vulnerable to one or another criticism), I have settled on a particular concept of irreversibility – consequential path dependence – to capture the rationale for considering the future options that might be foreclosed by today's choices (Chapter 5). In a complex system, a regime change that raises effective barriers to reversion would count as an instance of strong irreversibility. Yet, strong irreversibility is hardly a requirement for taking foreclosed options seriously – any commitment to a path that changes the prospects of the system consequentially and imposes non-trivial costs of reverting to the prior path raises concerns about foreclosed options.

It is hard to imagine an instance of great harm that would not involve consequential path dependence. A system that survived an event that caused great harm would, at the very least, experience a serious set-back. Recovery may take a long time, and require great sacrifice during that time;

and there is no general assurance that the *status quo ante* can be restored. The most likely prospect for such a system is that it finds itself on a new and different path which, at least initially and perhaps for a long time, will deliver opportunities that are less fulsome (by whatever measure) than the prior path.

Now, consider *chance*. The simplest concept of chance is Knightian risk, where outcomes are generated by stable random processes, which implies that the outcome set and associated probabilities are knowable (as in games of chance, where outcomes probabilities can be calculated precisely). This kind of chance is about the system, not about us. If we have done our homework, we can predict the odds of various outcomes and the expected value of a trial – our inability to predict the actual outcome of a single trial is due not to lack of knowledge, but to lack of clairvoyance.

If we don't fully understand the system that generates outcomes, we face serious impediments to knowing the outcome set and associated probabilities. In the best possible case, we face Knightian uncertainty where the outcome possibilities are known but not their probabilities. If we cannot specify the complete set of outcome possibilities, we are beyond uncertain; we are in a state of gross ignorance, facing Rumsfeld's "unknown unknowns" (Chapter 3). We are more likely to find ourselves in this kind of situation when the system itself is complex and/or non-stationary, which implies that outcomes are less predictable and, in the extreme less imaginable, than they are in stationary random processes. Genuine surprises, even for the well-informed, are possible and perhaps likely. These kinds of chance are about the system *and* (typically, I would conjecture) about us. In complex systems, chance is not a matter of simple frequency, and knowledge means less (e.g. knowing that things are in considerable degree unpredictable) and is more difficult to acquire. System outcomes may not be predictable (especially outcomes a few steps down the road), and we are likely to have inadequate knowledge and understanding of the system.

Knightian risks of modest harm are manageable with ORM. No surprise here – ORM was invented for just such risks. As argued in Chapter 5, ORM, being constructed around the case of stylized games of chance, is inadequate and in extreme cases misleading when applied to risks beyond that case – the possibility of great harm and our inability to specify the outcome set and assign probabilities are warning signs. So, we would want to direct a coherent PP toward the cases that have one or both of these characteristics, i.e. cases that raise *serious threats*, defined as cases where the likelihood of serious harm is non-trivial.

Uncertainty. Most PP formulations are premised on the uncertainty of harm. Uncertainty, of course, invokes the idea of chance and, as you have surely noticed, I have settled on *threat* (defined as chance of harm) as the most serviceable damage concept for our purposes. Immediately above, two kinds of chance are distinguished – chance because outcomes are unpredictable in some objective sense (not everything we need to know is knowable), and chance because we do not know everything that can be known. Distinct as these sources of uncertainty are, we recognize a tendency for both kinds of chanciness to increase with increases in complexity – there is a sense in which less is knowable and that which is knowable is harder to know, in complex systems.

Nevertheless, there is value in maintaining the conceptual distinction between chance due to the unpredictability of outcomes, and uncertainty due to our failure to know everything that is knowable. Assigning the uncertainty in the real world to the damage concept – chance of harm – allows us to treat the remaining uncertainty, due to the incompleteness of our knowledge of the systems that generate outcomes, as a knowledge issue.[1] The knowledge concept we will use is *evidence*. The concept of evidence is not about outcomes and likelihoods, it is about our knowledge of outcomes and likelihoods.

There are three major issues that should be addressed in an evidence criterion.

First, the evidence that would justify a precautionary interruption of business as usual should be scientific and credible – one cannot take seriously a PP that can be triggered by unfounded panic. The evidence underpinning decisions should reflect accurately what is broadly accepted in the scientific community, what controversies remain active and why, and what remains uncertain or unknown.

Second, science and the institutions that support it should have adequate defenses against distortions (including inflated threat-claims that may induce unfounded panic, and unwarranted insistence that there is nothing to worry about) and the cynical exploitation of cognitive biases in service of various interests.

The third issue is, given scientific uncertainty, how much credible evidence of threat is enough to trigger a precautionary response? We should perhaps entertain the prospect that the acceptable amount and quality of evidence might logically be related to the magnitude of potential harm. We may take precautions against catastrophic harm even when we are quite unsure if it might be experienced in the default (without precautions) case.

In very general terms, it makes sense that a coherent PP should be activated only in those cases where there is *scientifically credible evidence* of plausible serious threat.

Action. It took a little work to settle on *threat* as our concept of potential harm (incorporating the elements of chance in real-world outcomes), and *evidence* (addressing the uncertainties introduced by our lack of knowledge) as our knowledge concept. We can decide on the appropriate concept of action more readily, I think. In the context of the PP, action means *remedy*: given credible evidence of plausible threat, what remedy is appropriate?

Several kinds of considerations are relevant to our choice of remedy.

First, given the objective to explore the coherence of a PP that would make a distinct contribution beyond ORM, the set of appropriate remedies surely must include some that are stronger (in some sense) than those that would be prescribed by ORM. The standard instruments of ORM may well have roles in a precautionary policy package, but a meaningful PP would not be bound to using only the ORM toolkit and using it only in ways consistent with ORM.

Second, compared with ORM a PP is more likely to invoke *precautionary* remedies in advance, to head-off uncertain threats. Again, this is a matter of going beyond ORM – the ORM toolkit includes techniques and procedures for evaluating the risks associated with novel interventions, yet these are not implemented routinely and consistently prior to release of the novel organism or substance, or adoption of the new technology. For example, in the US, new pharmaceutical drugs intended for human use are tested (too exhaustively and rigorously, some critics contend) prior to general release. In contrast, synthetic chemicals are released into the environment without serious oversight; any harmful effects are discovered belatedly and debated extensively before remedies are invoked. By that time, the substances have become embedded in the business-as-usual economy, with the effect that remedies are expensive and disruptive. PCBs, and more recently MTBEs for use as octane-enhancers in gasoline, are examples (see also Box 5.4, sketching the case of asbestos, which is not synthetic).

In the case of novel outcomes from overstressing systems in the course of business-as-usual, opportunities for pre-release testing are rare. However, precautionary approaches may still deviate from ORM by emphasizing early warning, which is likely to be enhanced by research and investment, and perhaps lowering the barriers to implementation of remedies.

Box 7.2 A stylized iterative, sequential release protocol

1. Conceptual evaluation and pre-screening (chemistry, biology, genetics, etc.)
2. Laboratory testing *in vitro*
3. Laboratory testing with whole organisms
4. Release protocol with iteratively less restrictive quarantine
   - Step 1
   - Step 2
   - Etc.
5. Release for general use (conditional on what, if any, restrictions?).

Third, PP remedies may be designed to enhance scope for research and learning, to reduce ignorance, narrow the uncertainties, better specify the possible outcomes and probabilities, and develop and test strategies for avoidance, mitigation, and adaptation – in the best case, gross ignorance may be reduced to manageable risk.

Fourth, serious PP proposals are likely to place high priority on the quest for affordable remedies, which are helpful in building and sustaining coalitions in support of solutions among contemporaries, and inter-generational commitments to solutions (UNESCO 2005).

Placing high priority on scope for learning and affordable remedies points us toward sequential, iterative remedies. Iterative procedures are likely to reduce the up-front cost commitment to precaution, and generate knowledge to support the sequential decision process. For example, a novel intervention (say a genetically modified organism, GMO) might be taken through a sequential process such as outlined in Box 7.2, with decision points (stop/ proceed to the next step) at the end of each step. Ideally, serious harm can be prevented, while introduction of benign GMOs would proceed with only modest delay and modest cost for research and testing.

Fifth, because precaution may impose costs and economic disruption – especially in cases where the threat has become embedded in the economy or emerges from overstressing systems in the course of business-as-usual – remedies should include specific policies to reduce or mitigate disproportionate negative impacts of precaution on particular locations and/or socio-economic groups (UNESCO 2005).

In general terms, a coherent PP should address cases where there is scientifically credible evidence of plausible serious threat, invoking *remedies that reach an appropriate threshold of potency.*

An ETR framework

To summarize, I propose to advance the quest for a meaningful and coherent precautionary principle – one that has more force than a soft norm, but stops short of an imperative to avoid all risks – by addressing the allegedly weak connections between the three key elements – harm, uncertainty, and action. To this end, consider an **ETR** framework:

If there is evidence stronger than **E** that an activity raises a threat more serious than **T**, we should invoke a remedy more potent than **R**.

A PP of this form would focus on the key issues: what sorts of threats might invoke precaution, what sorts of evidence might justify a precautionary intervention, what sorts of remedies might be appropriate, and how might these key elements, **E**, **T**, and **R**, interact? The agenda for Chapters 8 and 9 is to begin answering these crucial questions.

NOTES

1   Note that, by defining the knowledge issue in terms of the incompleteness of our knowledge of the systems that generate outcomes (and distinguishing earlier in this chapter between lack of knowledge and lack of clairvoyance), I am suggesting a different view of knowledge and information than that found, e.g. in the quasi-option value and real options literatures. These literatures contrast *ex ante* and *ex post* knowledge, so that if *ex ante* we knew the outcome set and associated probabilities perfectly we still would not know the *ex post* outcome. The wait for more information that looms so large in this literature is waiting for nature to roll the dice. This literature performs a useful service in emphasizing the costs of premature commitment – if we have two alternatives and only one of them is relatively serviceable regardless of the next-period outcome, that characteristic raises the value of the more flexible option. The problem with the concept of waiting until informed, as I see it, is that the wait for certainty in the *ex post* sense is never over – the future is always ahead of us, and there is no assurance that tomorrow will bring less uncertainty than today. We would be better-off, I conjecture, to work at learning more about the workings of the system(s) that generate outcomes, so that we can better characterize outcome possibilities and their likelihoods, and use that information effectively in risk management.

The knowledge issue as defined here has more in common with the perspective of Gollier *et al.* (2003), who contrast chance in the real world and scientific uncertainty. They write of managing the wait for better information, but they acknowledge that the wait may change what we know, not how the real world works.

8 Threat and evidence

The ETR framework for a coherent precautionary principle relates evidence, threat, and remedy (Chapter 7). Among the desiderata for a coherent PP, the most basic are that it be neither foolish nor redundant. To avoid redundancy, PP remedies should include some that go beyond ordinary risk management (ORM); it follows that some (but, one would hope, not all) PP remedies may be costly and intrusive. Given that invoking the PP in any particular case may be a big step, two kinds of foolishness readily can be imagined: the injunction to avoid all risks is foolish because it is impossible in the real world, and even approaching it would be paralyzing; and a PP that can be invoked by unfounded panic would be obviously foolish.

In this chapter, these issues are addressed directly. I start with the *threat* (the chance of harm), asking what kinds of threats might justify precautionary remedies. Given that PP remedies include some that go beyond ORM, it makes sense that the PP focus on threats that are in some sense beyond the ordinary, that is, involve some combination of non-trivial chance and extraordinarily great possible harm. If the PP is directed to these kinds of threats, it is far from an injunction to avoid all risks.

We made a conceptual distinction (Chapter 7) between two kinds of chance – chance because real-world outcomes are unpredictable in some objective sense (not everything we need to know is knowable), and chance because we do not know everything that can be known. The first kind, chance in the real world, is assigned to the damage concept, *threat*; and the second kind, chance due to our lack of knowledge, is assigned to the knowledge concept, *evidence*. The concept of evidence is not about outcomes and likelihoods, it is about our knowledge of outcomes and likelihoods. An appropriate evidence criterion needs to be calibrated to avoid susceptibility to unfounded panic and to unwarranted complacency.

It is *prima facie* plausible that the threat and evidence criteria may be linked in various ways. For one thing, it makes sense that the evidence criterion be related to the magnitude and likelihood of the threat – for example, if the threat is horrific we may want to invoke precaution on the basis of even relatively weak evidence. Furthermore, we recognize a tendency for both kinds of chanciness (due to real-world unpredictability, and to the incompleteness of our knowledge) to increase with increases in complexity – there is a sense in which less is knowable and that which is knowable is harder to know, in complex systems. The following discussion of threat and evidence addresses the unique issues of each separately, and the interactions between them.

Threat

It makes sense to focus the PP on threats that are in some sense extraordinary. These are exactly the kinds of threats that pose difficulties for ORM, which is better suited to situations where outcome possibilities are of modest magnitude and normally distributed with modest variance. To evaluate threats, we are interested in two aspects of the probability distribution: the magnitude and the likelihood of harm. We start with a baseline case (Figure 8.1). Outcome values are on the horizontal axis, and outcome probabilities are on the vertical axis. The thin bell-curve depicts a normal distribution of outcomes, with fairly narrow dispersion (extreme outcomes, good and bad, are quite unlikely), centered on the neutral outcome. The expected value of this lottery (or project) is exactly zero. In a world with ideal incentives, it would be hard to find anyone advocating this project strongly. In the real world, there may be advocates among local and/or sectoral interests expecting to gain at the expense of the broader society, but benefit–cost analysis would be sufficient to expose the lack of expected net benefits of such a project.

A more relevant case is depicted by the thicker-lined bell-curve: the expected value of outcomes is positive, yet there is a substantial probability of negative outcomes. Decision makers guaranteed many opportunities to play this lottery are likely to act in a risk-neutral manner, but risk-aversion might be observed among players who cannot be sure they will have repeated opportunities. This is the paradigm case of insurable risk – under ideal conditions, insurers will be willing to take-on a large portfolio of such risks and people who are not assured of multiple chances (e.g. automobile owners) will be willing to pay insurers a little more than the expected value of their losses to do so. ORM is well able to deal with risks like this.

Because benefit–cost analysis will identify prospects that do not have expected net benefits, and ORM is able to deal with risks that are readily insurable, a defensible role for a coherent PP must be found elsewhere. To get

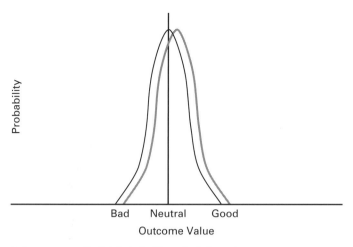

Figure 8.1   Outcomes normally distributed with modest dispersion

started, we confine our search to cases with positive expected net benefits. From there, it makes sense to focus on threats that involve extremes of magnitude and/or likelihood of harm. The extremes of magnitude and likelihood of harm are captured by the adjectives disproportionate and asymmetric, respectively.

Disproportionate addresses the magnitude of possible harm, and describes the case where the outcome set includes possibilities of harm, even if not very likely, that is disproportionately greater than the relevant prospects for good. So, what exactly are the relevant prospects for good? Two plausible concepts of "relevant prospects for good" are the expected value of outcomes, which we already have stipulated is positive, and the mode (i.e., the single outcome value that is most likely) which will be positive for most kinds of distributions that generate positive expected value. In Figure 8.2, the outcome distribution (the thick dashed bell-curve with widely dispersed outcome possibilities) is normal – and thus symmetric around the mean, median, and mode – and expected value is positive. We can think of the outcome distribution as continuous (in which case we would represent it with an unbroken curved line), or discontinuous with a few discrete possible outcomes (as illustrated). For comparison, the baseline case (Figure 8.1) – a compact normal distribution around a modest expected net gain, where potential losses are readily insurable – is reproduced as the thin bell-curve. Given a normal but widely dispersed distribution of outcome values, there is a possible outcome very much worse than the most likely outcome is good. Statistically, there is a possible outcome far out on the negative tail of the distribution.

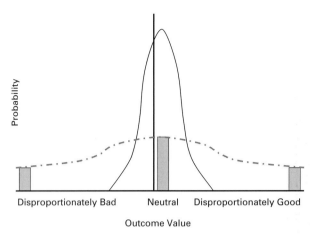

Probability

Disproportionately Bad   Neutral   Disproportionately Good

Outcome Value

Figure 8.2   Catastrophic possibilities with a normal outcome distribution – highly dispersed outcome possibilities

If the harm threatened is horrendous, or if it is merely very bad and we are not guaranteed repeated trials, a risk-averse posture may be reasonable. The non-trivial possibility of disproportionate harm may be reason enough to reject this prospect, even though there is also the possibility of a highly beneficial "nirvana" outcome. A non-trivial possibility of a disproportionately bad outcome is a plausible trigger for a coherent PP. A focus on disproportionate threats responds to the commonsense admonition, "Don't risk great harm in pursuit of modest benefit," where the mode – the most likely outcome – offers modest benefit.

While we have shown that disproportionately harmful outcomes may be possible with normally distributed outcome values, intuition suggests that disproportionate-harm outcomes are more likely to emerge from non-symmetrical outcome distributions. *Asymmetric* is an adjective describing likelihood – specifically, the disproportionately harmful outcome is more likely than we might expect if we applied the common default assumption that the outcome possibilities are distributed normally (as in the bell-curve) or symmetrically. Statistically, the probability distribution exhibits skewness and/or kurtosis such that great harm is more likely than it would be if outcomes were normally distributed. Weitzman's discussion of climate change (2009 – see also Chapter 5) addresses such a situation.

Figure 8.3 illustrates the concepts of disproportionate and asymmetric threat. All three diagrams are anchored on the neutral (no net harm or benefit) outcome. As in Figure 8.2, a normal distribution, with a modest net benefit as the most likely outcome and with relatively low variance, is provided

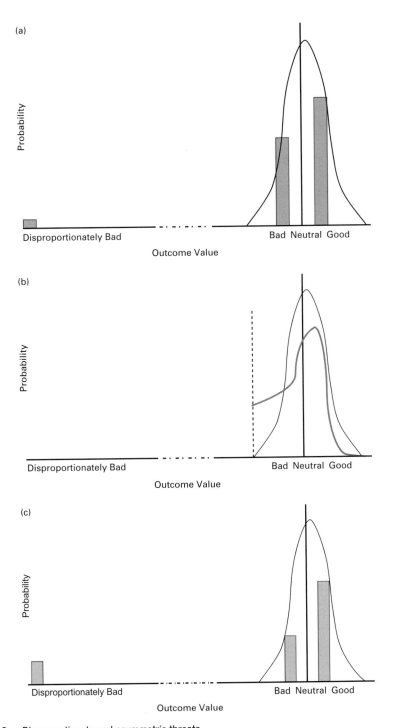

Figure 8.3   Disproportionate and asymmetric threats

for comparison. In Figure 8.3a, three discrete outcomes are possible: the most likely is a modest net benefit; modest net harm is also fairly likely, and extreme net harm has a low but non-trivial probability. That is, the outcome set includes a non-trivial possibility of disproportionate harm. This prospect involves a *disproportionate threat* of harm.

In Figure 8.3b, a continuous distribution of outcome possibilities (truncated at outcomes that are clearly bad but not disproportionately so) is illustrated, and compared with the normal distribution. Again, the most likely outcome is a modest net benefit. However, the distribution is asymmetric and is skewed toward harmful outcomes. Substantial (but, by assumption, not disproportionate) harm is more likely than it would be if outcomes were symmetrically distributed. This prospect can be said to involve an *asymmetric threat* of harm.

In Figure 8.3c, we return to the case of three discrete possible outcomes. In this example, a disproportionately harmful outcome is asymmetrically likely. Therefore we describe this prospect as involving a *disproportionate and asymmetric threat* of harm.

Cases where disproportionate harm is non-trivially likely pass a test of relevance for invoking the PP; asymmetric likelihood of disproportionate harm adds weight to the case for invoking PP (Box 8.1). Intuition suggests that D threats are likely also to be A – i.e. D threats are more likely to emerge when the distribution of outcomes values is skewed toward harmful outcomes – but there is no claim here that this is a general proposition. However, to reduce clumsiness in the exposition, I routinely use the phrase "disproportionate and asymmetric" to describe the sorts of threats that interest us most, rather than the more precise "disproportionate and, in many cases, asymmetric."

What kinds of threats are likely to be disproportionate and asymmetric?

Perhaps some things can be said about the sorts of threat that are likely to be disproportionate and asymmetric. To get started, consider the choice of an individual to participate in a clinical trial. Suppose that the individual has a disease that threatens grim prospects if left untreated, and standard treatments are unsatisfactory and relatively ineffective. The experimental treatment is considered promising but risky, and it has been through all the standard steps in testing prior to testing with human subjects. Participation in the trial is voluntary and the individual is well informed.

Should the individual invoke a personal precautionary principle and decline to participate in the trial? One can imagine a variety of reasons why

Box 8.1 PP-relevant threats – disproportionate and asymmetric?

A PP addressed to extraordinary threats might apply to situations where disproportionate harm is non-trivially likely – again, "Don't risk great harm in pursuit of modest benefit." Requiring that the threat be disproportionate (D) and asymmetric (A) dials-up the threat threshold a notch: disproportionate harm is more likely than it would be if outcome values were normally distributed. This raises a question: should we require that threats be both D and A in order to qualify as PP-relevant?

To begin, stipulate that the expected net benefit (of a proposed novel intervention, or of continuing on a business-as-usual course that may over-stress the system) is positive, $E(gain) > 0$. ORM would filter-out any proposals that did not meet this minimal condition. Then, we need to specify what it is about an extraordinary threat that would make it a candidate for PP-relevance. Plausible benchmarks for gain are $E(gain)$ and the net benefit of the most likely (i.e. modal) outcome – these are identical in the case of symmetrical outcome distributions, including the normal distribution.

Regarding the threat, four cases cover the relevant range of possibilities:
1. There is a harmful outcome that is non-trivially likely.
2. There is a harmful outcome that is *asymmetrically* likely.
3. There is a non-trivially-likely *D* outcome much worse than $E(gain)$, or modal gain, is good.
4. There is a *D* and *A* outcome much worse than $E(gain)$, or modal gain, is good.

Implications:
1. For the *ordinary harm* case, symmetrical distributions typically will not support invoking PP. Positive $E(gain)$ and symmetrically distributed outcome values implies that the harmful outcome possibilities are no worse than counter-balanced by the chance of good outcomes.
2. For the *ordinary harm* case, asymmetrical likelihood of harm will not in general support invoking PP. The limited nature of possible harm implies the likelihood of surviving a bad outcome and being rescued eventually by the positive $E(gain)$.
3. Where a *disproportionately harmful* outcome is non-trivially likely, PP may be justified despite symmetrically distributed outcome values and positive expected (or modal) net gain. If a *D* outcome would end the game or leave its participants with hugely diminished prospects going forward, it may be reasonable to invoke PP despite the counter-balancing chance of a very good outcome. This implies that PP should not be ruled-out for *D* cases, even in the case where probabilities are well-specified. This conclusion is contrary to the fairly common claim that uncertainty (i.e. a chancy situation where probabilities cannot be specified) is a necessary condition for invoking PP; but it is consistent with the earlier conclusion that utilitarian decision theory under risk fails to offer convincing responses to the low-probability high-damage case (Chapter 5).

4. Where a *disproportionately harmful* outcome is *asymmetrically* likely – more likely than would be the case with symmetrically-distributed outcome values – the *D* justification for invoking PP is strengthened by the *A* likelihood of the *D* outcome.

Conclusion, and a note on language: Given D, A is never truly necessary to justify invoking PP but it always adds weight to the case for invoking PP. Furthermore, intuition suggests that the D but not-A case (Figure 8.2) will be rare – most but not all D cases will also be A. Rigor suggests that the criterion for threats that are in some sense beyond the ordinary should be "disproportionate and mostly but not always asymmetric," which is correct but something of a mouthful. I beg the reader's indulgence henceforth to use the not-quite-rigorous term "disproportionate and asymmetric" as shorthand.

the potential subject might decline to participate, and a variety of reasons why he or she might accept this opportunity. But the threat of disproportionate and asymmetric harm is not likely to figure among these reasons – the potential participant may face a risk of serious harm from the treatment, but the risk of serious harm applies also to the alternative of foregoing the trial. Choices between potentially devastating afflictions and risky and intrusive treatments are literally awful, but the hazards are not disproportional and asymmetric.

Might a public policy response prohibiting the trial for precautionary reasons be justified? I think not, again because it is difficult to identify any disproportionate and asymmetric threat presented by the trial. Public policy may well have other valid roles. For example, policy may require that the treatment has been subjected to a detailed pre-release testing protocol prior to trials with human subjects (Box 8.2). Policy may reasonably require that participants have the indicated affliction, perhaps that they have exhausted other available remedies, that they be fully informed, and that they have consented voluntarily to participation. The concepts of full information and voluntary consent seem simple enough, but their application is not always simple and obvious, again suggesting a role for policy.

Suppose instead that the drug has been approved for general use and has been prescribed widely, as was the case with thalidomide in several countries at the beginning of the 1960s (Box 8.3). Note that patients in that situation enjoy much weaker safeguards than human subjects in clinical trials. They are treated as though, and are likely to behave as though, the treatment has been thoroughly tested and found to pose no extraordinary risks – official approval conveys explicit or implicit promises regarding safety. Accordingly,

Box 8.2 Novel outcomes and scope for pre- and post-release remedies

Thus far, we have drawn a distinction between novel outcomes that arise from novel interventions and those arising from over-stressing natural systems in the course of business as usual (Chapters 3, 5, 7, and 8). This distinction has important implications for remedies: pre-release remedies may be applicable to novel interventions, but not for surprise outcomes of business-as-usual.

There is also a third category: novel outcomes caused by interventions that were novel when they occurred but have long since diffused throughout the natural and economic systems. Asbestos (Box 5.4), thalidomide (Box 8.3), PCBs, and MTBE are examples. Serious damage is attributable to a clearly identified agent, but the time for pre-release remedies has long passed. The cause of harm is a novel intervention but, because it has already happened, the available remedies are limited to post-release measures.

Cause of novel outcomes	Available remedies
Novel interventions (ex ante)	Pre-release, post-release
Novel interventions (ex post)	Post-release only
Business-as-usual	Post-release only

one might expect much less attention to fully informing the patients and obtaining their consent.[1]

Certain specific birth defects increased promptly and sharply, and were traced to thalidomide (Box 8.3). The threat posed by thalidomide to pregnant women and their fetuses was clearly disproportionate and asymmetric – after all, the drug was prescribed for morning sickness (not typically a debilitating condition). The manufacturer promptly withdrew thalidomide from the market. It might be argued that withdrawal of thalidomide was not exactly precautionary, because the threat had been clearly demonstrated and the cause determined, whereas the PP is often recommended for cases where harm and causation are thoroughly uncertain.

Withdrawing thalidomide from the market was an *ex post* response, and it has proven impossible to rectify (or even to compensate for) all of the human damage that occurred. It can be argued that the thalidomide episode demonstrated a failure of pre-release testing in those countries where it was approved for general use. It was not approved in the US because one persistent scientist on the FDA staff reasoned that it might harm the fetus,

Box 8.3 Thalidomide – a novel intervention gone bad

Thalidomide (patented by the German pharmaceutical company Grunenthal in 1954) was found to act as an effective tranquilizer and painkiller, and was proclaimed as a "wonder drug" for insomnia, coughs, colds and headaches. Soon it was being used by thousands of pregnant women in Europe, Japan, Australia, and Canada to treat morning sickness. At the time, it was not thought likely that any drug could pass from the mother across the placental barrier and harm the developing fetus. Yet, about 10,000 children around the world were born with severe birth defects such as missing or shortened limbs because their mothers had taken the drug during early pregnancy. When doctors traced these devastating birth defects to thalidomide in 1961, it was withdrawn from the market.

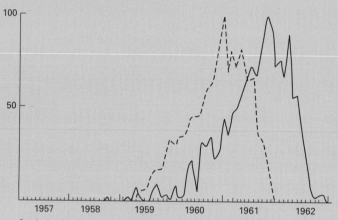

Graph showing the relation between the malformations of the thalidomide type and the sales of thalidomide (figure for Germany excluding Hamburg).

- - - Thalidomide sales (January 1961 = 100)

——— 845 abnormalities of the thalidomide type (October 1961 = 100)

Birth defects followed thalidomide sales closely, in Germany (www.health.org.nz/thalid.html)

Compensation settlements varied widely, with victims in Germany receiving only a fraction as much as their counterparts in Britain, and those in Italy and Spain getting no compensation at all. An estimated 3,500 victims are still alive today and are finding life increasingly difficult as they get older and their parents, their principal caregivers, become infirm or die. Some victims' advocacy groups, claiming that the original settlements were totally inadequate, are seeking to re-open the compensation claims (www.reuters.com/article/idUSL0286587320080403).

To summarize, a newly patented drug was released for general use and soon was widely prescribed in several countries. Serious harmful effects were soon evident, and the offending agent was withdrawn from the market. In retrospect, pre-release testing in the affected countries was woefully inadequate, and the task of addressing the damage post-release remains incomplete.

and its approval should at least be delayed to permit more exhaustive testing. The thalidomide episode led to changes in drug approval law and policies in many countries (Box 9.4).

Had pre-release testing exposed the threat entailed in prescribing thalidomide to pregnant women, a strong case could have been made for *ex ante* prohibition of its general use, and it seems likely that would have happened.

An argument can be made, instead, for releasing thalidomide for general use, provided that the risks involved were communicated clearly to physicians and their patients. With full information, the decision might be left in the hands of individuals and their physicians. However, this hypothetical policy response would likely have little effect in practice, because the manufacturer had strong incentives to decline to market the drug, given the prospect of poor sales, damage to the firm's reputation, and substantial liability exposure.

It seems clear that thalidomide was withdrawn from the market (whether by the manufacturer's self-interested decision or by policy action) because the risks involved were disproportionate and asymmetric to any benefit from relief of morning sickness. There is in fact some support for this hypothesis – thalidomide has subsequently been approved for use in treating certain much more serious afflictions, subject to a very strict oversight program (Box 9.9). If I am right in the conjectures immediately above, the record reveals a precautionary approach in the case of banning thalidomide for treatment of morning sickness, but a willingness to defer to informed choice in the case of using it to treat much more serious afflictions.

Suppose that individual exposure to the threat is strictly involuntary, as would be the case where a treatment is, say, added to the public water supply. First, the case for a public policy response is even stronger, because the exposure and the threat are collective. Second, it seems that collective threats from novel outcomes are more likely to be disproportionate and asymmetric. A collective threat might plausibly involve a chance of catastrophic harm, but it seems less plausible that the alternative (precautionary) action of prohibiting exposure would involve a similar threat. More likely, a precautionary prohibition may increase morbidity and/or mortality fractionally or, perhaps, the opportunity for a fractional decrease in mortality may be foregone (more likely, postponed). In cases of collective exposure, the typical outcome from precautionary action is not binary – literally life or death – but modest differences in the chance of life or death.

Involuntary exposure can arise from lack of valid information about the risks, as surely as it can from damage to systems upon which we are dependent.

For example, it can be argued that exposure was effectively involuntary, for the pregnant women who were prescribed thalidomide, not because thalidomide was added to the public water supply (it was not), but because they were not provided the necessary information to make an informed choice.

To summarize, disproportionate and asymmetric threats are likely to be concentrated among the class of threats that are collective in at least one of two senses: individual exposure is involuntary, and/or the threat impacts a larger system to which we are linked inextricably. This position has been developed above in the context of clinical trials and prescribed treatments for medical conditions, but it applies with at least as much force to the case of complex systems overstressed (e.g. by unsustainable harvests or pollution loads) in the course of business-as-usual.

Certain characteristics of threat situations seem more likely to pose the possibility of asymmetric and disproportionate harm

Here, complexity, novelty, and large spatial and/or temporal scale are highlighted.

Complexity. The resilience of complex systems – their tendency, following perturbations, to return toward their prior trajectory; and/or their capacity to tolerate disturbances while retaining their structure and function – may be undermined by sudden anthropogenic shocks that precipitate regime shifts, or by sustained anthropogenic pressure (e.g., harvest, or effluent inflows) that reduces resilience and increases vulnerability to regime shifts (Holling 2001, Folke *et al.* 2004; see also Chapter 5). Because regime shifts change the system in unpredictable ways (Folke *et al.*), the threats introduced may be disproportionate and asymmetric. Among complex systems, the least stable and resilient are more vulnerable, and it is harder to take effective avoidance/ mitigation actions for those that signal early warnings only weakly.

Novelty. New and untested phenomena (things and events) may introduce disproportionate and asymmetric threats. We have better knowledge of outcomes and/or probabilities associated with familiar phenomena and it is likely that research and experience already have mitigated some of the risks and eliminated the extremely harmful possibilities, which implies that the remaining risks are more likely to be manageable with standard tools.

Large spatial and/or temporal scale. If the effects of an action cannot be confined readily in space or in time, then the chances are exacerbated that threats will be disproportionate and asymmetric. Uncontrolled dispersion of an innovation that is novel and incompletely understood exposes us to the risk of large-scale damage, delayed detection and response and, eventually, very expensive and disruptive remediation. Confinement in space permits quarantining the innovation until we can learn more about any harm it may cause, and confinement in time permits destroying it before general release should its adverse effects raise sufficient alarm. These safeguards allow us to approach a program of innovation more confidently, because each potential innovation can be tested extensively under low-risk conditions (Box 8.2) prior to decisions about general release.

Are uncertainty and irreversibility essential characteristics of PP-relevant threats?

Scholarly publications (e.g., Arcuri 2007, Sunstein 2006) and official reports often specify uncertainty and irreversibility as essential characteristics of situations that call for precautionary intervention. It turns out that neither is essential, but for different reasons. An uncertainty requirement would rule out all cases where probabilities are known, including the high damage, low probability cases for which ORM alone does not have convincing answers. The problem with irreversibility concerns the ambiguity of the term itself (Chapter 5). Note also that the French Committee on Precaution proposed dropping irreversibility as a condition justifying PP on the grounds that irreversibility is inherently a prediction yet irreversibility is not always predictable (Noiville *et al.* 2006).[2] Nevertheless, it remains a sound intuition that the case for precaution is strengthened if reversion to something approaching the baseline state would be impeded by high costs and/or high thresholds of one or other kind.

Box 8.4 Focusing on disproportionate and asymmetric threats resolves some PP controversies

Reserving the PP for disproportionate and asymmetric threats resolves several major issues in the literature, including Sunstein's (2005) general charge of meaninglessness and several controversies about whether the PP is serviceable in various particular applications.

The PP is meaningless and self-defeating (Sunstein 2005). Sunstein's charge that PP is meaningless and self-defeating hinges on the claim that PP demands that all risks be avoided. A PP addressed to disproportionate and asymmetric threats is immune to this criticism. Note also that Sunstein's complaint is an extreme version of a rather common PP criticism – the PP does not take risk–risk issues seriously enough (Manson 2002). A PP aimed at disproportionate and asymmetric and threats cannot be dismissed so easily; in fact, Sunstein (2006) followed-up his 2005 anti-PP broadside by proposing a PP targeted at catastrophic risks.

Does PP apply to clinical trials? The PP seems not well adapted to guide decisions about the permissibility of clinical trials (Peterson 2007). Suppose participants are fully-informed, self-selected volunteers, each of whom has the condition for which the experimental treatment is indicated. With such a group, the threats related to treatment are less likely to be disproportionate to their individual defaults, which include grim possibilities if the ailment can be fatal or debilitating. They face hard decisions, but most likely not disproportionate and asymmetric threats. Suppose also that the public expects net benefits from the knowledge gained from clinical trials in aggregate, even if this particular trial turns out badly. It seems clear that this situation does not call for a precautionary prohibition, but it does call for vigilance that the experimental treatment has undergone exhaustive testing prior to experiments with human subjects, and that participation is limited to fully informed and consenting volunteers among those with the indicated condition.

Does PP apply to medical decisions for individuals? For individuals facing hard decisions about risky medical treatments, PP offers little guidance – again, the individuals involved face hard choices but most likely not disproportionate and asymmetric threats.

Does PP justify the "war on terrorism"? Serious authors have wondered whether the PP might endorse pre-emptive military strikes against "rogue states" believed to harbor terrorists (Wiener and Stern 2006). The threat of terrorism and the remedy of pre-emptive strikes against rogue nation-states would not qualify under this PP – where is the disproportion and asymmetry? A terrorist strike is a very bad outcome, but so too is provoking a war. Bronitt (2008) discusses use of deadly force to deal with serious aviation incidents, which seems to be a clearer case of asymmetric risk. A pre-emptive strike against non-state terrorist actors in remote locations (at the time of writing, the paradigm case is Osama bin Laden's suspected hide-out in the hills near the Pakistan–Afghanistan border) might represent an intermediate case where disproportionate and asymmetric threat is plausible, depending on the particulars. If the strike is ineffective and/or Osama's organization and alliances are decentralized, effective capacity for retaliation might survive a strike. Details are important.

Evidence

The concept of damage adopted here is threat, defined as chance of harm; and we have argued that a role for the PP is most likely to be found in the context of disproportionate threats (especially disproportionate and asymmetric threats). Our knowledge concept, evidence, addresses the matter of chance directly. Two kinds of chance can usefully be distinguished – chance because real-world outcomes are unpredictable in some objective sense (not everything we need to know is knowable), and chance because we do not know everything that can be known. To put it succinctly, the first kind of chance is about the world, and the second kind is about us.

Chance because the world is unpredictable. Much of the literature (e.g. Arrow and Fisher 1974, Gollier *et al.* 2003) focuses on the chance that remains because nature has not yet rolled the dice, that is, *ex post* outcomes are not revealed *ex ante*. In Knightian risk, which is the classical context for this kind of chance, the outcome set can be specified *ex ante* and the probabilities of each outcome can be calculated precisely. In that sense, we have perfect knowledge of the system that generates outcomes – our inability to predict the *ex post* outcome of a single trial is due not to lack of knowledge, but to lack of clairvoyance.

As noted earlier, this literature performs a useful service in emphasizing the costs of premature commitment – if we face two alternative courses of action and only one of them is relatively serviceable regardless of the next-period outcome, that characteristic raises the value of the more flexible option. Nevertheless, this concept of chance is limited, perhaps unduly so. The problem is that the wait for certainty in the *ex post* sense is never over – the future is always ahead of us, and there is no assurance that tomorrow will bring less uncertainty than today.

The more interesting kind of chance about the world arises because the system that generates outcomes is complex, perhaps non-stationary, and perhaps irreducibly unpredictable. These are the situations that give rise to uncertainty, gross ignorance, and the possibility that even the well informed will be surprised.

Chance because we do not know all that can be known. This kind of chance can, in principle, be reduced by investing time and resources in learning more about the workings of the system(s) that generate outcomes, not in a futile quest for clairvoyance, but so that we can better characterize outcome possibilities and their likelihoods, and use that information effectively in risk management.

While recognizing the inevitable interactions with chance because the world is unpredictable, the prime focus of our knowledge concept, evidence, is on chance because we do not know all that can be known. The overarching question regarding evidence is: Given that investing time and resources in learning tend to increase our knowledge but there are limits to what we can reasonably expect ever to know, how much evidence is enough to act upon?[3]

Not only is evidence costly, there are also costs of getting the decision wrong; and there are two ways to get to it wrong: committing to unnecessary precaution, and ignoring a threat of serious harm that eventuates. Obviously, we have a strong interest in finding an appropriate balance between costs of evidence and costs of wrong decisions.

For a coherent PP framework, the evidence criterion may be conceptualized as credible scientific evidence of plausible threat. The challenge is to put some flesh on the idea of credible scientific evidence.

To operationalize this criterion, we need to address the following key issues:

- The evidence underpinning decisions should reflect accurately what is broadly accepted in the scientific community, what controversies remain active and why, and what remains uncertain or unknown.
- Science and the institutions that support it should have adequate defenses against distortions (including inflated threat-claims that may induce unfounded panic, and unwarranted insistence that there is nothing to worry about) and the cynical exploitation of cognitive biases in service of various interests.
- Given scientific uncertainty, how much credible evidence of threat is enough to trigger a precautionary response?

Accurate reflection of the state of scientific knowledge

The evidence underpinning decisions should reflect accurately the state of scientific knowledge. We should be able to identify what is broadly accepted in the scientific community, what questions remain contentious and why, and what are the relevant topics where uncertainty or ignorance prevail. To do this, we need to sort through a cacophony of claims and counterclaims, as scientists jockey for attention abetted sometimes by media operating on the "man bites dog" principle, and interested parties pursue their agendas sometimes with insufficient attention to facts and reason. Yet, I am relatively optimistic that we, collectively, have ways of sorting things out.

Commonsense notions of what constitutes credible scientific evidence

It helps that there are commonsense notions of scientific credibility. There are commonsense distinctions between conjecture, hypothesis, theory, and scientific law, and I believe these distinctions are fairly well understood by the educated public. Testing against evidence from observation and experience, replication, and peer review are among the things that add to the credibility of scientific truth-claims. The credentials (training, accomplishments, and reputation) of the scientists making the claim, or reporting the result, provide some (albeit imperfect) indication of its credibility. It helps also, if the scientists have no obvious conflicts of interest. Consensus among the scientific peer group carries weight, yet attention should also be paid to qualified and respected alternative opinion.

In the case of a particular study, I believe the educated public attends to whether the researchers have appropriate credentials (training, accomplishments, reputation, institutional support), well-specified hypotheses have been tested, the methods used have been tested (the error rate is known, etc.), the data and analysis have been made available for review, the results have been replicated (ideally by independent researchers), the study has been peer reviewed, and respected peer scientists find the results and conclusions credible.

These commonsense notions of scientific credibility owe a lot to the received view of scientific method. Among the educated public, there is some deference to scientific authority, but it is leavened with an understanding that scientific claims are always tentative, and not all conjectures and preliminary results will stand the test of time.

Jurisprudence

US courts have addressed the issue of scientific credibility in contexts ranging from ordinary civil liability to issues of regulatory authority.

What are appropriate standards for admissibility of scientific and technical evidence in court? In two civil liability cases, *Daubert* regarding a prescription drug marketer's responsibility for birth defects and *Kumho Tire* which dealt with a tire manufacturer's responsibility in a fatal road accident, courts affirmed the admissibility of expert scientific testimony. The courts ruled that there are some hallmarks of what is credible in scientific testimony (the evidence and the methodology have been tested, the results have been peer reviewed and/or published, the potential rate of error is known, the evidence is generally accepted in the scientific community), and courts should look for these in judging admissibility.[4] The *Kumho Tire* decision extended the reach of *Daubert* by refusing to distinguish scientific and technical evidence, thereby applying *Daubert* to both.

Must regulatory actions be based on an objectively-sound scientific rationale? US courts have addressed the scientific foundations for regulatory action in a series of 1990s cases where plaintiffs have challenged environmental and safety regulations on the grounds that regulatory authorities have acted without adequate scientific reasons and evidence. The 1980 *Lead Industry Association* ruling had limited the role of the courts, when reviewing agency rule-making, to determining whether the regulator's policy choices were supported by the record.[5] From a plaintiff's perspective, this standard poses a formidable obstacle to challenging regulatory rule making.

However, in the 1999 *American Trucking Associations* case, the Court of Appeals for the District of Columbia opened the door for closer scrutiny of regulatory rule-making. The court struck down EPA's air quality standards for ozone and particulate matter after concluding that EPA failed to articulate an "intelligible principle" to serve as a foundation for setting environmental standards.[6] This decision suggests that courts may scrutinize regulatory rule making to ensure that rules are based on an objectively sound scientific rationale.

How much scientific evidence is enough to justify regulatory actions? In *AT&T Wireless*, the City Council of Virginia Beach, VA had denied an application for a conditional use permit under the city's zoning code for the construction of two 135-foot mobile phone antenna towers on the grounds that local residents had objected on aesthetic and related grounds.[7] Among other things the court ruled that, to meet the "substantial evidence" criterion, evidence marshaled to justify denying a permit need not be overwhelming: "more than a scintilla, but less than a preponderance" of the evidence is required. In *Cellular Telephone*, the court reaffirmed the *AT&T Wireless* view of what constitutes sufficient evidence to justify regulation, and added a "reasonable person" benchmark: rather than requiring a large or considerable amount of evidence, it required "such relevant evidence as a reasonable mind might accept as adequate to support a conclusion."[8]

While *Daubert* and *Kumho Tire* were thought by some commentators to raise relatively high barriers to science-based regulation, the *AT&T Wireless* and *Cellular Telephone* courts endorsed the legitimacy of regulation despite scientific uncertainty. That is, the court was reluctant to hold regulatory decisions at the frontiers of technology to evidentiary standards appropriate to areas where the science is more settled.

Must admissible evidence represent the scientific consensus? While courts commonly suggest that consensus among peers scientists adds weight to scientific evidence (for example, the *Daubert* court listed "the evidence is generally accepted in the scientific community" among the hallmarks of credible scientific testimony), there has been at least one quasi-judicial ruling that explicitly denies that consensus among scientists is essential. In 1998, Canada requested consultations with the European Community regarding measures imposed by France prohibiting imports of asbestos and products containing asbestos. The World Trade Organization Appellate Body ruled that member states are not obligated automatically to follow what, at a given time, may constitute a majority scientific opinion, but may rely, in good faith, on scientific sources which at that time may represent a divergent but qualified and respected opinion (Shaw and Schwartz 2005).

Bottom line

This brief review has affirmed that commonsense notions of scientific credibility are fairly well established, and that US court decisions have tended to endorse that commonsense view. This is not to claim that scientific controversies do not exist, or that they exist but are readily resolved in every case. Nor is it claimed that the scientific community is quick and unerring in its evaluation of novel scientific claims. None of those things is true. The claim here is more along the lines that, in the fullness of time, science tends to get it right.

At the very heart of the PP lies a sense that certain kinds of threats require a policy response now, not in the fullness of time. The PP is all about the justification for precautionary action to prevent uncertain harm. The court decisions cited above do not tell us what to do in the face of each new threat, real or imagined. But they do provide not only benchmarks for credible scientific evidence, but a clear endorsement of the legitimacy of regulating threats at the frontier of technology despite substantial scientific uncertainty (*AT&T Wireless* and *Cellular Telephone*).

The locus of wisdom about risk: experts or the public?

There is a vocal strand of scholarly opinion that is inclined to view the public as unreliable in the face of risk – overly sensitive to novel and emerging threats, and susceptible to cynical exploitation of cognitive biases to promote an exaggerated sense of concern about certain emerging threats. Sunstein (2005) cites behavioral research to argue at length that ordinary people simply get risk wrong (e.g. misperceive probabilities and make irrational choices under risk), and Wexler (2006), among others, has argued that "public interest" groups exploit cognitive biases – e.g. the salience of new versus familiar risks – to promote an exaggerated sense of concern about certain emerging threats. We are invited to conclude, therefore, that public decisions regarding risk should rely on expert risk assessment.

Sunstein (2008), citing the work of psychologists Kahneman *et al.* (1982) and Slovic (2000), highlights the following cognitive biases that, he argues, lead ordinary people to overreact to risk, especially new and emerging risks.

Loss aversion. People evaluate prospects relative to their *status quo* baseline, and tend to strongly prefer avoiding losses to acquiring gains. This would imply that, in risk situations, people are more impressed by the threat of loss than by the chance of gain.

Familiarity bias. People are much more willing to tolerate familiar risks than unfamiliar ones, even if they are statistically equivalent.

The availability heuristic. People tend to overestimate the magnitude of risks when examples come readily to mind.

Salience. People are more impressed with harms they have seen first hand (as opposed, say, to harms they have read about), and more impressed with harms experienced recently than those that happened some time ago. For example, people are more likely to buy flood insurance if floods have occurred recently.

All of this adds up to an argument that, in risk situations, people are more impressed by the threat of loss than by the chance of gain, but they do not and cannot grasp the full extent of risk in the world, and they systematically overstate new and exotic risks, salient risks, and risks that come easily to mind. To Sunstein, this argument serves two purposes: it attributes the motivation for precautionary policies to cognitive biases, that is, to systematic failures of human rationality; and it underpins the case that, in matters of policy toward risk, we should trust the experts rather than the public.

These findings from experimental psychology are not controversial – what is controversial is the meaning we attribute to them. Loss aversion is perhaps the most thoroughly confirmed, empirically, of these effects. It is less clear, however, that it should be considered a bias. If we assume that people's standard of living is precarious (as it has been for most of our history), the law of large numbers offers little reassurance to individuals – even if the odds favor a net gain over many trials, people with few reserves of resources are not assured many trials. From an evolutionary perspective loss aversion is fairly easy to explain, even if it is perhaps less serviceable to affluent individuals.

The remaining effects – familiarity, availability, and salience – are unsurprising at one level. Would we not expect that familiar risks might lose their shock-value, and that non-specialists (people who by definition are occupied mostly by other concerns) might focus most readily on "new" risks and risks that have caught their attention? Discussing familiarity bias, Sunstein (2008) suggests road accidents as a familiar risk that generates less concern than it seems to deserve. Certainly, road accidents have lost some of their shock value. But it is hard to argue that we have taken our eye off the ball – we continue to support policies that devote enormous expenditures to keeping road accidents on their current modestly downward trajectory.[9]

The claim that ordinary people overstate new and unfamiliar risks often lacks context, it seems to me. If the new risk is offered along with an explicitly offsetting reduction in some familiar risk, one might expect a degree of reluctance to make the trade (for one thing, people may worry that the experts have underestimated the threat involved in the new risk). Much more commonly, it seems, people perceive that they are being asked to accept a new risk with no explicit risk–risk trade-off. Reluctance to accept a new and unfamiliar risk as a net addition to our risk portfolio seems a reasonable response.[10]

Our collective memory includes more than enough cases where expert reassurances that "we have nothing to worry about" turned out to be false. Initially, experts grossly understated the risks of thalidomide, nuclear radiation, PCBs, MTBE, and C8 (used to manufacture Teflon®), to provide just a few examples. People have learned to be skeptical of bland reassurances from men in white coats (Willis 2001) – even well-meaning men in white coats tend to be overly optimistic about the beneficence of technology. Furthermore, there have been enough blatant cover-ups over the years (e.g. the tobacco industry and health effects of smoking) to keep the fires of public suspicion smoldering.

Kahan *et al.* (2006) have offered a new and interesting interpretation of the well-replicated "biases" in risk cognition.[11] Basically, they argue that it is not that people get the facts of risk wrong; rather, we (the researchers) misinterpret what people are telling us – they are answering a different question than the one we think we are asking. The argument is that "culture is prior to fact" – that what appear as incoherent risk preferences and irrational choices are really conflicts over worldview, i.e. a clash of cultures. For example, people with strong feelings in support of gun-owners' rights systematically underestimate the probability of death or injury from accidental shooting. What they are really trying to tell us, Kahan *et al.* argue, is "I don't think the probability of accidental shooting death should be a consideration in crafting laws about guns."

The import of the Kahan *et al.* argument is not that people get risk systematically wrong (and therefore it should be left to the experts), but that risk management institutions should engage the ordinary public more deeply and pay more attention to sorting out the rich web of input they are offering. This is consistent with the customary argument for public involvement – people tend to resist what they do not understand – but goes some considerable way beyond it. Kahan *et al.* do not shy from the fundamental implication of their argument: the inescapable role that risk regulation plays in adjudicating disputes between competing cultural groups over whose worldview will be institutionalized in laws and regulations.

Sunstein (2008) concludes by arguing that, even if ordinary people can be excused for the cautionary biases in the way they think about risk, this kind of thinking is inappropriate for governments. This amounts, implicitly, to an argument that government risk policy should be guided by the law of large numbers and the expected value criterion.[12] Ordinary people can be excused for being less impressed by this argument. Government by the EV criterion offers them no protection against catastrophe (which is uninsurable by definition) and no systematic insurance against harm to individuals.

Bottom line

For several reasons suggested above, I reject the Sunstein arguments that the motivation for precautionary policies can be attributed to cognitive biases among the ordinary people and, in matters of policy toward risk, we should trust the experts rather than the public. People's risk cognition and attitudes are more complex than EV utilitarians comprehend, and many of their alleged cognitive biases can be attributed reasonably to unwillingness to add new risks of uncertain gravity to the considerable portfolio of existing risks, and to the intuition that while the law of large numbers offers assurance on average it provides no certainty to individuals.

Arguing for attitudes and policies more respectful of ordinary people's intuitions about risk is the easy part. As Kahan *et al.* imply, there is much more work to be done before we can distil policy implications from ordinary people's understanding of risk, and there is little reason to think these implications can be cleanly separated from the cultural worldviews that sustain them.

Politicization and defense of science

Credible scientific evidence requires that science and the institutions that support it have adequate defenses against distortions (including inflated threat-claims that may induce unfounded panic, and unwarranted insistence that there is nothing to worry about) and the cynical exploitation of cognitive biases in service of various interests.

A goodly share of the purposeful distortions of scientific reasoning and evidence emanate from a continuing campaign to politicize science and reduce scientific discourse to an ordinary cultural quarrel. Manifestations include:

- "Muddying the waters" and "manufacturing uncertainty," that is, attempting to create scientific controversy, and manufacture or exaggerate uncertainty about the scientific evidence (Michaels and Monforton 2005).[13]
- Charges of "junk science" (junkscience.com).
- Promoting a false sense of balance, so that it seems only elementary fairness that "both sides" should be respected in the law and taught in the schools ("teaching the controversy"). This sort of thing is familiar in the public discussion of evolution and climate change, but it appears also in ordinary regulatory disputes.[14]

Perhaps false balance is the key concept in this unsavory mess. Muddying the waters, manufacturing uncertainty, and charges of "junk science" are aimed at creating a false sense that there are competing theories of equal credibility, or empirical records that supply factual credibility to competing views of the truth and conflicting policy agendas. If theories with vastly different implications are competing on equal grounds, and vastly different accounts of the facts are equally credible, we are free to believe what we want to believe and to craft theories and fact claims that support whatever policies are consistent with our cultural worldview. This goes well beyond the Kahan *et al.* argument that cultural worldview shapes people's perceptions of the facts; it is a claim that theory and empirical fact should be treated as malleable in the service of some greater good.

One way to think about false balance is that it is a fallacious application of the argument from ignorance – if we can list the potential outcomes, but we know nothing about their probabilities, then it makes sense to suppose that each is equally likely. The fallacy is that merely posing an alternative to a well-accepted scientific theory does not make the two equally likely.

While this campaign may have its small victories it is unlikely to succeed completely, because science has some strong defenses against politicization. The whole culture of *scientific detachment* and the political independence of science itself, and the self-policing and self-correcting tendencies built into the institutions of science sustain a considerable degree of interpersonal reliability in what counts as scientifically plausible and credible. The public and the courts willingly concede substantial deference to science as an institution in matters of scientific judgment, in effect according credibility to individual scientists to the extent that they and their work conform to scientific norms (*Daubert, Kumho Tire*). Nevertheless, the public has to be brought along. "Just as consultation breeds trust in expert risk regulators, the perception that (they) are remote and unaccountable erodes it" (Kahan *et al.* 2006, p.1104).

How much credible evidence of threat is enough to trigger a precautionary response?

Economists seeking utilitarian decision rules (Gollier *et al.* 2000, Gollier and Treich 2003, Barrieu and Sinclair-Desgagné 2006) have addressed scientific uncertainty and how response decisions might be adjusted in light of emerging scientific information. Modeling scientific uncertainty and the response to new information is an interesting and potentially fruitful line of inquiry, but the decision rules developed thus far remain highly stylized and limited by their utilitarian foundations.

The *AT&T Wireless* standard for scientific evidence to justify regulation of uncertain threats – less than a preponderance but more than a scintilla – is imprecise, and intentionally so (it is clear that the court intended to allow considerable regulatory discretion). However, it is consistent with the concept of a principle (rather than a rule). It leaves room for case-by-case judgment, considering the principles that come into play and the facts of the case. Nevertheless, the proposed evidentiary criterion would specify a clear lower bound on acceptable evidence: scientifically credible evidence of plausible threat.

Interactions of threat and evidence

Intuition suggests that the evidence criterion should be related to the nature of the threat. Perhaps, for example, we may decide to relate the standard of evidence to the magnitude of threatened harm – other things being equal, the greater the threat of harm, the more likely we may be to invoke a precautionary response despite substantial scientific uncertainty. Yet, this sensible intuition leaves a lot of details unanswered. Would a regime switch in dynamic simulation output provide reason enough for precautionary intervention? What about a regime shift in simulation output and empirical observations consistent with early warning indicators identified by the simulation exercise? Is any regime shift threat enough, or should we require evidence that the regime shift would be devastatingly harmful and prohibitively costly to reverse? Of course, in these I am offering questions rather than answers to the original problem, but I would argue that they are the right sort of questions.

Frankly, the insights that arise from considering the interaction of threat and evidence are rather modest, and for good reason. The costs of precaution – which is, after all, the reason why we would be ill-advised to invoke precaution in every instance of threat – depends very much on the nature of the precautionary remedy. We will see in Chapter 9 that for certain major categories of threats, remedies can be designed that are iterative and incremental, and in the process generate information that enables sequential re-evaluation of the threat and the remedy. Then, we will be ready to re-frame the question to consider interactions among threat, evidence, *and* remedy.

NOTES

1 This point can be debated, but the concept of "doctor's orders" held sway at the time (and still has some currency) and patients may have been reluctant to challenge a physician's decision to prescribe the drug.

2 Viscusi (1985) models decisions in the face of a continuum of probabilities of "downward" and "upward" irreversibility.

3 An important related question is deferred until Chapter 9: Can we devise *remedies* that enable us to calibrate our commitments while generating additional evidence, in order to arrive ultimately at better decisions?

4 *Daubert* v. *Merrell Dow Pharmaceuticals*, 509 U.S. 579 (1993); and *Kumho Tire Co. v. Carmichael* (97–1709) 526 U.S. 137 (1999).

5 *Lead Industries Association* v. *EPA* 647 F.2d 1130 (DC Cir. 1980).

6 *American Trucking Associations* v. *EPA* Nos. 97–1440 and 97–1441. (D.C. Cir. May 14, 1999).

7 *AT&T Wireless PCS, Inc.* v. *City Council of the City of Virginia Beach*, 155 F.3d 423 (4th Cir. 1998).

8 *Cellular Telephone Co.* v. *Town of Oyster Bay*, 166 F.3d 490 (2nd Cir. 1999). Commenting on the *Cellular Telephone* decision, Cranor (1999) notes correctly that courts have accepted different standards of proof for different purposes, e.g. for criminal and civil cases. However, the weaker standard for civil cases still demands a preponderance of the evidence, whereas the *Cellular Telephone* court required something less than a preponderance to justify regulating uncertain hazards.

9 In pursuit of safety, we accept intrusive regulation of road use, and state and local expenditures on highway safety and enforcement in the US that amounted to $14.8 billion in 2006 (*Highway Statistics* 2007). This is merely the tip of the iceberg – it does not include private and NGO expenditures on safety education, and it is dwarfed (I conjecture) by the on-going expenditure on safety features of highways, roads, and motor vehicles.

10 I am reminded of the familiar complaint that a volcanic eruption makes a mockery of attempts to control air pollution and/or greenhouse gases. Again, there is no meaningful trade-off: we are being asked to compare an occasional volcanic eruption with an occasional volcanic eruption *plus* business-as-usual emissions day after day.

11 Note that Paul Slovic, whose research results were cited in support of Sunstein's (2008) position is among the authors.

12 Sunstein makes the point quite explicit in particular cases, e.g. his argument that the risks prevented by pre-release drug testing should be balanced against the lives potentially saved by earlier access to new drugs.

13 While the US Chamber of Commerce has cited the MTBE fiasco (MTBE became widely used as a substitute for tetra-ethyl lead in gasoline before it was recognized as a potential human carcinogen) as an example of EPA's failure to employ "sound science" in regulatory decision-making, Garrity's (2004) analysis suggest that the industry itself is largely to blame. For example, the industry launched a major effort to circumvent an EPA rule requiring "time consuming and expensive" testing under the Toxic Substances Control Act. He observes that law and regulatory procedure can unwittingly provide regulated industries with incentives to choose ignorance (i.e. to deflect demands for more testing and to produce data from tests already conducted), and to manufacture uncertainty.

14 The Junk Science website has its roots in the Coalition for Sound Science, a since disbanded advocacy group that initially was funded in large part by tobacco companies seeking to undermine the science relating tobacco use and health.

9 Remedy

In the context of the precautionary principle, our action concept is *remedy*: given credible evidence of plausible threat, what remedy is appropriate? Given the objective to explore the coherence of a PP that would make a distinct contribution beyond ordinary risk management (ORM), the set of appropriate remedies surely must include some that are stronger (in some sense) than those that would be prescribed by ORM. The standard ORM risk management tools – prohibiting or regulating the drivers of the threat; restoring and/or remediating any damage; accommodations such as avoiding, mitigating, and/or adapting to the threat; and insurance, self-insurance, and self-protection in its many forms – may well have roles in a precautionary policy package, but a meaningful PP would not be limited to the ORM toolkit and committed to using it only in ways consistent with ORM.

The distinctions between ORM and PP remedies are likely to be matters of timing and degree. Consistent with *pre*caution, remedies may be implemented in advance to head off uncertain threats; and they may be calibrated to include safety margins, themselves a matter of degree because safety margins appear in ORM policy practice, too.

Precautionary remedies – must they always involve prohibition?

Critics often focus on a caricature of the PP, in which novel interventions or long-standing practices flagged as risky are prohibited in response to unsubstantiated threats of harm. Applied to a particular case, such a PP may well nip a potential intervention in the bud in response to a claim that it threatens harm, regardless of the benefits it may bring. For example, Turvey and Mojduszka (2005) report that PP-based objections to international food aid on the grounds that it contained genetically modified organisms (GMOs) invited certain disaster for the very poor in certain east African countries, as the presumably acceptable cost of avoiding a more speculative and plausibly avoidable risk.[1] Applied systematically to proposed innovations that arouse fears of possible harm, such a PP would stifle science, innovation, and economic growth, with huge attendant opportunity costs to welfare. Applied in response to fears that business-as-usual practices risk overstressing the systems upon which we depend, inducing regime shift and systemic collapse, such a PP would obligate huge expenditures on prohibition, elimination, and remediation, again with huge opportunity costs to welfare. When the agent believed responsible for the threat is well integrated into the economy and environment, prohibition and remediation can indeed be dauntingly costly. In each case, it is claimed, the PP requires these huge direct and opportunity costs without regard to: the risks inherent in substitutes for the prohibited intervention or innovation; the risks inherent in familiar on-going practices for which future innovations may substitute; and the risk reductions that could have been obtained had the funds expended been used elsewhere.

Hand in glove with the claim that the PP demands excessive remedies – prohibition of threatening activities regardless of the cost – goes the claim that such draconian remedies can be triggered on the flimsiest of evidence of threat. See for example the following statement of the Social Issues Research Center (www.sirc.org/articles/beware.html):

But the principle goes much further than seeking to protect us from known or suspected risks. It argues that we should also refrain from developments which have no demonstrable risks, or which have risks that are so small that they are outweighed, empirically, by the potential benefits that would result. In the most recent application of the doctrine it is proposed that innovation should be prevented even when there is just a perception of a risk among some unspecified people ... The burden of evidence and proof is taken away from those who make unjustified and often whimsical claims and placed on the scientific community which, because it proceeds logically and rationally, is often powerless to respond. This is what makes the principle so dangerous.

In contrast to these rather intemperate charges, economists Gollier and Treich (2003) – whose sympathy with the PP agenda is restrained by their commitment to the utilitarian framework of economics – define a precautionary measure as "a temporary and flexible decision that is taken in face of the lack of current scientific evidence." A recurring theme of this chapter will be to explore the implications of this definition. Under what circumstances can a genuinely precautionary measure be temporary and flexible? Can precautionary protocols be developed that not only deal effectively with limited information but serve to actively encourage the generation of more information? To foreshadow my conclusion, yes we can identify cases where precautionary measures are information generating, flexible, and perhaps temporary. Nevertheless, a serious PP may require prohibitions when the level of threat justifies them.

Distinguishing three kinds of threat cases

As early as Chapter 3, we distinguished threats from novel interventions (the Hippocratic Oath example, where the intervention could be stopped *ex ante* if it was viewed as sufficiently threatening) and novel outcomes from business-as-usual (the rivet-popper example, where a pattern of continuing exploitation raised concerns of eventual harm from cumulative stress). It is clear that these cases have different implications for the menu of available remedies and the costs entailed. Proposed novel interventions can be subjected to a pre-release testing protocol, with the option of abandoning the intervention should a threat of harm be confirmed. By the time business-as-usual stresses are recognized as potential threats to system stability, the stressor is integrated into the economic and environmental systems with the effect that reducing or eliminating the stressor and remediating past, present, and future damage may be very costly and disruptive.

At this point, we need to formalize a third case, first suggested in Box 8.2 – interventions that were novel once, but have become integrated into the economic and environmental systems so that damage may be widespread before the cause is recognized, and prohibiting further production and use of the stressor and remediating the damage may be very costly and disruptive. In these respects, novel interventions found to be harmful *ex post* resemble overstress from business-as-usual. However, the stressor is typically a single agent, which may simplify elimination and remediation, compared to the case of greenhouse gases generated in the course of business-as-usual, which is attributable to a complex matrix of stressors. The three kinds of sources of potential threats are defined, with examples, immediately below (see also Box 9.1).

NI_1: novel intervention *ex ante*. A novel intervention is proposed, offering the possibility of pre-release testing for any adverse effects. This case is most readily adapted to flexible, iterative pre-release testing protocols that generate information useful in evaluating the threat and potential remedies even as they provide protection (Box 7.2). In this process, empty threats are identified and the intervention allowed to proceed, manageable risks are identified and the intervention allowed to proceed perhaps subject to continuing regulatory

Box 9.1 Threat cases – availability of pre- and post-release remedies

Threat		Available Remedies	
Category	Example	Pre-release	Post-release
NI_1: Novel intervention (ex ante) may pose a threat	Request to approve a new drug for general use	An iterative and incremental program of pre-release testing	Follow-up studies of users. Drug can be withdrawn if serious risk of harm is determined
NI_2: Novel intervention (ex post) is found, after wide dispersal, to pose a threat	MTBE, introduced to replace ethyl lead, is found to be carcinogenic after wide dispersal in ground-water, streams, and lakes	None	Prohibit production and use of MTBE; reduce or eliminate MTBE from environment; remediate damage
BAU: Overstress from business-as-usual threatens harmful regime shift	Sharp increase in atmospheric carbon threatens climate change	None	Reduce or eliminate greenhouse gas emissions; mitigate damage; adapt

oversight, and in the relatively few cases where unacceptable threats are confirmed the proposed intervention can be abandoned pre-release.

Examples that fall potentially into the NI_1 category include new drugs, purposeful releases of non-indigenous species, GMOs, and synthetic organic compounds. The word "potentially" is crucial – for practical purposes, cases fall into the NI_1 category only if full advantage is taken of the opportunity for pre-release testing. The US Food and Drug Administration (FDA) does in fact handle new drugs as NI_1 cases, but in many countries thalidomide was prescribed to pregnant women with disastrous consequences (Box 8.3) – thalidomide was NI_1 in the US (Box 9.4) but NI_2 in many other countries. In the US, new synthetic organic compounds tend to default into the NI_2 category.

NI_2: Novel intervention *ex post*. The NI_2 category refers to novel interventions that are released without serious pre-release testing, but damage is identified after production and use has become integrated into the economy and environment. The pre-release testing option is no longer available, and we are

Box 9.2 Novel interventions gone bad: (i) PCBs – one from the regulatory "dark ages"

From the 1920s to the 1970s, PCBs (polychlorinated biphenols) were produced and used as coolants and insulating fluids, plasticizers in paints and cements, stabilizing additives in flexible PVC coatings of electrical wiring and electronic components, pesticide extenders, reactive flame retardants, lubricating oils, sealants, adhesives, wood floor finish paints, water-proofing compounds, casting agents, surgical implants, and in carbonless copy paper. While it is unlikely that a full inventory of global PCB production will ever be accurately tallied, known production was on the order of 1.5 million tons.

PCBs are persistent organic pollutants and have become widely dispersed throughout the environment through use, disposal, and environmental transport at a global scale. Their commercial utility was based largely on their chemical stability, which has been responsible also for their continuing persistence in the environment. PCBs are likely carcinogens having the potential to adversely impact the health of humans and a wide range of biota.

The toxicity of PCBs and related synthetic organic compounds was recognized by the early 1930s following a variety of industrial incidents. A number of scientific publications referring to the toxicity of various chlorinated hydrocarbons were published before 1940. However, PCB manufacture and use continued with few restraints until the 1970s, when production was banned.

Despite extensive regulatory actions beginning in the 1970s, PCBs still persist in the environment and remain a focus of attention. In the US, hazardous waste sites are remediated under the Superfund program authorized in 1980. Cleaning up of hazardous waste sites is expensive, averaging about $40 million per site in today's dollars. PCB site remediation figures prominently among Superfund projects, and it is estimated that total Superfund clean-up expenditures from the early 1980s through 1994 were in the $20 billion to $30 billion range. In the US, PCB site remediation remains a work in progress.

left instead with the prospect of damage that is often systemic and remedies that can be dauntingly costly. Examples include asbestos (Box 5.3) and PCBs (Box 9.2). MTBE (Box 9.3) is also an example, but Garrity (2004) argues that it need not have been – environmental regulation had become sufficiently sophisticated by the 1980s, and the US EPA's authority was strong enough (at least, on paper), to have required serious testing prior to general release if the political and regulatory will had been strong enough. The MTBE case is interesting also in that it was a risk undertaken to reduce and eventually eliminate a confirmed environmental threat, ethyl lead in gasoline.

Box 9.3 Novel interventions gone bad: (ii) MTBE – by the 1980s, we should have known better

In the 1980s and 1990s, MTBE (methyl tertiary-butyl ether) became the petroleum industry's additive of choice to replace tetra-ethyl lead in gasoline. Yet by the end of the 1990s, MTBE had leaked from tens of thousands of underground storage tanks across the country polluting groundwater and eventually streams and lakes, precipitating a large-scale environmental crisis. MTBE has been identified as an animal carcinogen with the potential to cause cancer in humans.

Garrity (2004) argues that the US EPA had five distinct opportunities to require additional safeguards before MTBE became widely used and dispersed throughout the environment. It did not examine seriously the risk–risk implications of replacing ethyl lead with MTBE, and it passed up several opportunities (including the fuel additive waiver, the Toxic Substances Control Act testing agreement, the Underground Storage Tanks implementation regulations, and the reformulated gasoline requirements) to require serious testing prior to general use of MTBE. Garrity notes that US approaches to environmental law often permit precautionary approaches, but in practice they seldom are required or implemented.

BAU: Overstress of systems in the course of business-as-usual, threatening harmful regime shift. Like NI$_2$, there is no pre-release testing option, and the threat concerns damage that is often systemic and remedies that can be dauntingly costly, because the foundations of the economy and the environment are undermined. Compared with NI$_2$, elimination and remediation of BAU threats may be even more complicated, expensive, and disruptive, because many BAU threats are attributable to a complex matrix of stressors. In that sense, some BAU threats may pose the ultimate risk dilemmas – cases where the threat is potentially catastrophic but so too is the sacrifice required to eliminate the threat.

Examples of BAU threats include north Pacific salmon (Box 9.5), where a variety of stresses with their origins in the modern economy and demographics threaten native salmon varieties, but effective protections for the salmon may be viewed as excessively expensive and disruptive of the regional economy; and climate change, which can be controlled only by dramatic reductions in fossil fuel use worldwide.

In these risk dilemma cases, there is extensive debate about diagnoses, and solutions and their costs. Are the costs of serious remedies really prohibitive? Some commentators claim that significant progress can be made at relatively

> **Box 9.4 The thalidomide case led to stricter approval procedures in the US**
>
> Thalidomide, a newly patented drug, was marketed to thousands of pregnant women in Europe, Japan, Australia, and Canada to treat morning sickness. About 10,000 children around the world were born with severe birth defects. When doctors traced these devastating birth defects to thalidomide in 1961, it was withdrawn from the market (Box 8.3).
>
> The USA avoided the thalidomide disaster. Approval of thalidomide in the USA had been delayed mostly because Dr. Frances Kelsey of the Food and Drug Administration was concerned about the development of peripheral neuropathies and reasoned (correctly, as it turned out) that such a drug might distort fetal development. Kelsey took the position that there was insufficient proof of the drug's safety in humans. Soon reports of fetal deformities linked to thalidomide led the German government to withdraw the drug from the market, and worldwide withdrawal followed quickly.
>
> Dr. Kelsey's role in preventing a thalidomide disaster in the USA was reported in major newspapers. Public recognition that institutionalized FDA procedures had not offered adequate systematic protections – protection was provided, instead, by one skeptical and persistent scientist – led to passage of the Kefauver-Harris Amendments (1962) to the Federal Food, Drug, and Cosmetic Act of 1938, strengthening the FDA's control of drug experimentation on humans and making the approval process for new drugs more rigorous. For the first time, applicants for approval of new drugs were required to demonstrate their effectiveness as well as safety. So, the extensive post-release harm in countries where thalidomide was used widely motivated US legislation to strengthen pre-release testing of new drugs.

modest expense, and that remedies have off-setting benefits like reduced air pollution that should figure into the calculation (Quiggin 2007).

Do adaptation and mitigation count as remedies for climate change? Are they really cheaper than greenhouse gas reduction? Do we really have a choice, when it comes to radically reducing carbon dependence – surely we understand that the carbon economy is inherently unsustainable?

Looking more closely at remedies: 1. Novel interventions

Compared with ORM, a PP is more likely to invoke precautionary remedies in advance, to head off uncertain threats. Again, this is a matter of going beyond ORM – the ORM toolkit includes techniques and procedures for evaluating the risks associated with novel interventions, yet these are not

Box 9.5 North Pacific salmon – overstressing a system in the course of business-as-usual

Stresses on native Pacific salmon, originating in the modern economy and demographics, have caused population declines around the north Pacific Rim, and have endangered or threatened several salmon species and an even larger number of distinct locally and regionally adapted varieties. Habitat loss and overharvest are major drivers of decline for salmon in the southern parts of their range, as is the proliferation of land-based fish hatcheries and ocean salmon farming operations (which tend to homogenize the genetic stock). Salmon in the northern latitudes of their range – northeastern Russia, British Columbia, and Alaska – are more likely to have healthy habitat, but suffer from legal and illegal overharvest in both the ocean and freshwater spawning rivers.

In their range, salmon are the biological foundation, or keystone species, of coastal ecosystems and human economies. It is no coincidence that the largest remaining populations of apex predators such as brown bears and eagles occur where salmon runs are still healthy.

Effective protections for salmon and their habitat will be expensive and disruptive of the regional economy. Already, billions of dollars have been spent on salmon restoration efforts, with only modest success. Some observers argue that protecting wild salmon is not necessarily futile. Past efforts have had disappointing results, it is argued (www.wildsalmoncenter.org/about/whySalmon.php), because they have been too little, too late. Intervention has been attempted only after salmon population decline was well advanced. Symptoms have been treated rather than causes – e.g. (i) replacing the native, locally-adapted genetic stocks with hatchery-bred salmon, and (ii) implementing temporary fixes, such as engineering stream habitat. Long-term solutions, e.g. protection of in-stream flows and existing habitat, have been neglected.

Better approaches may include finding and protecting the remaining intact habitat; making permanent investments, focusing on the rivers where the chance of achieving watershed-level habitat protection are best; and in the southern portion of their range (where economic and demographic pressures are greatest), focusing on smaller, more manageable watersheds. An ultimate goal might be a coordinated multi-national approach – a Pacific Rim-wide system of protected, or mostly protected, salmon sanctuaries.

Pacific salmon make an excellent case study in BAU threats. Salmon are themselves an integral component (more than that, a keystone) of a large and complex regional natural system that is pressured by a large and growing human system. Protecting the salmon will require large and systemic adjustments in the human system, the expense will be substantial, and success is not assured.

implemented routinely and consistently prior to release of the novel organism or substance, or adoption of the new technology.

The distinguishing feature of *precautionary* intervention is that it is undertaken in response to uncertain harm, which includes harm that has yet to occur, but also harm that has yet to be detected and its cause established. The core notion suggested by the prefix is intervention before we really know (but not always before the damage is done).

PP critics warn of the benefits that would be lost due to premature prohibition in particular cases and, should the PP become institutionalized, the innovation and economic growth that would be stifled by the resulting pattern of premature prohibitions. With NI_1 cases, there is opportunity for pre-release testing, which enhances the degree of precaution and reduces both the threat of harm and the disruption of innovation. In the US, there is a clear contrast between the handling of new pharmaceutical drugs intended for human use and new synthetic organic chemicals. The FDA requires systematic pre-release testing which, despite the apparent wide popular support, draws flak from utilitarian critics who argue that innovation is delayed and lives lost due to excessive pre-release testing.[2] In contrast, despite laws and regulations that permit a stronger precautionary stance by EPA (Garrity 2004, and Box 9.3), synthetic chemicals are released into the environment without serious pre-release testing; any harmful effects are discovered belatedly and debated extensively before remedies are invoked. By that time, the substances have become embedded in the business-as-usual economy, with the effect that remedies are expensive and disruptive. PCBs (Box 9.2), and more recently MTBE (Box 9.3) for use as an octane-enhancer in gasoline, are examples (see also Box 5.4, sketching the case of asbestos, which is not synthetic). The ORM argument for this approach to synthetic chemicals, one presumes, parallels the utilitarian critique of the FDA approach – surely the benefits in aggregate from a continuing stream of newly introduced synthetic chemicals would more than compensate for the damage caused by the relatively few that turn out to be harmful.

Yet it is not at all clear that the choice is between precaution that is typically costly and disruptive of the economy and scientific and technological advance on the one hand, and costly and disruptive post-release remedies for the novel interventions that turn out badly. While one can find plenty of concern about the inflexibility of precaution in the utilitarian literature, it also offers a quite different perspective. Gollier and Treich (2003) characterize a precautionary measure as a temporary and flexible decision taken in response to admittedly inadequate current scientific evidence. Earlier writings in the option value tradition (Arrow and Fisher 1974, Henry 1974, and

Pindyck 2007), without endorsing precaution, emphasize the costs of premature commitment – the option that allows more flexibility at a future decision point should enjoy something of a premium today for that reason alone. Gollier and Treich write explicitly of precaution as managing the wait for better scientific information. So, there is a utilitarian tradition that values maintaining flexibility while we wait to learn more.

Waiting to learn more strikes me as only part of the story, and a rather passive part at that. What are we waiting to learn? If we are waiting for nature to roll the dice, that would resolve the uncertainty in a particular sense, but not always to our benefit. Rolling the dice converts an *ex ante* outcome set into a particular outcome, and it is this resolution that seems to be on the minds of the option value authors. However, it has a Russian roulette quality – the uncertainty is resolved but the catastrophic outcome, should it occur, may be irreversible. It would be so much better, in the real world, if we could learn more about how the system works. What outcomes are possible, how likely are they, what would it take to avoid, mitigate, or adapt to the most harmful of the possibilities?

Suppose we can not only wait to learn more, but actively manage the process of learning more.

Perhaps we could stick a toe in the water, i.e. find ways to gather information while risking only a small part of our endowment. We could learn more about the proposed novel intervention, perhaps in the laboratory; model the system to identify possible reactions to the intervention and to identify indicators that might provide early warning of harm; perhaps even conduct limited trial releases under controlled conditions that allow revocability (pulling the plug on the experiment, and containing and eliminating any further harm); all before exposing the system to the risks entailed in general release.

Consider the idea of quarantine and stepwise release (QSR) as a stylized representation of the kind of pre-release process we have in mind, and a metaphor for a whole class of pre-release research and testing programs. QSR is feasible if the effects of an innovation can be confined in space and time.[3] Beginning with testing under laboratory conditions, the innovation goes through a stepwise release process with monitoring, study, reassessment of the threat and the remedy, and adjustments in remedy as warranted by emerging evidence, at every step – a process that may be iterated perhaps many times. Each step ends with a continue-to-next-step/terminate decision, terminating the process only when the evidence suggests unacceptable risks in the next step. Notice that the unacceptable risk criterion assumes that some risks, presumably manageable risks, are acceptable – this suggests that research should focus on mitigation

Box 9.6 Stylized pre- and post-release strategies for threats from novel interventions

Imagine a new genetically modified organism with attractive commercial prospects. However there is a credible threat of plausible harm.

Pre-release (continue/terminate decision at each step)   Test in isolation for
1. Conceptual evaluation (chemistry, biology, genetics,   potential harm
   etc.)
2. Laboratory testing *in vitro*
3. Laboratory testing with whole organisms
4. Release protocol with iteratively less restrictive
   quarantine – proceed to next step only if harm is
   below a threshold of concern
   • Step 1
   • Step 2
   • Etc.
5. Release for general use (conditional on what, if any,
   restrictions?)

Post-release   Determine pathways to
1. Follow-up research (perhaps using epidemiological   harm in environment
   methods)
2. If signs of harm
   • Conceptual evaluation (chemistry, biology, genetics,
     etc.)
   • Laboratory testing *in vitro*
   • Laboratory testing with whole organisms
   • Testing in confined environment with intensive
     monitoring
3. If it is established that the harm was caused by the
   novel intervention
   • Prohibit, restrict, regulate further use of substance
     or organism
   • Mitigate, adapt, remediate damage

and adaptation, as well as harm. Should evidence of unacceptable risk fail to arise after several iterations, general release may be undertaken with much more assurance than if we had simply rolled the dice at the outset.[4] The QSR pre-release phase would be followed by a program of post-release follow-up research to check for unexpected harmful consequences – possible but less likely now, because extensive pre-release testing should have revealed the more likely harmful possibilities (Box 9.6). In addition to mitigation and adaptation, post-release research should include remediation.

Potential for learning applies not only to the extent of the threat but also to methods of managing it. Sinha *et al.* (2008) highlight lifecycle management procedures for cadmium-telluride photovoltaics as an alternative to the PP. It makes more sense to see the development of lifecycle management procedures as an integral part of an appropriate PP remedy. Followed by research, development, and testing of lifecycle management procedures for this particular material, a precautionary prohibition would be relaxed should the research succeed in developing feasible management technologies and institutional–organizational arrangements that ensure their effective implementation. A precautionary pause that in due course turns a serious threat into manageable risk is not an alternative to the PP but a victory for the PP.

This discussion suggests that PP remedies can, and ideally should, be designed to enhance scope for research and learning, to reduce ignorance, narrow the uncertainties, better specify the possible outcomes and probabilities, and develop and test strategies for avoidance, mitigation, adaptation, and remediation. Ideally, this process identifies and eliminates the unacceptably risky interventions before harm becomes widespread while, for the majority of proposed interventions, reducing gross ignorance to manageable risk with only modest delay and modest cost for research and testing. Reducing the costs of precaution makes it more likely that precaution itself will not induce extreme threats, in which case the choice set includes actions that induce disproportionate and asymmetric threats (plowing ahead), and actions that do not (pause-study-reassess).[5]

Serious PP proposals are likely to place high priority on expanding the scope for learning and promoting the quest for affordable remedies, which are helpful in building and sustaining coalitions in support of solutions among contemporaries, and inter-generational commitments to solutions (UNESCO 2005). The virtues of this approach are obvious in specific cases of novel interventions, but even more so when we consider an on-going program of innovation (Box 9.7). While we cannot rule out *a priori* the case where we are unable *ex ante* to distinguish the more hazardous prospects among a stream of innovations, that case is likely to be relatively rare. More often, we can expect to be able to identify more and less hazardous classes of innovations or, better yet, learn some things about particular innovations prior to their general release. Ideally, from a precautionary standpoint, we may be able to implement fully the QSR procedure. The argument of Box 9.7 offers some reassurance that the PP can be implemented in ways that do not systematically stifle the process of innovation.[6]

Box 9.7 Innovation and the PP

The explorers and pioneers were adventurers, but most were not fools – they used scouts, brought goods they expected would be useful in trade and bargaining with the locals, and had contingency plans that could be invoked if things went badly.

Given that exploring the unknown has upside possibilities, critics have worried that PP would stifle innovation and growth. It turns out that many innovations yield modest net losses that lead to their abandonment, but a minority of innovations are winners. Occasionally a truly novel innovation may cause harm that is disproportionately greater than the benefit of the typical benign innovation, but assume that the expected value of a long sequence of innovations is positive. There may even be occasional upside surprises such as the laser, which turned out to have beneficial uses not imagined at the time of its discovery. Provided we can save enough from the gains that we can bear the infrequent disasters, we would want to keep on innovating. But the disaster may happen on any trial and, whenever it happens, it will be a huge set-back. If it happens early in the sequence, recovery will be difficult, perhaps impossible. Would the PP prohibit innovations?

Consider four cases.

1. Suppose we can never learn anything about the chances of a specific innovation being disastrous until the die is cast, and we cannot contain the disaster or mitigate it when it occurs. Then, our PP deliberations must focus on the program of innovation. **T** is large, and **E** is clear (we know that some innovations are disproportionately harmful, and *ex ante* we know nothing specific about the threat in any particular trial). It is reasonable that admissible **R** would include prohibition (but prohibition will not necessarily be the chosen **R**).

2. Suppose, instead, that we know some things *ex ante*. Then we can sort prospective innovations into *ex ante* more and less hazardous classes, and confine extreme remedies to cases that are *ex ante* more than ordinarily prone to generate serious threats. For example, we may know that:
   - Increasing novelty of the innovation and complexity of the systems impacted increase the chance of surprises.
   - This proposed innovation belongs to a class that has experienced more than its share of harmful outcomes.
   - This proposed innovation is in a domain where people tend to be strongly averse to downside surprises (e.g. medical/pharmaceutical).

3. Suppose we can learn some things about each innovation before implementation. Then, we can sort the proposed innovations with more confidence, and quarantine those that **E** suggests are more likely to be disastrous. For example, perhaps we have:
   - Lab results suggesting a plausible serious threat.

- Modeling results (better yet, consensus results from several well-calibrated and extensively examined models) suggesting a plausible serious threat.
- Theory sufficiently well developed that we can make calculations demonstrating that particular threats should/cannot be taken seriously. Manhattan Project scientists made calculations showing that nuclear explosions of the magnitudes contemplated for Japan in 1945 could not trigger chain reactions that would blow up the planet. Had the calculations gone the other way, using the weapons would have been unthinkable.

4. Suppose we are not limited to binary remedies (implement/prohibit). Perhaps we can implement each innovation stepwise, relaxing the degree of revocability following each step that reveals no unacceptable risks. Then, if **E** generated by this QSR procedure signals alarm early in this process, implementation can be aborted and disaster contained.

Case 1, where all innovations must be treated as equally likely to turn out disastrously and prohibiting the whole program of innovation is an admissible remedy, seems unlikely. Case 2, where all we can do is sort potential innovations into *ex ante* more and less hazardous classes, is likely to be rare and good policy and practice would aim to make it more so. In cases 3 and 4, the PP serves the learning function envisioned, and provides (it can be argued) needed protections as we venture into the unknown – and these protections are directed not against innovation generically but against particular innovations identified as especially risky.

Consider the case of genetically modified (GM) crops. A research program of global dimensions, in which the corporate role has come to dwarf that of universities and research institutes, has demonstrated the capacity to produce a continuing stream of potential commercial innovations. In addition to risks of harm to human health and the environment, concerns have been raised about impacts on the structure of the agricultural industry and associated socio-economic effects, and a threat to public trust generated by reluctance of industry and some governments to label GM foods as such (FAO 2000). Below, a stylized pre- and post-release strategy is applied to the health and environmental threats from a stream of innovations in GM crops.

A stylized case study: genetically modified crops

GM crops offer a variety of potential benefits, including, higher yields, resistance to diseases and pests, specific characteristics desirable to consumers (e.g. nutritional enhancements, and perhaps disease-fighting properties), and characteristics that reduce production costs (e.g. resistance to weed-control chemicals). However, specific threats have been raised. Among them, food safety and other effects on human health, gene flow and other effects (e.g. toxicity to non-target species) on biodiversity, and development of resistance in targeted weeds, pests, and diseases (superbugs and superweeds) are addressed here.

We proceed by examining these three categories of threats one by one.

Food safety and human health

1. Case 1 (Box 9.7), where we are unable to learn about the chances of a specific innovation being disastrous prior to its general release, is quite unlikely.
2. We can learn some things *ex ante*. For example, by chemical assessment, analysis of pathways, etc., we should be able to predict cases that increase the likelihood of toxicity and food allergies.
3. Testing in the laboratory should distinguish *ex ante* some of the cases where release would be risky.
4. QSR applies quite readily – analysis, modeling, laboratory testing, limited and controlled trials with animals and eventually human volunteers, and eventually general release with follow-up review and assessment. Even for GM foods etc. judged safe, individual exposure does not have to be involuntary – labeling can provide individuals the opportunity to choose.

Biodiversity

1. Case 1 (Box 9.7) is quite unlikely.
2. Conceptual analysis may be fruitful – we know some important things *ex ante*. For example,
   - We can distinguish open-pollinated species, where risk of gene flow (spread to the non-GM population) is higher, from others.
   - We know something about susceptible species and varieties and their roles in the host environment, and we can model the impact of the proposed intervention on host ecosystems.
3. If the results of conceptual analysis are inconclusive, QSR may apply quite readily – ecosystems modeling, limited and controlled trials, and eventually general release with follow-up review and assessment.
4. If it is decided to permit commercial use of GM species with higher risk of gene flow, the choice is between quarantine and general release.

Quarantine may be implemented in commercial operations by emphasizing containment. In the case of general release, the emphasis must be on post-release review and assessment and dealing with the damage, if any, after it has occurred. Quarantine arrangements in commercial production, being expensive, would be concentrated on high-value crops and varieties. This implies that, for low-value crops, the options may be limited to prohibition and general release with mitigation, adaptation, and remediation of any damage.

Resistance

1. We know *ex ante* that evolutionary processes favor mutations exhibiting resistance, and that evolution proceeds more rapidly among simpler kinds of organisms. Nevertheless, the natural selection that drives evolution requires fairly broad exposure to the resistant crop. This consideration suggests only limited opportunity to learn anything prior to general release about the chances of a specific innovation being especially risky in this regard.

2. Nevertheless, we have at least a little *ex ante* knowledge. For example, factors relevant to gene flow (the biodiversity discussion, above) may be relevant also to development of resistance.

3. Modeling may help distinguish *ex ante* the cases where general release is likely to stimulate development of resistance. However, there seems to be only a limited role for lab testing.

4. If it is decided to permit commercial use of GM species with higher risk that resistance will develop, the choice is between quarantine and general release. Quarantine may be implemented in commercial operations by emphasizing containment, and is plausible in the case of high-value crops. In the case of field crops, commercialization implies general release, and the emphasis must be on post-release review and assessment and dealing with the damage, if any, after it has occurred.

Where might PP prohibitions apply?

In the case of GMOs, prohibitions are most likely to apply in the QSR domain, where results in the early stages suggest aborting the process before general release. The argument for PP prohibitions always requires careful assessment of the evidence, threat, and remedy (ETR) conditions in the particular case. However, we can identify some kinds of cases where resort to PP prohibitions is more plausible.

Food safety and human health
- Lab testing demonstrates toxicity or allergenic properties.
- Limited and controlled trials demonstrate toxicity or allergenic properties.
- Post-release review and assessment demonstrates toxicity or allergenic properties.

Biodiversity
- High-risk GMOs may be restricted to operations capable of effective containment.
- General release may be prohibited if effective containment cannot be demonstrated, or is economically infeasible (e.g. low-value field crops).

Resistance
- High-risk GMOs may be restricted to operations capable of effective containment.
- General release may be prohibited if effective containment cannot be demonstrated, or is infeasible economically (e.g., for low-value field crops).[7]

The GM crops case has served, among other things, to emphasize the importance of containment, i.e. the ability to confine a new innovation in space and time while we learn more about the risks entailed.[8,9] The QSR process, where applicable, adds substantially to the information base for decisions, given the limited capacity of science-based risk assessment to predict effects in complex systems.[10]

Is routine pre-release testing too costly?

Economists argue frequently that routine pre-release testing of innovations is too costly, and that the costs that really matter are the hidden ones: the benefits forgone when innovation is delayed. In the US, the Food and Drug Administration has become the poster child for this argument, as economists highlight the costs in lives lost and afflictions suffered due to delays in the release of promising new drugs (for the most part these costs are assumed rather than documented, see footnote 5). Yet the FDA operates as it does in response to clear political intent – more rigorous pre-release testing of new drugs was mandated following the thalidomide disaster in the early 1960s (Box 9.4).

The FDA's approval procedure follows laboratory and animal testing with three phases of testing with human subjects, each phase involving more subjects and conditions closer to actual clinical practice than its predecessor. Typically the developers of the new drug submit tests they have conducted; the FDA reviews the results, and has the options of requesting more tests, and tests by independent researchers, prior to making its decision. If the drug is approved, the FDA does post-market surveillance, analyzing outcomes from use among the general population. The approval process may take around eight years, long enough to motivate complaints that innovation is stifled and its benefits delayed, but short enough that it may fail to identify long-term harmful effects. Even with this rather exhaustive pre-approval testing, mistakes occur.[11]

Given the utilitarian form taken by the economists' critique – the benefits of harm avoided by a relatively strict pre-approval testing regimen are likely to be much smaller than the benefits foregone by delayed approval of new drugs – it is fair to pose the question directly: Do we really want the FDA to apply a maximum expected value (EV) criterion? Do we really want the FDA to interpret the Hippocratic injunction as "Do no net harm, on average"? Again, it seems we encounter the disconnect between individuals and populations, when it comes to the law of large numbers. The population may be better off on average if the FDA implemented an approval process that maximizes expected value, but individuals who may not get many rolls of the dice typically seek more assurance than the law of large numbers offers.

In addition, there are legitimate behavioral concerns. When it comes to treatment of medical conditions, ordinary people have little choice but to defer to the judgment of the medical and pharmaceutical establishments – the professionals wield the authority to prescribe, as well as the soft power of expert knowledge. Submission to treatment involves inconvenience, perhaps pain and limited activity while recuperating, the risk that the treatment will be ineffective, and perhaps a chance that it will do more harm than good. Why submit to treatment, then, is an obvious question and I suspect many of us ask it. The answer, most likely, comes couched in overt appeal to the professional authority of the experts. We are asked to trust their judgment and, in return, most of us demand assurance that they, collectively, have eliminated the unacceptable risks in the recommended treatment. Without that assurance, we might expect reluctance to submit to professional judgment, unwillingness to undergo prescribed treatments, and increased resort to folk remedies. The healthcare system we have relies on trust and deference to qualified professional authority, and the costs of undermining that authority could be much greater than the direct increase in harmful outcomes (as well as beneficial outcomes) as we implement the EV criterion.

Manski (2009) does not pursue the utilitarian critique (the FDA drug approval procedures forego too much in the way of benefits in pursuit of safety).

> ### Box 9.8 Factors influencing the welfare-optimal combination of pre- vs. post-release remedies for threats from proposed innovations
>
> In the spirit of Manski's (2009) suggestion that we strive to find and implement a more nearly optimal combination of pre-release testing and post-release surveillance, here we identify the key factors influencing the comparative welfare effects of pre- and post-release testing.
>
> The welfare advantage of pre-release testing (PRT) increases with:
> - magnitude of damage without PRT relative to PV of benefits of the innovation;
> - probability of damage without PRT;
> - time elapsed before without-PRT damage is discovered, the causal path established, and post-release remedies implemented;
> - precision of QSR (fewer false positives and false negatives – both are costly).
>
> The welfare advantage of pre-release testing diminishes with:
> - time taken to complete pre-release testing (assume that innovations become obsolete inexorably, so that time in QSR delays the benefit stream and perhaps reduces its duration);
> - its cost.

Rather, he asks whether the FDA has settled on the optimal combination of pre-approval and post-market research (Box 9.8). He proposes a shift in the mix – new drugs would reach the user population more quickly but follow-up surveillance of users would be more systematic. Quicker release would increase risk for all early adopters of new treatments, while the benefits would be concentrated among those with serious afflictions. So, it would make sense to accelerate availability not across the board, but for new treatments for serious afflictions, and to direct early post-market use toward patients with serious cases of the indicated condition. Manski frames his proposal as a change in the phase-3 trial process. Phase-3 trials would involve more subjects, increasing the chance that individuals needing the treatment would get it sooner; and systematic follow-up of this group would enrich the data sets for post-market surveillance. Phase-3 outcomes would be reviewed annually, with possible outcomes of withdrawal, approval, and continue testing. Compared with current practice, the drug approval process would be more continuous, giving the patients with greatest need earlier access to potentially beneficial drugs while encouraging more systematic long-term studies of users.

Note that Manski's is a welfare argument – he makes no mention of the PP. It follows from our construction of the PP – disproportionate and asymmetric

Box 9.9 Thalidomide redux – new uses, strict protections

In 1998 the FDA approved the use of thalidomide, despite its troublesome history, for the treatment of lesions associated with leprosy. Studies are also being conducted to determine the effectiveness of thalidomide in treating symptoms associated with AIDS, Behçet disease, lupus, Sjögren syndrome, rheumatoid arthritis, inflammatory bowel disease, macular degeneration, and some cancers. In 2006, the FDA granted accelerated approval for the use of thalidomide in combination with dexamethasone to treat newly diagnosed multiple-myeloma patients.

Because of thalidomide's potential for causing birth defects, the distribution of the drug was permitted only under tightly controlled conditions. To prevent fetal exposure to thalidomide, the FDA required implementation of an oversight program, which came to be called System for Thalidomide Education and Prescribing Safety (STEPS). Only physicians who are registered may prescribe thalidomide to patients and those patients, both male and female, must comply with mandatory contraceptive measures, patient registration, and patient surveys. Thalidomide may be dispensed only by licensed pharmacists who are registered in the STEPS program and have been educated to understand the risk of severe birth defects if thalidomide is used during pregnancy.

Despite the well-documented risks associated with thalidomide, it has been approved for treatment of certain ailments, and research continues to determine its effectiveness in treating a number of additional conditions. Two observations are relevant. First, most of these ailments are serious and unpleasant, much more so than morning sickness, which suggests that risk–benefit considerations played some role in the approval decisions. Second, the required oversight program is quite rigorous. Given the decision to approve a treatment known to be risky, the FDA proceeded to require rigorous safeguards to minimize the chance of harm.

threats call for remedies stronger than can be justified by ordinary welfare considerations – that, when the PP is invoked in cases of proposed novel interventions, it would call for greater than the welfare-optimal effort in pre-release testing.

Recent developments regarding thalidomide illustrate some elements of the Manski proposal. Thalidomide was prescribed originally for nausea and morning sickness, rather mundane afflictions, and the resulting serious birth defects were judged to be disproportionately harmful. However, new applications for much more serious afflictions – where the patients' prospects are grim in the absence of treatment – have been approved, subject to rigorous safeguards to minimize the chance of harm (Box 9.9). Perhaps the

Box 9.10 Uses and limits of quarantine as a remedy

1. Consider a decision about introducing a new risky activity assuming that we can confine its effects in space and time, that is, we can quarantine and eventually destroy the activity and its effects.

   Quarantine and stepwise release, QSR, is all about learning in relative safety. At the outset, we do not know the potential for harm or our ability to manage it, but we can continue research under quarantine conditions. Stepwise release is invoked when what we learn at each step tends to calm our fears. QSR cannot eliminate all risk – as it proceeds iteratively toward general release, capacity to confine the effects is diminished. The remaining risk in QSR is that harmful effects emerge too late to completely confine and eliminate them.

2. Now, assume that our capacity to confine the effects is time-limited. The confinement facility has a long but finite life expectancy.

   To the risks in (1) are added the risk of persistent harmful effects beyond the life expectancy of the confinement facility:
   - In the event something else destroys our society first, the threat of harm from this source is irrelevant – so, worries about very long-term risks are contingent on our chances of surviving all other threats in the interim.
   - Worst-case harm is reduced or eliminated; in the event we learn how to avoid, mitigate, and/or adapt to it in the interim – the QSR process allows learning about the threat and how to manage it; and in the worst case, buys time.
   - The present value of harm is trivial, even in the worst case, if we discount the welfare of distant-future people.
   - Worst case harm (present value or otherwise) may be very large if (i) we never learn how to avoid, mitigate, and/or adapt, (ii) we would otherwise survive everything else that may threaten us, and (iii) we impose no positive pure time preference.

   The ethical case, incomplete as it is, for introducing this kind of activity is best founded on faith that learning in the interim will solve the problem of avoidance, mitigation, and adaptation. As Parfit (1984, 1988) points out, there is no ethically defensible reason for betting against disastrous possibilities, even if unlikely.

3. Assume now that the activity that generates the threat already is ongoing, and we are quite sure the effects are harmful, as in case of nuclear waste. We can quarantine it, perhaps for a long time, but it will persist.

   This case is all about quarantine. Because we have the waste and we are sure about harmful effects, there is no need for reference to worst-case harm and no role for stepwise release. The case for an isolation and storage facility project is strong. An existing threat would be reduced sharply for a long time, during which we may learn how to better secure the facility and mitigate any damage; and we should be able to solve the problem of minimizing and compensating for disproportionate local impacts.

4. The real-world issue of storage facilities for nuclear waste question is complicated by the likelihood of continued additions to the nuclear waste stockpile:

- If we committed to creating no more nuclear waste, case 3, above, applies.
- However, a long-term storage facility could be designed with capacity much greater than required for the existing stockpile of waste. It is reasonable to expect that the excess capacity would encourage creation of additional nuclear waste. Then the question is answered in two steps: first, there is a strong case for secure storage of existing waste and, second, the case for creating a continuing and perhaps increasing stream of new waste is founded most securely on faith that learning in the interim will solve the problem of avoidance, mitigation, and adaptation (as in case 2).

FDA's response to this situation reveals one of America's few fundamentally precautionary institutions exhibiting some sensitivity to the utilitarian critique.

The QSR process applies most completely to NI_1 cases, proposed novel interventions. But perhaps quarantine is applicable more broadly (Box 9.10). Case 1 is a standard QSR case. In case 2 the capacity for effective quarantine is limited in time, as we might expect of a nuclear waste isolation and storage facility, introducing intergenerational issues. In case 3, we define the threat as nuclear waste explicitly, and we have no doubt that it is harmful. Given that considerable quantities of nuclear waste have been produced already, the quarantine decision is something of a no-brainer, and the duty to strive to learn how to better secure the facility and mitigate any damage seems clear, as is the duty to minimize and compensate for disproportionate local impacts. In case 4, where the existence of an effective nuclear waste isolation and storage facility is likely to encourage creation of more nuclear waste, the question is answered in two steps: first, there is a strong case for secure storage of existing waste, but the case for creating a continuing and perhaps increasing stream of new waste is contentious and founded ultimately on faith that learning in the interim will solve the problem of avoidance, mitigation, and adaptation.

These details are interesting, I think, but we should not lose sight of the main point: while QSR in its complete form applies to NI_1 cases, there is a role for quarantine as a remedy to some kinds of NI_2 threats.

Looking more closely at remedies: 2. BAU – Overstress from business-as-usual

The cumulative effects of exploitation, habitat encroachment, and pollution in the course of business-as-usual may eventually overstress systems, threatening damage that may range from gradual deterioration to full-blown regime shift. On the surface, the set of appropriate PP remedies looks much like those offered by ORM. They include prohibiting or regulating the actions or business-as-usual stresses that drive the threat; restoring and/or remediating any damage; accommodations such as avoiding, mitigating, and/or adapting to the threat; and insurance, self-insurance, and self-protection.

Various authors have linked the PP and sustainability (Deblonde and Du Jardin 2005). Economists often assume that there is a broad domain in which business-as-usual stresses can be managed by systematic implementation of policies to correct market failure. This involves getting the prices right throughout the economy – to internalize externalities, optimize provision of public goods, and the like – and through time to ensure that resource rents are re-invested. Such business-as-usual weak sustainability policies and institutions may be adequate for many natural resource and environmental sustainability problems, but Randall (2008) argued that they should be back-stopped by PP-justified strong sustainability exceptions in particular cases where such remedies are inadequate, or simply too late (the time for them has passed). For Australia, he identified climate change, endangered species and ecosystems, and dryland salinization as likely requiring more than weak sustainability remedies. Complexity theory and modeling tend to reinforce these concerns. They alert us to the importance of hysteresis (system response to stimuli is determined not only by current conditions but also by the path the system has been taking), and the possibility of sudden, drastic, and perhaps irreversible regime shifts that can be explained *ex post* but not always predicted.

The essence of *pre*cautionary intervention is that it is undertaken in response to uncertain harm which, in the BAU case, would take the form of on-going and perhaps accelerating harm that has yet to be detected and its cause established. This business of detecting harm and establishing its cause is more complicated than it seems at first glance. Typically, the harm that is visible today is tolerable. What raises the alarm is the perception of a rising trajectory of harm – that what we see today is just the tip of a future iceberg.

Projections of future trajectories and attribution of cause are both inexact and prone to controversy, as we see in the cases of climate change and north

Pacific salmon. Furthermore, the suspected business-as-usual causes are embedded in the human system (economy and society), and remedies therefore are likely to be costly and disruptive. The facts are objectively difficult to establish but, in these circumstances, controversy is exacerbated by a tendency among partisans to treat facts as malleable in service of policy positions.

So, in the BAU case the foremost concerns are possible regime shift, which may be unexpected and perhaps irreversible; uncertainty and perhaps controversy about causes; and the cost of remedies and the disruption of business-as-usual, given the likely social and political pressure to keep costs and disruption within tolerable bounds.

The concern that cumulative stress on systems will induce regime shift places a premium on learning more about how the system works, to get a better sense of the possibilities, and perhaps to identify some of the warning signs of impending harm. *Modeling* the system and empirical validation of models, to get a sense of its dynamics, stability, and resilience, will be a priority. It may be possible to identify thresholds of significant change and *early warning* signals of impending regime shift. Bussiere and Fratzscher (2008) emphasize the crucial role of early warning in risk management, and encourage enhanced research and investment in early warning systems. In this context, complex systems modeling may allow us to predict some regime switches; and it may allow us to identify some observable variables that we can monitor in order to predict some regime switches.

With early warning, feasible remedies may include measures to reduce the stresses that threaten regime shift and/or implement compensating measures in order to stabilize the system. Intuition suggests that stabilizing the system to maintain the *status quo ante*, if feasible, will be less expensive and probably more effective, than attempting to restore the *status quo ante* in the event we are unable to forestall regime shift. Note that restoration is not a hold-harmless solution, because even if the system eventually recovers fully, interim lost use[12] is experienced during the intervening period of reduced service flows. If mitigation and adaptation are included in the remediation package, it is likely that early warning would also reduce their costs and perhaps increase their effectiveness.

At this early stage, the science of early warning in complex natural systems is promising perhaps, but not consistently reassuring. Brock and Carpenter (2006) provide evidence that, in the case of shallow lake ecosystems, sudden increases in the variance of certain variables that can be monitored relatively easily provide early warning of potential regime shift. This optimistic finding is tempered by the observation of Brock *et al.* (2008) that the prospects of early warning are much less favorable for some other types of complex eco-systems. If early warning means early enough to allow effective policy and management response, what is early enough varies widely depending on the nature of the system and the required response. Meaningful response takes time, to generate a sense of political urgency and implement effective policy and management actions. Perhaps three-year's warning may be early enough in the case of impending collapse of a lake sport fishery, if restrictions on angler effort would be an effective response. If reductions in nutrient flow from the surrounding agricultural and residential land uses are required, three years seems much too little warning. In the case of climate change, we now have plausible predictions of temperate increases several decades hence, but that hardly constitutes early warning if we believe it will take several decades to make the systemic changes in the global economy and society that will be necessary to change the trajectories of the major climate stressors, and for these changes to have a noticeable effect on temperatures.

Recent research suggests that large increases in the indicators tend to occur only when a regime shift has begun, often too late for management to avert a shift (Biggs *et al.* 2009). If indicator-change signals come too late for corrective policy response, we might be better advised to focus research on defining critical indicator levels. Biggs *et al.* develop a new indicator with critical levels related to switches in ecosystem attractors. Even if indicators along these lines provide warning consistently earlier than indicator-change signals, these authors worry about the need to develop policy processes that enable society to respond more rapidly to information about impending regime shifts.

Early warning matters, and the latest science suggests reasons for cautious optimism, at best, that we will become better at forestalling impending regime shifts. Even with adequate warning, pragmatic decision makers may well frame society's choices as speculative damage sometime down the road versus certain, costly, and disruptive restriction of the human economy and society beginning immediately. Who can blame them for seeking to hedge their bets, and gravitating toward remedies that seem manageable in terms of cost and disruption?

Adaptive management frames remedy as a stepwise process – plan, implement, monitor, adjust plan, etc. (Box 5.3) – designed to increase opportunities for learning, as well as make progress toward reducing the threat. It is tempting to think of adaptive management as the paradigmatic "baby steps" approach to remedies for BAU cases (just as QSR is, for NI_1 cases). It allows us to experiment with remedies by trial and error. Where relatively small and easily-bounded systems are involved, it may be feasible to run different

experiments in parallel. Where conditions are favorable for adaptive management, it allows us learn about remedies "on the job" (so to speak) – in
the best cases, identifying opportunities to substitute effective but cheaper
and less intrusive remedies – and to make progress toward remedy relatively
cheaply in terms of cost and disruption. But one worries that such remedies
may be quite incomplete. Can we really forestall regime shift using adaptive management approaches? Perhaps we can, but only if the warning comes
early enough and the system is resilient enough. Following a regime shift, can
we really restore the *status quo ante* using adaptive management approaches?
Perhaps we can, but only if the barriers to reversion are low enough.

It seems obvious that adaptive management is best suited to the less
urgent threats, but perhaps it is also well-suited to the "hopeless" cases: those
where there is no realistic hope of forestalling regime shift or of restoring
the *status quo ante*, and the pragmatic objective is to learn how to survive
and perhaps thrive in the new regime.[13] For this assignment, *mitigation
and adaptation* loom large among the feasible remedies, and adaptive management seems well-suited to on-the-job learning about effective and relatively non-disruptive ways to mitigate the damage and adapt to the changed
environment.

Even where mitigation and adaptation are not central to the portfolio of
remedies, they may have a role to play. Seldom will it be possible to stabilize the system completely, or to restore the *status quo ante* completely and
without interim lost use, which implies that real-world remedies will typically include an element of adaptation. It is conceivable, too, that mitigation
and adaptation may be central to remedies in cases to which they are not
well-suited. If, facing the threat of dramatic regime shift, we dismiss drastic
restriction of the activities that drive the stressors as too costly and disruptive, we may in effect be choosing to take our chances with regime shift in
this case too, pushing mitigation and adaptation to the fore.[14]

Risk dilemmas – Is it ever too late for precaution?

Risk dilemmas are those situations that have a "doomed if we do, doomed if
we don't" flavor – disaster is hugely costly, but so is preventing it or restoring
the *status quo ante* (Jablonowski 2007). Risk dilemmas describe situations
that are already out of hand – it is too late for inexpensive and effective pre-
emptive actions to prevent uncertain harm. While the threat may be huge
thereby suggesting a role for PP, if the costs of averting it also are very large,
PP offers no guidance distinct from ORM (Box 9.12).[15]

Box 9.11 Can we take adaptive management seriously, in the case of climate change?

Regarding climate change, the immediate instinct is to assume that remedies will be hugely costly and only grudgingly effective (Weitzman 2009). But there is on-going debate about the extent of the threat and the costs of effective interventions. Here, we contrast two positions, each of which has attracted the support of some prominent economists.

High costs do not justify inaction. Weitzman examined the predictions of a set of most credible climate models. He observed that while we could perhaps adapt to the most likely predicted temperate increase, there remained a non-trivial chance (around 7 percent probability) of catastrophic climate change. The level of threat, he argued, is sufficiently great that we should be willing to bear very high costs for reducing GHG emissions (Chapter 5). Barro (2009) estimated society would willingly forego 20 percent of GDP to eliminate economic disasters, which (if even roughly accurate) suggests a much greater public tolerance for economic costs of disaster-avoidance than many of us suspected.

The costs of effective action are more tolerable than we may think. Others argue that real reductions in GHG emissions can be obtained relatively cheaply, and that the costs are offset at least in part by the environmental and health benefits of reduced air pollution (Quiggin 2007, Krugman www.nytimes.com/ 2009/12/07/opinion/07krugman.html). Furthermore, some observers are optimistic about the more traditional economic benefits – green technologies and green jobs – that might flow from climate action. If all social costs were considered, fossil fuels are not such a bargain even in the absence of threats to climate.

So, does adaptive management have a central role among the remedies for climate change?

- The second position (that the costs of effective action are really not so daunting) is potentially compatible with adaptive management. With more modest costs and substantial off-setting benefits of fairly familiar kinds, the case for making a modest but serious beginning is much stronger. That kind of approach allows for an element of trial and error, and for tilting the mix of remedies toward those that generate visible benefits fairly quickly.
- The first position is all about justifying drastic remedies, which suggests strongly that adaptive management is not the remedy of first resort. Nevertheless, there would be substantial roles for mitigation and adaptation, administered first to the economic shocks unleashed by drastic action on climate, and then to the changed environment even with drastic remedies (which will surely be unable to freeze in place the environment as we know it).

The two positions about the costs of climate remedies contrasted here suggest very different roles for adaptive management. So what should we do? Obviously, that depends on what we believe about the costs of effective climate remedies, which is why there is such lively controversy about remedies and time-frames for action, as well as the extent of the threat.

Box 9.12 Clarifying risk dilemmas

Jablonowski (2007) defines risk dilemmas as "doomed if we do, doomed if we don't" situations – disaster is hugely costly, but so is preventing it or restoring the *status quo ante*. This definition has its clearest implications in the case of what might be called damage dilemmas: cases where disaster is certain *and* the cost of preventing it is roughly the same as the value of damage to be avoided. Benefit–cost thinking is clear about such cases: choose the lesser of the evils; but, either way, welfare will suffer.

Of course, there usually is uncertainty about both the value of damage and the cost of avoiding it, and in both cases the uncertainty pertains to outcomes and to likelihoods. Often it is assumed that we know more about the cost of avoidance than the value of damage – frequently, the case analyzed involves uncertain damage and certain cost of avoidance. In this case, the recommendation of ORM depends on the degree of risk aversion. To avert an uncertain threat with certainty, ORM would endorse spending up to EV of damage if society is risk-neutral, and as much as the value of worst-case damage if society is sufficiently risk-averse to use a minimax-loss criterion – and this is true for any risk problem involving uncertain harm and certain costs of avoidance, not just for risk dilemmas.

What, then, is the special import of risk dilemmas? It seems clear that, like irreversibility, risk dilemma is not a binary concept but a continuum: categories can be defined but the definitions are inherently arbitrary. Likelihood matters – the possibility of great harm that is relatively unlikely generates a disproportionate threat; if the great harm is more likely than a normal distribution of outcomes would suggest, the threat is disproportionate and asymmetric; and if great harm is certain we have one of the conditions for a damage dilemma. The damage dilemma case makes it clear that cost of avoidance also matters – great harm cheaply averted is no dilemma. So, it makes sense to think of risk dilemmas as situations that approach damage dilemmas. Worst-case damage is great, and the dilemma becomes more pressing as cost of avoidance approaches the value of worst-case damage and the likelihood of the worst case approaches certainty.

A huge meteorite hurtling in the general direction of our planet would constitute a risk dilemma, but most risk dilemmas result from much more ordinary circumstances. Asbestos and PCBs present damage dilemmas, because the harm is great and the identity of the causal agent is effectively certain, and the remedy is enormously expensive; and it is clear that these situations resulted from belated recognition of the threat, which greatly increases the damage and the cost of the remedy as the causal agent becomes embedded in the economy and society. Risk dilemmas share these characteristics, but to a lesser degree. Ordinary NI_2 and BAU cases become risk dilemmas when the threat is recognized only slowly and the causal conditions are widespread and deeply embedded in the economy and society.

So, risk dilemmas are situations where it is, in a meaningful sense, too late for precaution. The situation is similar to that of the individual facing a choice between potentially devastating afflictions and risky and intrusive treatments (Chapter 8). At this stage, PP offers little unique contribution to the awful decision that must be made. But preventative care and early diagnosis have their roles in human healthcare, so there are things that individuals can do to avoid their own personal health risk dilemmas (but not to eliminate them). So it is with society. We can avoid many risk dilemmas by adopting a precautionary stance, seeking to reduce the occurrence of NI_2 cases, and address BAU cases early enough that adaptive management approaches offer fairly good prospects of averting the threat (Box 9.13).

Of course, there is not always a consensus as to whether we are in the grip of a risk dilemma. The debate between those who believe great expenditures to reduce greenhouse gas emissions are justified and those who argue that significant progress can be made without great economic disruption (Box 9.11) can be cast as a debate between those arguing that we are already in a climate risk dilemma and those who do not think so.

Remedies – a summary comment

A precautionary perspective puts high priority on remedies that can be implemented in advance to head off uncertain threats. The feasibility of preemptive remedies depends very much on the nature of the threat, and we have distinguished among novel interventions *ex ante*, novel interventions *ex post*, and novel outcomes from cumulative stresses due to business-as-usual exploitation, habitat encroachment, and/or pollution. NI_1 cases offer the possibility of screening with pre-release testing of those that pose non-trivial threats. For novel interventions that are sensitive (because they are known to pose non-trivial threats, or because we have low risk-tolerance regarding the systems they impact – new drugs for human use may fall into this category), for a desired level of precaution it may be possible to optimize the combination of stepwise processes that include pre-release testing and post-release follow-up. For NI_2 and BAU cases, pre-release testing is not possible. Early warning may allow remedies that avert the threat, restore the *status quo ante*, or get a head start on mitigation and adaptation. The longer it takes to recognize the threat and generate the political will to act, the more likely it is that available remedies are limited to mitigation, remediation, and adaptation. Risk dilemmas, by definition, present only very undesirable

Box 9.13 Risk dilemmas – can we avoid this kind of mess in future?

If you don't know how to fix it, please stop breaking it! (Martin 1997)

PP cannot offer a unique contribution to risk management once a risk dilemma is in place. For example, global warning may cause horrendous damage, yet abating it might be hugely costly (Box 9.11). All PP can do is chime in to the ORM debate on the side of strong risk-aversion (footnote 14).

It may be useful to ask whether systematic inclusion of the PP in risk management policy and practice can be expected to reduce the occurrence of risk dilemmas. ORM typically proceeds on the assumption of "safe until strong evidence of harm is established" – most of the weight is placed on the side of avoiding false positives regarding harm. When ORM methods are used to forecast risk, modeling approaches typically are reductionist and often linear in logic and assumption, and thus not well suited to complex systems. We might expect this sort of analysis to underestimate systematically the chance of surprises in complex systems (May *et al.* 2008) and, in practice, too often harm has occurred long before the science catches up (Murphy 2009). If ORM is applied again and again, to threat after threat, the path is toward an increasing aggregation of risk. Policy driven by risk assessment practices that systematically underestimate risk exposure, coupled with the "safe until proven harmful" null hypothesis, can be expected to result in the systemic accumulation of risks and hence to risk dilemmas (Jablonowski 2007).

Risk dilemmas are confined to cases where post-release remedies are the only kinds available. That is, we may encounter risk dilemmas in NI_2 and BAU cases but not in NI_1 cases. PP thinking would suggest the following approaches to avoiding risk dilemmas:

- Adopt the PP evidence criterion: credible scientific evidence of plausible threat. This would restore a degree of balance to the weight given to null and alternative hypotheses regarding harm.
- Be more systematic about screening of proposed novel interventions, and pre-release testing of those that pose non-trivial threats.
- Adopt complex systems thinking – alertness to path-dependence and the possibility of surprises; systematic modeling to identify indicator variables for impending regime shift.
- Seek to incorporate early warning, scope for learning, affordable remedies, QSR for NI_1 cases and adaptive management for NI_2 and BAU cases, and policies to mitigate disproportionate negative impacts.
  - QSR addresses credible threats earlier, when solutions are less expensive; and tests avoidance, mitigation, adaptation strategies on a limited scale under controlled conditions prior to more general implementation.
  - When precautionary intervention is not prohibitively urgent, intervention may take multiple forms (avoidance, mitigation, and adaptation) and may be implemented in adaptive management processes that may reduce the expense of the precautionary policy.

options – a serious likelihood of disastrous harm, and remedies that are disastrously expensive – and occur only when it is too late for inexpensive and effective pre-emptive actions. Risk dilemmas cannot always be avoided – a huge meteorite hurtling toward our planet would be an example – but the intuition of many PP proponents is that our dedication to ORM approaches to risk exposes us to too many risk dilemmas.

A comprehensive precautionary policy is sensitive to the need for:

- Affordable remedies, which are helpful in building and sustaining coalitions in support of solutions among contemporaries, and intergenerational commitments to solutions (UNESCO 2005).
- Scope for learning, to reduce ignorance, narrow the uncertainties, better specify the possible outcomes and probabilities, and develop and test strategies for avoidance, mitigation, and adaptation – in the best case, gross ignorance may be reduced to manageable risk (Sinha *et al.* 2008).[16]
- Together, the above two considerations encourage "slow down and learn" strategies: screening, pre-release testing, and QSR approaches to NI_1 cases; and early warning and, to the extent feasible, adaptive management approaches to NI_2 and BAU cases. Such strategies reduce the costs of remedies and are designed to create opportunities for learning, but they are feasible only if implemented before things get out of hand.
- Explicit recognition that precaution may impose costs and economic disruption, especially in cases where the threat has become embedded in the economy or emerges from overstressing systems in the course of business-as-usual; and remedies that include specific provisions to reduce or mitigate disproportionate negative impacts of precaution on particular locations and/or socio-economic groups (UNESCO 2005, Dickson 1999).

Linking evidence, threat, and remedy

Intuition suggests interdependence among evidence, threat, and remedy in action. For example, our willingness to address a threat might depend in part on the menu of available remedies; and we might adjust our notion of credible evidence depending on the magnitude of the threat. The extensive discussion of QSR and adaptive management in this chapter makes a point that should receive added emphasis here: evidence applies to remedies as well as threats. Response processes that encourage learning augment evidence about the extent of the threat and the nature, effectiveness and cost of available remedies. Where stepwise remedies are implemented, evidence, threat, and

Box 9.14 Threats from novel interventions: E, T, and R in an iterative implementation process

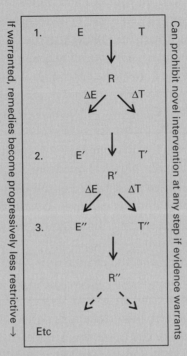

Consider an iterative process that responds to evidence of threat by implementing a remedy, **R** – perhaps quarantine, research, and assessment – that provides protection against the spread of a potentially harmful agent while enabling some learning about the nature of the threat and the effectiveness of the remedy. As a result of this learning process, the evidence and the threat are re-assessed. This new understanding, **E′** and **T′**, suggests a modified remedy, **R′**. If **E′** and **T′** are more reassuring than the original **E** and **T**, **R′** may relax the quarantine restrictions a little, to expand the scope of potential learning about the behavior of the agent. But if **E′** and **T′** are more alarming than the original **E** and **T**, **R′** may be even more restrictive than **R**; if warranted, the novel intervention may be prohibited. Evidence gained from implementation of **R′** provides a new understanding of the evidence and threat, **E″** and **T″**, and suggests another modification of the remedy, **R″**. And so on …

In this kind of process, all three components, **E**, **T**, and **R**, interact iteratively. Evidence, threat, and remedy are all re-assessed in light of new information generated in an iterative process designed to promote learning.

remedy are all re-assessed in light of new information generated in an itera-tive process that promotes learning as well as providing more decision points and thus less up-front commitment (Box 9.14).

In this section, the objective is to think a little more systematically about how evidence, threat, and remedy might be linked in a coherent decision framework. An intuitively appealing goal is to attain proportionality in some meaningful sense among the criteria we impose regarding evidence, threat, and remedy.

For evidence (**E**), threat (**T**), and Remedy (**R**), the relevant attributes include:

- **E.** The criterion for invoking the PP is credible scientific evidence of plaus-ible threat. So, the practical question is how accurate, precise, complete, and well-validated must **E** be? For the sake of this discussion, suppose we can create an index that captures these attributes and ranks the available evidence along a single **E** dimension of less to more.
- **T.** We define threat as chance of harm. The relevant attributes are the mag-nitude of harm and the chance of it occurring. Suppose threats can be indexed and ranked from smaller to larger on a single **T** dimension.[17]
- **R.** Remedies are not so readily indexed. Remedies may avert the threat, restore the system, mitigate/remediate the damage, and/or help us adapt to the new world we find ourselves in. For each of these tasks, remedies may be more or less costly and more or less effective. For **R**, we are interested in the continuous dimensions of less to more costly and less to more effective; and also on the qualitative distinction between those that can be implemented stepwise and those that are implemented in binary (all or none) fashion.

To get started, we consider pairwise links between **E**, **T**, and **R**:

- **T** and **R**:
  - Assuming effectiveness of **R**, the larger is **T** the more likely we would be willing to undertake more expensive **R**.
  - Assuming effectiveness of **R**, the more stepwise is **R** the more likely we would be willing to invoke **R** for smaller **T**.
  - Doubts about effectiveness of **R** undermine willingness to invoke costly all-or-none **R**, especially for smaller **T**.
  - The more stepwise is **R**, the more likely we are to start the **R** process even if we have effectiveness concerns, because we can learn more about both **T** and **R** as we proceed, and we have the option to discontinue **R** at any step.
- **E** and **T**:
  - The larger is **T** the more likely we are to sound the alarm on less **E**, because the risk entailed in doing nothing looms large.

- **E** and **R**:
  - The more expensive and disruptive is **R**, the more **E** we might require before invoking **R**.
  - The earlier that **R** can begin, and the more stepwise the **R** process, the less **E** we might require before invoking **R**.
  - Doubts about effectiveness of **R** undermine willingness to invoke costly **R** given modest **E**.
  - With stepwise **R**, we are more likely to start the **R** process on modest **E** even if we have effectiveness concerns.

Now, we consider the three-way links among **E**, **T**, and **R**. The key conclusion is that the earlier **R** can begin, the more stepwise the **R** process, and the more likelihood that the **R** process will generate more **E**, the smaller is the **T** and the lower is the **E** standard we might require before invoking **R** even if we have concerns about its effectiveness. Implications include:

- With stepwise **R** we acquire more **E** about both **T** and **R** as we proceed, and we have the option to discontinue **R** at any step. It follows that:
  - We may require smaller **T** and/or lower **E** standards to initiate pre-release **R** in NI_1 cases, and to activate adaptive management in NI_2 and BAU cases.
  - We may be willing to invoke pre-release **R** in NI_1 cases and activate adaptive management in NI_2 and BAU cases, even if we have doubts about the effectiveness of **R**.
- With all-or-none **R**, we must take the cost and effectiveness of **R** as fixed attributes of a decision to invoke **R**. Implications include:
  - For a considerable range of **T**, we would require larger **T** and/or higher **E** standards to invoke more costly **R**. But these relationships are not linear:
    - For daunting **T**, we might invoke **R** on less **E**, because the greater risk lies in doing nothing.
    - But as **R** approaches **T** in cost, we might require higher **E** standards to invoke **R** (i.e. we would want to be fairly sure about **T** and **R**), because we are in a risk dilemma, just trying to make the best of a really bad pair of alternatives.
  - Doubts about effectiveness of **R** undermine willingness to invoke costly **R**.

A note on cost considerations in the PP context. Cost of remedy considerations have emerged explicitly at several points throughout this chapter. For example, exploring the idea of proportionality among **E**, **T**, and **R**, we find ourselves considering the likely cost and effectiveness of all-or-none remedies, and valuing sequential and iterative remedy processes for the opportunities they provide to reassess our commitment to remedy in light of emerging information. Once we are in a risk dilemma, it is too late to invoke the PP – the options have a "doomed if we do, doomed if we don't" character and decisions about remedies are likely to be driven by cost minimization: are we worse-off living with the disaster or committing huge expenditures to prevent it? Given this sensitivity to costs of remedy, one might ask, how is this PP differentiated from, and in what ways does it go beyond, ORM (with its benefit–cost foundations)?

Costs always matter, even to PP proponents. One of the recurrent arguments for precautionary approaches points to the enormous costs of remediation and restoration in NI_2 cases – the clean-up and restoration expenses for PCBs, MTBE, and C8 (used in manufacturing Teflon®), to give just a few current examples, would cover the costs of testing a lot of new synthetic organic chemicals prior to release. Cost-effectiveness is always a consideration in the choice of R. It seems reasonable to argue that, because the tendency of PP is to invoke remedies to more threats and to invoke them earlier than ORM, the PP places if anything a higher priority on cost-effectiveness – resources are not unlimited. In these things, differences between PP and ORM positions are mostly matters of degree.

Nevertheless, the PP departs from ORM on matters of cost in several ways. The PP is not committed to utilitarian criteria such as benefit–cost, expected value, or expected utility. PP thinking recognizes the complexity of the real world and the unpredictability of complex systems, and worries that ORM risk assessment systematically underestimates threats. PP thinking is less enamored with the law of large numbers than ORM – catastrophe takes us out of the game, and disaster wipes out resources so that starting-over does not guarantee catching up: this time, we start later and with less. If we concede that utilitarian solutions to certain classes of problems (infinite prospects, high damage but unlikely prospects, etc.) are unconvincing, PP proponents argue, it would make little sense to insist that policies addressed to disproportionate and asymmetric threats must pass a utilitarian test.

Accordingly, the PP commits us to invoke remedies when faced with credible scientific evidence of plausible disproportionate threat, i.e. before the threat and its causes are firmly established. In effect, this becomes a commitment to act earlier (and, one would expect, more often) than ORM, which suggests that precaution can be costly; but early action also has its cost-reducing benefits in many cases. For proposed novel interventions that pose threats above the PP threshold, pre-release testing looms large among the remedies that may be invoked; and for NI_1 cases that can be quarantined, prohibition readily defaults to quarantine and stepwise release which, as we have seen, provides a sequential decision process that allows us to tailor the remedy to the threat as we learn more about both. For novel interventions *ex post*, earlier action means rigorous post-release surveillance. Withdrawal from the market and remediation are likely remedies should a serious threat be confirmed. For overstress from business-as-usual, earlier action means developing and implementing early warning systems and invoking remedies should the alarm be signaled. For both NI_2 and BAU cases, adaptive management may play an important role in restoration, mitigation, and adaptation; and for BAU cases, if remedies are invoked early enough, adaptive management may figure in remedies to avert the threat. Again, the PP impetus to early action is combined with sensitivity to costs and a bias toward remedy processes that provide sequential decision points and encourage learning.

NOTES

1 The issue was that peasants may save some of the GMO-food offered for seed, thus introducing GMOs into future crops and thereby putting exports from the affected countries at risk of being banned by the European Union. Donor counties offered to mill the grain involved, which would eliminate that particular risk.

2 The FDA has been sensitive to this criticism, and has fast-tracked promising drugs for the worst sorts of afflictions.

3 The protection afforded by confinement was recognized as early as 1975, in the context of recombinant DNA research (Berg *et al.* 1975), along with the notion that the security of required confinement should be related to the potential risk posed by the organism, and the hope and perhaps expectation that subsequent research and experience would lead to a more optimistic reassessment of the risks entailed in such research.

4 Thomas and Randall (2000) outline a protocol along these lines for the case of purposeful introduction of a non-indigenous species.

5 If, on the other hand, there is a non-trivial chance that aliens would destroy us while we research and dither, the threat is no longer asymmetric and disproportionate – but there are plenty of asymmetric and disproportionate cases, I suspect.

6 I cannot offer any systematic evidence that the benefits foregone, as pre-release scrutiny and testing delays implementation of the whole stream of innovations, are likely to be relatively modest, but my intuition suggests that this is the case. I do note, however, that there is very little empirical evidence in support of the utilitarian argument that pre-release testing required by the FDA comes at a substantial net cost in affliction and death that could have been saved by quicker access to new drugs. Apparently, this is one of those arguments that economists think is too self-evident to require empirical support.

7 Nevertheless, the routine administration of antibiotics in the feed of healthy livestock in confined animal feeding operations continues in the US, despite fears that it will contribute to development of antibiotic resistant human pathogens.

8 Many countries review and/or regulate GMO crops and/or foods, incorporating some of the procedures sketched in the stylized case study (above). For example, the US FDA maintains a voluntary consultation process in which it reviews tests (typically theoretical and *in vitro* – animal studies are rare) conducted by developers of GMO foods and, if satisfied (the substantive standard is that they pose no greater risk than non-GMO foods), issues a letter stating that they have no further questions. Developers apply to the US Department of Agriculture for non-regulated status, and a US DA agency reviews risk factors and solicits public comments before making a determination. GMO crops with pesticidal properties must be registered, and the US EPA conducts a risk assessment and invites public comment before making the registration decision. Post-release, all three agencies have the authority to remove GMO products from the market if new, valid data demonstrate serious threats to consumers or the environment (www.agbios.com/static/cscontent/REGUSACAN-USAEN_printer.html). The European Union regulatory framework, being designed for GMOs, is more comprehensive and consistent. All foods and feeds containing non-trivial proportions of GMOs or GMO derivatives are regulated via a one-stop authorization procedure (http://europa.eu/legislation_summaries/agriculture/food/l21154_en.htm). A risk assessment is conducted, and the authorization criterion is that the product must be determined, by tests using the most advanced knowledge and technology available, to be as safe to humans, animals, and the environment as their conventionally derived counterparts. Consumers, farmers, and businesses must be given the freedom to either use or to reject authorized products made from GMOs, a goal that leads to requirements for GMO labeling, traceability, and co-existence (GM plants must be grown and handled so as to prevent uncontrolled mixing with conventional products).

9 The US regulatory process is less complete in several dimensions than that sketched in the stylized case study. Nevertheless, Fedoroff *et al.* (2010) argue that US pre-release screening and testing procedures amount not to too little regulation but too much. One of their points is that corporate biotechnology shows little interest in raising production in the lowest income tropics, leaving that market segment to government and university programs that cannot afford the regulatory burden.

10 The ORM risk analysis model attempts to calculate the mathematical likelihood that any new technology or substance will cause harm to the public or the environment. The trouble is that it has not been very effective in predicting effects within complex systems. Too often, harm has occurred long before the science catches up (Murphy 2009).

11 Consider the case of Vioxx, a Merck product prescribed as an anti-inflammatory following approval in 1999. Post-market surveillance revealed increased incidence of strokes and heart disease among users, and Merck recalled Vioxx in 2004 and set aside almost $5 billion to settle legal claims. It has been argued that the phase-3 testing of Vioxx was inadequate (despite FDA approval) because the subjects were not representative of the population likely to use it post-approval (Manski 2009).

12 "Interim lost use" is a technical term in natural resources damage assessment, and refers to the value of resource services lost in the time interval between the onset of damage and the accomplishment of full restoration.

13 To complete this picture, adaptive management is least-suited to situations that call for urgent, drastic, and decisive action.

14   We see some of this thinking in the US discussion of policy responses to threatened climate change.

15   The fact that many ORM practitioners argue for no more than modest degrees of social risk aversion should not blind us to the fact that strong risk-aversion is admissible in ORM. In this situation all PP can contribute is to argue for a relatively high degree of risk-aversion. Such a stance may be appropriate, but it would not represent a distinct contribution of PP thinking.

16   At least one judicial body has ruled that commitment to continuing research is a hallmark of good faith in applying the PP. The World Trade Organization Appellate Body (in the EC – Hormones case) ruled that a pivotal point in determining the legitimacy of a measure based on the precautionary principle is that the member state putting such a measure in place must continue its scientific research and perform serious reviews of the precautionary measure to show evidence of its good faith (Shaw and Schwartz 2005).

17   ORM offers the expected value of damage and the expected utility of damage criteria to serve this purpose. To suppose an index of threat can be constructed does not commit us to either of these ORM formulations.

10   Precaution for utilitarians?

The precautionary principle developed in Chapters 7 – 9 departs from ordinary risk management in several ways. It is more likely to prohibit a proposed novel intervention when faced with a specific NI_1 that presents a disproportionate threat; and it is more likely to prescribe a pre-release testing regime for a whole class of NI_1 innovations if some of its members have presented disproportionate threats in the past (e.g. new drugs, synthetic chemicals), or theory and/or experience suggest that the class has the capacity to generate some disproportionate threats (e.g. some groups of genetically modified organisms). Radically new technologies that present plausible scenarios of disproportionate harm but no basis for specifying its likelihood are obvious candidates for pre-release testing. Note that if the NI_1 can be quarantined, prohibition readily defaults to the quarantine and stepwise release process, which begins with pre-release testing, and can be discontinued at any time if it is determined that no serious threat exists. When a general release is approved, the precautionary principle (PP) is more likely than ordinary risk management (ORM) to prescribe rigorous post-release surveillance, and likely remedies should a serious threat be confirmed include withdrawal from the market and remediation of damage.

For novel interventions *ex post* and overstress from business-as-usual (BAU), the PP is likely to prescribe early warning systems and prompt remedial action should the alarm be signaled. For both NI_2 and BAU cases, remedies may include an important role for adaptive management.

So, our PP is more likely than ORM to prohibit some novel innovations and more likely to prescribe pre-release testing of individual NI_1 cases. It is tilted toward early action that includes developing and implementing early warning systems in NI_2 and BAU cases, and adaptive management strategies are likely to feature among the remedies. This PP is sensitive to costs and biased toward remedy processes that provide sequential decision points and encourage learning, but it is nevertheless open to remedies that go beyond those that would be endorsed by ORM.

Limits of utilitarian precaution

I have argued that the characteristic features of ORM are risk assessments that rely on simple reductive models of the systems that generate risk and are impacted by it, and utilitarian decision criteria based on the benefit–cost rule (Chapter 5). ORM is founded on the insurance model – the insurer relies on the law of large numbers and so uses expected values in its benefit–cost calculations, and individuals who are not assured of many draws from a stable distribution will buy insurance at a mark-up, using expected utility in their personal benefit–cost assessment of the transaction. With idiosyncratic risk, insurers are risk-neutral and individuals are risk-averse within limits derived from their preferences. Applied to public policy, ORM usually recommends that government use expected value criteria for a broad range of risk management decisions. Nevertheless, a literature emerged arguing that expected utility should have a role in certain specific public decisions under risk and uncertainty, motivating the lengthy utilitarian excursion into irreversibility (where the law of large numbers seemed problematic), and option value, quasi-option value, and real options thinking as vehicles for utilitarian risk aversion (Chapter 5).

Going back to the 1970s, at least, utilitarians (especially economists) have attempted to show that precautionary restrictions could be derived from utilitarian foundations. Having put a little flesh on the bones of the **ETR** framework for the PP, we can now make some progress at clarifying the relationship between the PP as framed here and various utilitarian-inspired arguments and proposals that tilt in a precautionary direction.

An important precursor to the PP was the "safe minimum standard of conservation" (SMS), proposed by Ciriacy-Wantrup (1968) to address conservation issues in biological systems. The classical model assumes, at least implicitly, a single species whose biomass grows in sigmoid fashion, i.e. slowly from a very low baseline, more rapidly in the mid-range, then slowly again as it approaches the carrying capacity of its environment, and eventually hits a ceiling at the Malthusian limit (Figure 10.1).[1] With a growth model of this kind, there is a level of biomass, S_{min}, below which the population will be unable to recover. Obviously, a crucial management objective is to maintain biomass above S_{min}. Now assume the level of the growth curve is stochastic – the growth curve experienced at a given time may be higher and it may be lower than usual – and if it were lower than usual, management strategies geared to maintaining at least S_{min} would not necessarily meet the conservation objective. If the dashed curve represents the lower-bound growth curve,

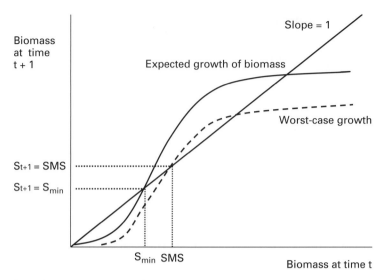

Figure 10.1   The safe minimum standard of conservation

a safe minimum standard of conservation would maintain biomass above SMS rather than S_{min}.[2]

The SMS can be considered a kind of precaution, because (i) the notion of *safe* minimum, i.e. a minimum level that is enough to assure conservation in even the worst of times, clearly involves *caution*, and (ii) the management objective is to avert a conservation crisis rather than to address one should it arise, thereby providing the *pre-* in this kind of precaution.

Economists (and some other utilitarians) found the SMS argument unconvincing for several reasons:

- Surely there are substitutes for the particular biomass system under stress, which would imply limits to the costs we would be willing to bear to conserve it.
- Economic solutions to inter-temporal decision problems in biological systems typically recommend efficient exhaustion of systems that fall below some minimum level of economic productivity. The economic solution requires sustainable management of those biological resources that are sufficiently productive, but there are limits to the sacrifice that can reasonably be expected to preserve relatively unproductive resources.
- Microeconomic thinking – which is mostly about making fine adjustments to management objectives in response to changes in prices and other variables exogenous to the firm – is generally uncomfortable with all-or-none decision rules such as the SMS that are unresponsive to relative prices.

These various objections all reflect the utilitarian intuition that an analysis that results in rigid decision rules such as the SMS must surely be assuming something odd about preferences or the way the world works. So, we see at the outset that the quest to justify utilitarian precaution will encounter serious obstacles.

There are two obvious avenues for a utilitarian attempt to justify precaution: (i) arguments from preferences, most commonly that risk aversion is sufficient to justify precaution; and (ii) arguments from the way the world works, i.e. that under certain non-trivial conditions response functions are discontinuous, with kinks, thresholds, etc, that would yield precautionary rules. We will review progress to date in both of these approaches to justifying utilitarian precaution.

(i) Arguments from preferences

Arguments from preferences explore the conditions under which risk aversion as ordinarily understood and catastrophe aversion are sufficient to generate optimal decisions to invoke precautionary measures.

PP as a rational implication of risk aversion. Early attempts at a utilitarian justification of the SMS went the preferences route, imposing extreme risk aversion in one guise or another, and often unconvincingly. For example, Bishop (1978) argued that the SMS could be derived as a maximin solution to an endangered species problem. In other words, the best of the worst-case solutions – and thus the one an extremely risk-averse decision maker would choose – must be the one that conserves this particular species (or biological system).

However, Ready and Bishop (1991) show that the maximin solution is not always a strict conservation rule. In the Ready and Bishop analysis, it might turn out that a chemical found in the species provides the cure to a dangerous disease. The maximin solution depends on the balance of the risks – species conservation is maximin when the cure is certain but the disease outbreak is risky, but it is not maximin when the outbreak is certain but the species' contribution to the cure is risky. This is yet another instance of a problem mentioned in Chapter 5: risk aversion yields ambiguous results when there is risk on both sides of the equation. One might predict a Kolstad-type (1996) ambivalence result when both risks are considered: the disease might/not come and the cure might/not work.

Utilitarian responses to catastrophic possibilities. Chichilnisky (2000) shows that the expected utility approach is insensitive to unlikely but potentially catastrophic events. By convention, EU is implemented with bounded utility functions to avoid the St. Petersburg paradox (Chapter 5). The effect of bounded utility is that lotteries are EU-ranked independently of the utilities of states (even catastrophic states) whose probabilities are lower than some threshold, the value of which depends on the particular lotteries being compared. She proposes a ranking criterion for potential projects or policies that gives weight to expected utility considerations and to the desire to avoid unlikely but catastrophic outcomes.

Barrieu and Sinclair-Desgagné (2006) offer a rather elaborate weighting formulation in an attempt to deal simultaneously with two key PP issues: scientific uncertainty and risk–benefit trade-offs. Scenarios are weighted: greater threat of harm increases the weight attached to a particular scenario, but the weights of all plausible scenarios are reduced when there are more of them. *Ex ante* benefits of taking the risky action are weighted, as are plausible damages. The scales are tilted toward harm-avoidance in two ways: more harmful scenarios are over-weighted and the benefits–harm trade-off is tilted in favor of harm-avoidance. The authors work through a couple of representative cases to provide a flavor of how their formulation works.

Chichilnisky (2000) and Barrieu and Sinclair-Desgagné (2006) clearly incorporate risk-aversion, and even a degree of disaster-aversion, into their formulations. For these authors, precaution takes the form of a thumb on the scales favoring avoidance of disastrous outcomes.

Gollier *et al.* (2000) and Gollier and Treich (2003) have used the concept of scientific uncertainty, a real options approach to managing the wait for better scientific information, and a Bayesian approach to learning from new information to identify conditions under which precautionary measures are efficient. Gollier *et al.* (2000) address scientific uncertainty via a Bayesian response to new scientific information. In Bayesian formulations, one's prior beliefs and the new information both influence one's posterior beliefs, and their relative influence depends on the weights given to each. These authors identify a class of quite restrictive but plausible conditions such that scientific uncertainties justify an immediate reduction of the consumption of a potentially toxic substance. More uncertainty justifies more conservation today (a quasi-option effect, Chapter 5). For BAU cases, where accumulation of stressors (e.g. greenhouse gases) threatens regime shift, they identified conditions that yield an unambiguous result with precautionary implications – more effort should be made to prevent future threats when the situation is more uncertain – but these conditions are quite restrictive.

Gollier and Treich (2003) define PP as a bias toward premature invest-ments in prevention of uncertain harm. They distinguish between *scientific uncertainty*, which is about us and what we know – scientific uncertainty is greater today if we expect scientific research to be more informative in the future – and *real risk*, which is about the real world. The structure of real risk remains what it is, as scientific uncertainty is perhaps reduced by an experiment. To Gollier and Treich scientific uncertainty, not real risk, is at the root of the precautionary motive. And because scientific uncertainty may be reduced over time, a precautionary measure is a temporary and flexible decision that is taken in the face of inadequate current scientific evidence. In short, to these authors, precaution aims at managing the wait for better scientific information.

Their decision maker is Bayesian, revising beliefs after each new input of scientific information. An action is called irreversible if undertaking it unambiguously reduces the set of choices available later on.[3] Gollier and Treich examine the link between irreversibility, the prospect of increas-ing information over time, and risk management. They identify conditions under which the PP is an EU-efficient economic guideline, and they identify an irreversibility effect – which favors retaining flexibility, i.e. a larger choice set, until more information is available – and a precautionary effect such that if today's consumption increases future risk, under certain fairly restrictive conditions involving risk-aversion, today's consumption should be reduced. In these ways, their work brings the notion of option value closer to that of precaution. All of this makes sense given that by PP Gollier and Treich mean a measured precautionary approach, i.e. a temporary and flexible deci-sion taken in the face of inadequate scientific information. In the end, their decision criterion is expected utility, and their explorations in precaution are all about conditions under which more or less preservation of options is EU efficient.

To summarize the take-home lesson from these several contributions to the literature, Chichilnisky (2000), Barrieu and Sinclair-Desgagné (2006), Gollier *et al.* (2000), and Gollier and Treich (2003) have all constructed cases where precautionary measures can be derived from utilitarian for-mulations under scientific uncertainty, given enough risk-aversion. For these authors, precaution takes the form of a thumb on the scales favor-ing avoidance of disastrous outcomes. But, because they remain true to the basic utilitarian framework, it is a circumstantial kind of precaution – at the end of all the weighting the scales are still there, and their reading drives the decision.[4]

Sunstein (2006) proposed a "catastrophic harm precautionary principle" (CHPP). He writes of buying a real option to avoid uncertain and perhaps unlikely catastrophic harm. This sounds promising in so far as it goes, but it remains undeveloped because Sunstein does not specify exactly what would trigger the purchase. Real options theory suggests a rule such as buy the option at prices less than V_1 (Boxes 4.2 and 5.2), i.e. if buying it passes an expected utility benefit–cost test. Even if the rule is to buy the option at prices less than aV_1, $a > 1$, where a is a risk-aversion parameter, it amounts to a benefit–cost rule with a risk-averse thumb on the scales. Under these interpretations, CHPP fits firmly within the utilitarian "circumstantial precaution" tradition. Only if the buy rule was simply "if the evidence is credible that the threatened harm could be disastrous, buy the option," would CHPP be a PP of the general kind framed here.

All of these utilitarian contributions fit comfortably within the ORM framework. Gollier (2001) argues that what is good and reasonable about PP (precautionary environmental savings, option value, learning-by-doing, concern for future generations) can readily be incorporated into the potential Pareto-improvement benefit–cost framework; and Farrow (2004) takes a similar stance. All of these utilitarian formulations will endorse precaution if the numbers work out that way. The point is that the PP as framed here goes beyond ORM in that it does not impose a benefit–cost filter in the face of threats sufficiently great to trigger precautionary remedies.

Farmer and Randall (1998) and Randall (1999) have questioned the necessity for such Herculean struggling in search of a utilitarian PP, given that there can be no serious claim that utilitarianism is a complete and convincing moral theory. Instead, there seems to be broad acceptance among philosophers that the contest among ethical theories is likely to remain inconclusive. While each contending theory has powerful appeal, each is incomplete in some important way, each remains vulnerable to some serious avenue(s) of criticism, and it seems unlikely that any one will defeat the others decisively. Each, also, is inconsistent with the others in important ways, so that a coherent synthesis is unlikely (Williams 1985).

One might argue that the task of the thoughtful moral agent in the policy arena is to find heuristics – rules for action – that can support agreement on particular real world policy resolutions. Agreement might be reached, for example, that real resources should be expended to protect natural environments, among people who would give quite different reasons as to why that should be so. Taking moral pluralism seriously encourages us to think of the policy process as a search for heuristics we can agree upon, and to accept that these heuristics are likely to incorporate insights from various moral theories.

If the search for the single true, complete, and internally consistent ethical theory is bound to be fruitless, exclusive allegiance to any particular moral theory is hardly a virtue; and it becomes coherent to resolve life's everyday questions according to utilitarian precepts, while addressing a (perhaps smaller) set of less-negotiable issues by reference to moral imperatives or rights that should be respected. In the end, there is no convincing argument against the idea that the scope for business-as-usual utilitarian ethics might coherently be bounded by non-utilitarian constraints (Farmer and Randall 1998, Randall 1999).

(ii) Arguments from the way the world works

Naevdal and Oppenheimer (2007) and Margolis and Naevdal (2008) suggest a different approach to utilitarian precaution. Perhaps we should be searching for the thresholds, kinks, etc. needed to derive utilitarian precaution in the way the world works (i.e., in the response functions) rather than in preferences. Thresholds, kinks, etc. in the way the world works are in fact suggested by the ideas of complexity, regime shifts, tipping points, etc. (Folke *et al.* 2004, Holling 2001).

Margolis and Naevdal have shown that precautionary prohibitions or pauses may be optimal from a utilitarian standpoint when the response relationships exhibit thresholds. The example of atmospheric ozone emissions is offered, in which we know that problems for human health are triggered when ozone concentrations become high enough, but we are not sure exactly where the threshold lies and exactly what rate of emissions will maintain concentrations above the threshold. In a static optimization model, thresholds in the way the world works may induce optimal SMS-type conservation constraints as corner solutions.[5] Several dynamic models enrich the set of cases and solutions, but do not change the basic message – SMS-type solutions may be optimal in a variety of cases. They claim that this result reduces the set of cases where utilitarianism and SMS are in direct conflict. I would argue that the policy recommendation of Margolis and Naevdal may be precautionary but, once again, it is circumstantial rather than principled, being driven by response functions that generate the efficient precaution result.

Naevdal and Oppenheimer motivate their analysis with the example of someone paid by the step to walk blind-folded toward a cliff an unknown distance away. What is the optimal stopping rule? Not surprisingly, "stop now" may be a rather robust rule. The "walking toward the cliff" problem that exercises these authors is climate change and the possibility that it will reverse the gulf stream abruptly, plunging northwestern Europe into a climate more like Siberia's. This, too, is a threshold problem, where we do not know the location of the threshold. The analyses quickly get more complicated, as the possibility of multiple thresholds is introduced and the problem is defined as the regulator's decision about allowable carbon dioxide emissions. Depending on initial conditions, they get various results including some where a rigid limit is placed on the acceptable rate of temperature rise, and some "stop right here" results.

Margolis-Naevdal and Naevdal-Oppenheimer have shown that, with thresholds and aversion to catastrophic risk, stopping rules and strict limits on pollution, harvest, etc. – i.e. rules that look like SMS and precaution in BAU cases – emerge as optimal utilitarian solutions. Margolis and Naevdal explicitly interpret their result as "reduc(ing) the scope for argument between proponents and opponents of SMS as a policy tool [by presenting] simple conditions for when a SMS is consistent with utilitarian calculus" (p. 408).

A bottom line on utilitarian precaution

Some utilitarian formulations endorse precaution, but it is always a circumstantial sort of precaution in that it always depends on the particulars: risk and/or catastrophe aversion, and/or kinks, thresholds, and discontinuities in the model of how the world works. If utilitarian thinking gets a precautionary result (as in Naevdal and Oppenheimer 2007), PP advocates would welcome that circumstance – it broadens the coalition for implementing precaution in that case. Likewise, if a precautionary policy passes a utilitarian test that is sensitive to potential catastrophe, or Sunstein's (2006) real option to avoid catastrophic harm passes a benefit–cost filter.

While utilitarians express surprise and (for some of them) pleasure that utilitarian formulations can be constructed that generate precautionary results, PP proponents worry that utilitarian formulations offer only an iffy sort of precaution (Box 10.1). Under any formulation of utilitarian precaution, one can imagine some disproportionate threats that would not trigger precaution. So, we arrive at the core question raised by utilitarian precaution: should we accept a utilitarian filter on precaution, i.e. invoke precaution only if it passes a utilitarian filter? If we concede that utilitarian solutions to certain classes of problems (infinite prospects, high damage but unlikely prospects, etc.) are unconvincing, it would make little sense to insist that

Box 10.1 The problem with a utilitarian filter on precaution

A utilitarian filter would invoke precaution only if it passed a benefit–cost test based on expected value, or expected utility if risk aversion is assumed. The following example illustrates the implications of a utilitarian filter.

Should a typical household take an action with *ex ante* probability of .9999 of gaining $101 and a .0001 chance of losing $1,000,000? The expected value of this action is positive (about 99 cents), and an EV filter would reject precaution. With even a modest risk-aversion factor the expected utility would be negative, and precaution would pass an EU filter. Applying a PP motivated by the eminently reasonable heuristic, "do not take inordinate risks for modest gain." the action would be rejected out of hand – no calculation would be needed. ORM rationality could endorse the first or second answers but not the third.

ORM rationality treats this lottery as a serious option and, because some utilitarian formulations (EV) would counsel participating in it, one can imagine debate among utilitarians about whether the action should be taken. A simple but reasonable PP simply dismisses this lottery – participating is not a serious option. One might expect that reasonable people, including many who invoke utilitarian criteria for a considerable range of choices, would do the same.

policies addressed to disproportionate and asymmetric threats must pass a utilitarian test.

Quantity restrictions and regulatory safety margins – precaution in action?

The decision rules that are interpreted as utilitarian precaution have a familiar appearance – strict limits on emissions or harvest, and laws and rules that prohibit particular behaviors, for example. In the real world, we encounter regulatory tools such as traffic rules (stop at the red light even when observation suggests no danger in proceeding), fishing catch limits, ambient pollution standards and limits on allowable emissions, and the like. Are they instances of the PP in action? Can they be interpreted as evidence that ORM practice invokes precautionary measures more commonly than its conceptual foundations would suggest?

While these rules, targets, etc. may look superficially a little like precautionary remedies, mostly they are just heuristics used for cognitive simplicity in on-the-ground implementation of policies chosen for the usual reasons. If the usual reasons include benefit–cost thinking, one can imagine the policy analysis generating a set of optimal shadow prices. Rather than implementing shadow prices directly, it often is simpler to implement and enforce quantity rules consistent with these shadow prices – do we really want drivers consulting tables of shadow prices (or bargaining on the fly with fellow road-users) as they approach intersections? It seems best to think of these quantity restrictions as quantities-for-prices heuristics chosen for ease of interpretation and enforcement.

Some quantity-based rules include substantial safety margins, i.e. the quantity restrictions imposed may be more restrictive than the benefit–cost EV optimum. Clearly caution is involved – the cost of erring on the side of stringency is borne willingly to reduce the possibility of harm – but such policies do not require a PP justification. They can emerge from ORM in the presence of risk-aversion.

Clarifying the relationship between PP and ORM

The forgoing discussion helps clarify the relationship between the PP and ORM. PP is distinct from ORM, in that it departs substantively from utilitarian decision criteria. To question a position approached by Gollier (2001) and adopted by Farrow (2004), PP is not just ORM done right.

A starting point might be that ORM is appropriate for manageable risks but PP should be reserved for extreme cases. This sounds good, if we know already that the threat is manageable (e.g. it is not disproportionate, and the law of large numbers applies), but a key lesson of Chapter 9 is that ORM practice undervalues pre-release testing, which would serve (among other things) as a way of determining which risks are manageable. So, we cannot recommend a simple division of labor between ORM and PP, or simply splicing PP onto the disproportionate-risk end of "ORM in the whole."

What we can suggest is an integrated approach to risk management. What does the PP bring to the table? In addition to its core contribution, a readiness to invoke remedies in response to uncertain but disproportionate threats, PP brings complex systems thinking; more systematic procedures for reconnaissance; and respect for pre-release testing, and sequential decision processes that promote learning while offering a greater degree of protection than ORM. What does ORM bring? Its core contribution is the insurance, self-insurance, self-protection paradigm, which it combines with respect for risk–risk trade-offs, costs, and welfare concerns. Not that PP has no respect for risk–risk trade-offs, costs, and benefits – it just does not regard them as decisive in cases where the threat is disproportionate. A big issue in integration is how much weight the final product should put on these considerations.

An integrated approach would be integrated substantively. Compared to ORM, it would tilt more toward pre-release testing, sequential decision points, and adaptive management; and it would invoke precaution for disproportionate risks without a strict benefit–cost filter. It would be integrated procedurally, too. Once we have decided on the details of substantive integration, then procedural integration is essential to make it all work in practice. We will address these issues in some detail in Part IV.

NOTES

1 Growth, in a two-period model such as this, is measured by the change in biomass year to year (i.e. $S_{t+1} - S_t$). If that measure is positive, biomass is growing.

2 Farmer and Randall (1998) took this analysis a step further, introducing a minimum required harvest of biomass such that the human population would be seriously deprived if the harvest fell below this minimum level. Note that this situation is a case of potentially overstressing a system in the course of business-as-usual (BAU). Their main result is that the need to maintain a given level of harvest moves the effective SMS yet higher (call it SMS* > SMS). Because the sacrifice entailed in maintaining biomass at levels above SMS* is relatively modest, there is reasonable hope that succeeding generations would make the effort. However, the sacrifice that would be demanded to restore biomass to sustainable levels should it fall below SMS* is unbearable by definition, and we would not be confident that SMS* would be restored. One of the virtues of early warning in BAU cases is that it often reduces the costs of remedies or at least it reduces the sacrifice required in any particular time period.

3 This concept of irreversibility is not entirely convincing to me. The typical action eliminates some future possibilities but introduces others. For example, we may lose nonmarketed natural resources, but gain monetized wealth; and it is the trade-off involved that animates the debate about choices like this – if the choice menu would be reduced unambiguously, what is there to debate?

4 Before moving on, I should credit Barrieu and Sinclair-Desgagné (2006), Gollier et al. (2000), and Gollier and Treich (2003) with having advanced, in the course of this work, the discussion among economists about how scientific uncertainty should be understood and modeled – a point that I confine to a footnote only because, if placed in the text, it would be something of a detour from the main argument.

5 Corner solutions are cases where the optimal price or quantity of something is settled rather firmly at a given value (often zero), and it may take a rather big change in underlying conditions (e.g. prices, technology, or constraints) to move it. Corner solutions are special cases, but are not especially rare in economics.

11   A robust and defensible precautionary principle

In this chapter, the objectives are to specify a robust precautionary principle drawing on the findings of Chapters 7 – 10, and to show that it is defensible, which I interpret as meaning that it withstands the challenges considered in Chapter 6 and summarized in Box 6.3.

The structure of a robust precautionary principle

It makes sense to apply PP to novel situations that generate a chance of extra-ordinary harm. Novel situations highlight the knowledge issue, and the PP is all about invoking appropriate remedies for uncertain harm. We have distinguished three kinds of novel situations that may involve a chance of harm (Chapter 9):

1. Novel interventions *ex ante*, NI_1 – proposed novel interventions.
2. Novel interventions *ex post*, NI_2 – novel interventions already implemented and in many cases widely dispersed and integrated into the matrix of business-as-usual.
3. Novel outcomes from overstressing systems in the course of business-as-usual, **BAU** – customary patterns of exploitation, pollution, etc., fully integrated into the matrix of business-as-usual, may threaten harmful regime shifts.

These situations have quite different implications for the knowledge issues that arise. For example, we may be able to pre-screen NI_1 cases for harmful possibilities, but with NI_2 and BAU cases the focus shifts from pre-screening to early warning indicators of harmful effects in the real world. They also have implications for the menu of feasible remedies. For example, we may be able to quarantine NI_1 cases that exhibit harmful possibilities, but with NI_2 and BAU cases the focus shifts to remediation, restoration, mitigation, and adaptation. NI_2 and BAU cases share the characteristic that they are already integrated into the real world and driving changes therein; but they differ in that NI_2 cases are often the result of a single stressor – e.g. asbestos (Box 5.3), PCBs (Box 9.2), and MTBE (Box 9.3) – whereas BAU cases are often driven by a complicated matrix of stressors, e.g. north Pacific salmon (Box 9.5). This distinction has consequences for knowledge issues and remedies: both are often but not always more complicated in BAU cases.

The goal announced in Chapter 7 is to advance the quest for a meaningful and coherent precautionary principle – one that has more force than a soft norm, but stops short of an imperative to avoid all risks – by addressing the allegedly weak connections between the three key elements – harm, uncertainty, and action (Manson 2002, Hughes 2006).

To this end, an **ETR framework** is proposed. The basic elements of a general-form precautionary problem are chance of harm, the state of our knowledge, and the action that should be prescribed.

Chance of harm – threat, **T**, is our chance of harm concept, where chance of harm is conceptualized as a property of the real world and the stresses that we impose on it.

Knowledge conditions – chance also arises because we do not know enough about the workings of the real world. If lack of prescience is our worry, we can always wait until the real world speaks to us, i.e. until it rolls the dice, in the "games of chance" analogy that serves as a foundation of rational decision theory. But that is the problem, not the solution – our motivating worry concerns the chance that we will be damaged by the outcome. Rather, we need to know more about how the world works, and how it might respond to the stressors that motivate our sense of threat.

We have defined threat as real, but our knowledge of it may range from deterministic certainty (we know exactly what will happen), Knightian risk (we can completely specify possible outcomes and their probabilities), Knightian uncertainty (we can completely specify the outcomes but not their probabilities), commonsense uncertainty (where we are unsure about the probabilities as well as the magnitudes of outcomes), and gross ignorance (in which the *ex ante* outcome set is unbounded).

Evidence, **E**, is our knowledge concept. Evidence is likely to take many forms, including theoretical, empirical, and derived from informal analogy or formal modeling exercises; and may involve some combination of these various forms.

Appropriate action – remedy, **R**, is our action concept. Remedy is a broadly inclusive term that applies to averting the threat, remediating the damage, restoring the damaged system, mitigating the harm, and adapting to changed conditions after other remedies have been exhausted; and usually involves some combination of these various responses. Remedies may be devised to serve two quite different functions: to provide protection from a plausible threat and, in so doing, to generate additional evidence about the nature of the threat and the effectiveness of various remedial actions.

The general conceptual form of the PP suggested in Chapter 7 is:

If there is evidence stronger than **E** *that an activity raises a threat more serious than* **T**, *we should invoke a remedy more potent than* **R**.

A PP of this form would focus on the key issues: what sorts of threats might invoke precaution, what sorts of evidence might justify a precautionary intervention, what sorts of remedies might be appropriate, and how might these key elements, **E**, **T**, and **R**, interact? Careful consideration of these questions (Chapters 8 – 10) suggests a tentative working definition of the precautionary principle, in an ETR framework:

Credible scientific evidence of plausible threat of disproportionate and (mostly but not always) asymmetric harm calls for avoidance and remediation measures beyond those recommended by ordinary risk management.

The call to action is triggered by scientifically credible evidence of a disproportionate and in many cases asymmetric threat, such that the loss from the worst case outcome (even if unlikely) is disproportionately large relative to the gain from the most likely outcomes, and the remedies indicated are not restricted to those that would pass a benefit–cost filter even if substantial risk aversion is built-in. This precautionary principle addresses plausible but uncertain harm, and it may call for approaches that consciously depart from ORM. It is simply not limited to figuring out how much risk aversion to front-load into a benefit–cost analysis.

This PP departs from ORM in at two distinct ways. First, its approach to risk assessment differs importantly from ORM. It is open to complex systems thinking, whereas ORM risk assessment models tend to be overly reductive. It is alert to the possibility of systemic risk, whereas ORM tends to be too willing to take refuge in the law of large numbers. And it is more even-handed in its stance toward diagnostic risks (balancing the desires to avoid false positives and false negatives regarding harm and threat thereof) and open to adjusting the evidence requirement to the severity of the **threat**, whereas ORM bends over backward to avoid false positives.

Second, PP explicitly denies that responses to credible scientific evidence of plausible disproportionate threats should be restricted to those that pass a benefit–cost filter (even one that incorporates explicit risk aversion). This frees PP to prescribe pre-screening and pre-testing procedures for NI_1 cases (perhaps whole classes of cases where the possible risks are high enough, or the exposed systems sensitive enough, to pose a serious threat), and to prohibit a specific NI_1 that presents a disproportionate threat. Note that if the NI_1 can be quarantined, prohibition readily defaults to a quarantine and stepwise release (QSR) procedure. Because QSR is an iterative process with sequential decision points, it has the potential to provide more protection against threats while keeping direct and opportunity costs of precaution relatively low – cases where early rounds of testing establish no reasons for alarm can be released promptly from quarantine and subject thereafter only to post-release surveillance as appropriate. For NI_2 and BAU cases, where it is (by definition) too late for pre-screening and pre-release testing, PP is more concerned than ORM with early warning indicators of threat, and more open to adaptive management remedies (which are applicable only before the threat reaches crisis stage). Given enough evidence of plausible threat, PP is open to more stringent regulation of the stressors than ORM.

This PP is defensible

In order to define and justify a coherent and meaningful PP, the task ahead was detailed in Chapter 6 in terms of twelve components (Box 6.3) – the point being that a strong case could be made for taking seriously a PP that satisfied these twelve goals. Progress made in Chapters 7–10 has accomplished items 1 through 10 on that list. Items 11 and 12, which are mostly about procedural issues framing and implementing a risk management framework that includes a PP, will be addressed in Part IV.

Here, the ten tasks accomplished thus far are listed, along with the reasons for considering them accomplished, in bullet-point form.

i. *Conceptualize and flesh-out a precautionary principle (PP) that avoids the charge of meaninglessness, by directing it toward risks that are in some sense unusually serious.*

   - Our PP is addressed explicitly to disproportionate, D (and in most cases asymmetric, A) threats which, by definition, are unusually serious. This resolves Sunstein's (2005) charge of meaninglessness (how can we avoid risk, when there is risk in every action and in no action?), by focusing precaution on a limited set of disproportionate threats.
   - Our PP is framed as a principle that, as is the nature of principles, needs interpretation, and needs to be mediated within a broader framework

for resolving cases where conflicting principles and values come into play. This resolves several criticisms leveled at PP – it is not a complete and coherent stand-alone decision rule; it has no normative content; how can it be taken seriously when there is a proliferation of versions in circulation; and it conflicts with other important values that come into play in particular cases.

ii. *Concentrate the search for a meaningful PP on the class of cases where conditions ideal for ordinary risk management (ORM) are absent.*
   • Our PP is focused on D (and in most cases A) threats; and it is well-established that ORM does not handle low-probability high-damage prospects well.
   • To the extent that D and A threats are concentrated in cases involving complex systems and/or systemic risk, they are concentrated in areas for which ORM is relatively ill-equipped. Our PP is open to complex systems thinking and the possibility of systemic risk, and it takes a more even-handed approach to threat diagnostics, whereas ORM risk assessment norms tend toward systematic understatement of risks.

iii. *Specify a PP that is more than a soft norm, in that it systematically relates appropriate remedies to the nature of the threat and the evidence of potential harm.*
   • The remedies endorsed by our PP are carefully and systematically related to the nature of the threat and the evidence of potential harm (Chapter 9). In contrast, a soft norm is little more than a statement of a widely honored value, in our case a well-intentioned endorsement of precaution.
   • As previewed in Chapter 10 and developed in Part IV, real PP remedies are specified and procedurally integrated with ORM remedies as appropriate to create a risk management framework that, again, is more specific, targeted, calibrated, and enforceable than a soft norm.

iv. *To avoid redundancy, specify a PP framework that is distinguishable from ORM both logically and practically.*
   • Our PP is focused on D (and A) threats which, by definition are unusually serious.
   • Standards of evidence for our PP depart substantively from those for ORM:
      • In assessing risk, our PP is more open to complexity, ORM is more reductive.
      • Where chance is involved, ORM puts most of the weight on avoiding false positives re harm, whereas our PP takes a more nuanced sense of what constitutes credible scientific evidence.

- Our PP invokes remedies that depart from ORM practice:
  - For NI_1, pre- and post-release testing and surveillance strategies; quarantine and stepwise release processes; serious post-release surveillance.
  - For NI_2 and BAU, early warning indicators of threat; adaptive management remedies, given sufficiently early warning matters.
- We have sketched (Chapter 10) how this PP and the elements of ORM that make sense can and should be integrated into a coherent risk management framework (elaborated in more detail in Part IV).
- Our PP is alert and committed to compensation for disproportionate adverse effects on groups and/or regions and places.

v. *Develop standards of evidence – typically higher than merely "crying wolf" but lower than are applied to empirical scientific propositions – for things and acts that plausibly could harm us.*
  - Evidentiary standards for our PP include:
    - Accurate reflection of the science – consensus where it exists, controversies where there are plausible but conflicting scenarios, unknowns where there are unknowns.
    - Adequate defenses of science against politicization and distortions that may tend to promote unfounded panic or unfounded confidence that there is nothing to worry about.
  - These evidentiary standards resolve several criticisms leveled at the PP – it is invoked by unfounded panic, and it tilts authority away from experts and toward ordinary people whose judgment about risks is not to be trusted.

vi. *Elucidate the relationships between scientific evidence and precautionary remedies, addressing the kinds of evidence that would justify invoking more or less drastic precautionary interventions.*
  - We have addressed the question of how much evidence is enough to justify invoking precaution, identifying some principles that are useful in thinking about particular cases:
    - It may make sense to invoke precaution on the basis of less complete evidence in cases where plausible threats are of greater magnitude.
    - Iterative remedies with sequential decision points encourage learning (acquisition of more evidence) and reassessment of threat and remedy, and make more likely the achievement of proportionality between the expense and disruption of precaution and the risks assumed by inaction in the face of threat.

vii. *Include provisions for mitigating risk–risk trade-offs.*
  • Remedies endorsed by our PP include mitigation.
  • The discussion of proportionality (item 6, above) also applies to risk–risk trade-offs.

viii. *Explore the design of approaches and procedures to minimize the intrusiveness and disruptiveness of precaution, while providing adequate protection from threats of harm.*
  • Our PP seeks remedies that minimize the intrusiveness and disruptiveness of precaution:
    • For NI_1, pre- and post-release testing and surveillance strategies; quarantine and stepwise release processes; serious post-release surveillance.
    • For NI_2 and BAU, early warning indicators of threat; adaptive management remedies, given sufficiently early warning matters.
  • For cases in all three classes, restoration, mitigation, and adaptation are taken seriously as components of a remedies package.
  • Nevertheless, where the case for precautionary protections is strong, our PP does not shrink from endorsing such protections.

ix. *Conceptualize and design precautionary remedies that are calibrated to provide precaution without erecting undue impediments to innovation.*
  • The remedies discussed in item 8, above, are innovation friendly.
  • Several detailed passages in Chapter 9 demonstrate our alertness to potential benefits of innovation: the discussion of upside possibilities (Box 9.7), the discussion of adjusting the balance between pre-release testing and post-release surveillance in US Food and Drug Administration procedures, and the stylized case study of GMO crops all demonstrate a serious concern for risk "on the other side," i.e. excessive caution may reduce welfare by foregoing NI and/or BAU benefits.

x. *Consider strategies involving a sequence of pre- and post-release filters, and iterative approaches that encourage learning and adaptation, and develop them in promising cases.*
  • Our PP invokes remedies involving pre- and post-release filters and iterative approaches that encourage learning and adaptation:
    • For NI_1, pre- and post-release testing and surveillance strategies; quarantine and stepwise release processes; serious post-release surveillance.
    • For NI_2 and BAU, early warning indicators of threat; adaptive management remedies, given sufficiently early warning matters.

- For cases in all three classes, restoration, mitigation, and adaptation are taken seriously as components of a remedies package.
- These approaches have been sketched in some detail in Chapter 9, for several promising cases: upside possibilities and innovation (Box 9.7), adjusting the balance between pre-release testing and post-release surveillance in FDA procedures, and application to proposed releases of new GMO crops.
- We have sketched (Chapter 10) how this PP and the elements of ORM that make sense can and should be integrated into a coherent risk management framework (elaborated in more detail in Part IV).

Given these considerable successes in addressing the "tasks ahead" identified in Chapter 6, we rest our case that the PP defined in Chapters 7 – 10 is defensible. It provides coherent principles for management of extraordinary risks, and offers the promise that they can be integrated with "the best of ORM," to produce a new and coherent risk management strategy. Of course, there are issues to resolve in application to any particular case or class of cases – but that is to be expected when we are operating at the level of principles.

Part IV

Precaution in action

12 Precaution: from principle to policy

The precautionary principle is framed as a principle and, as such, cannot be expected to be ready for implementation in particular policy and management situations. Principles are general statements of normative moral positions for a class of concerns. But, to call a statement a principle does not accord it priority over valid moral principles and intuitions – in difficult and contentious policy issues, important principles come into conflict and resolution requires a balanced judgment that considers seriously the principles involved and the facts of the case. Agreed principles provide not policies but touchstones to be organized into a frame for policy resolution that anticipates and accounts for competing and conflicting principles.

In what follows, we establish the role of principles in the policy environment, consider some moral intuitions that inform and support the PP, and begin constructing a framework for precaution. As Arcuri (2007) points out, a serious PP must be articulated in both substantive and procedural terms. So, we proceed to identify the procedural requirements for bringing a substantive precautionary tilt to risk management practice. An intuitively appealing way of integrating the insights of ordinary risk management (ORM) and PP into a coherent risk management framework might treat ORM as the default approach to risk, but provide a PP override in cases where the risk is extraordinary, or the threat is disproportionate. We develop some of the implications of that approach and conclude that, in addition to stern remedies in the face of disproportionate threats, PP brings other important contributions to an integrated risk management framework: a more serious approach to *ex ante* risk assessment, and sequential and iterative remedies that encourage systematic learning and re-assessment of threat and remedy even as we provide protection in real time. Integrated risk assessment must be more than just "ORM subject to a precautionary constraint."

What we mean by "principle"?

In this section, we consider in more detail a question raised earlier – what is the meaning of "principle," and what is the role of principles in policy and governance? What do we mean by principles in the policy context and what reasonably can, and cannot, be expected of a principle that informs policy and management? To begin, consider principles in moral reasoning. Principles are general statements of normative moral positions for a class of concerns. Principles can be formulated from moral intuitions and are, in that sense, logically prior to complete moral systems. Examples of moral intuitions that are honored widely include:[1]

Beneficence: People should help themselves and others, and avoid harming themselves and others.

Honesty: People should not lie, defraud, deceive, or mislead.

Fidelity: People should keep their promises and agreements.

Privacy: People should respect their personal privacy and the privacy of others, and maintain confidentiality.

Autonomy: Each rational individual should be allowed to make free and informed choices.

Fairness: People should be treated fairly and should treat others fairly, and society should treat each of its members fairly.

Utility: Pursuit of benefits and avoidance of pain and deprivation are morally valued for oneself, other people, and society.

There are several things about this list that are worthy of comment. First, all of these moral intuitions address to varying degrees personal morality, reciprocity, and ethics at the level of society.

Second, there remains some ambiguity in most of these intuitions as stated. For example, four distinct concepts of fairness come immediately to mind:
1. fairness as *process* (like cases should be treated alike, and unlike cases should be treated differently);
2. fairness as *desert* (people should get the rewards they deserve, e.g. people should be rewarded in proportion to the added value that they produce);
3. fairness as *opportunity* (people should have equal opportunity to engage in the pursuit of happiness);
4. fairness of *outcomes* (society should provide some guarantees to people regarding outcomes, not just opportunities; e.g. society should guarantee the basic needs of all its members).

Third, these moral intuitions as stated are unbounded. But perhaps there are limits on the good that one can be expected to do for others, the promises one can be expected to keep, and the topics about which we are obligated to tell the truth.

Fourth, we can readily imagine conflicts among moral intuitions, even within this incomplete and rather non-controversial list:

- Immanuel Kant famously was challenged about whether truthtelling could be a universal imperative when the truth you were asked to tell would expose another to great and undeserved danger.
- Maintaining confidentiality may require lying, or at least misleading a questioner.
- We may encounter people who would harm themselves if allowed to choose freely. Such situations may be still more complex: we may be uncomfortable in our parentalism – how can we be sure we have judged correctly the harm that would follow from such people acting autonomously?
- We may encounter situations where harm would arise from keeping promises or agreements made earlier when circumstances (including available information) were different.
- The quest for utility may conflict with fairness, autonomy, and perhaps even honesty and fidelity.
- Personal privacy may be challenged on grounds of societal utility.

Moral intuitions provide the building blocks of moral principles. The derivation of moral principles from intuitions is a matter of rigorous consideration of the bounds and limits of particular moral intuitions, and the resolution of conflicts among moral intuitions thought valid. One thing that rigorous consideration suggests is adding an additional moral premise –

Universality: What one believes is right for others is right also for oneself.

– and applying it to all of the other moral intuitions in the list. Now, consider the following two examples of principles derived from moral intuitions.

From beneficence and utility, we might derive: *Change that benefits some people while harming none is morally desirable* (called the Pareto principle in honor of the late-nineteenth-century philosopher and economist Vilfredo Pareto). Add autonomy interpreted strongly, and we get a stronger and more controversial Pareto principle: *No matter how great the benefits to others, society should refrain from imposing change upon people who would not choose it for themselves.*

From utility and fairness as opportunity, we may derive: *In assessing change at the societal level, we should pay close attention to its likely effect on the opportunities facing the least well-off among us.* Substitute a very strong outcomes interpretation of fairness, and we get: *The benefits per capita to society from change are strictly limited to the benefits that accrue to its least well-off member* (called the Rawlsian principle in honor of the late-twentieth-century philosopher John Rawls).

The potential for conflict between the strong Pareto principle and the Rawlsian principle is obvious – it is likely that the policy alternative that promises the greatest benefit to society's worst-off member will require some non-consensual sacrifice on the part of others – and underlies many of the clashes between economic liberals and conservatives over what seem on the surface to be matters of practical policy and governance. However, it is unlikely that a society would endorse simultaneously the Rawlsian and strong Pareto principles; more likely choices include one, the other, and neither. The following example is a case where conflict arises between two principles that could plausibly be endorsed simultaneously.

From utility, privacy, and autonomy, we might derive: *The policy alternative should be chosen that most closely approximates the choices that society's members would make for themselves.*

From autonomy, beneficence, utility, and our understanding of public goods, we may get: *Some policy alternatives involving public goods are so compelling that society may and should override individual autonomy to ensure their implementation.*

We may well be unwilling to abandon either of these principles. Instead, after thought and deliberation we may resolve the conflict along the following lines: *In the absence of overriding considerations, policy will be attentive first to the choices that society's members would make for themselves. But provision of public goods that pass some specified test (perhaps of value and/or essentiality) is a valid overriding consideration.* One way to resolve a conflict between accepted principles is to designate one (in this case, the normative significance of individual choice) as the default consideration, and the other (provision of public goods) as a valid overriding consideration. Of course, there are other ways, e.g. constructing some system of weights to apply to the virtues of individual choice, and benefits and necessity of providing worthy public goods, and other relevant principles and values.

When valid principles clash

To call a moral statement a principle does not grant it lexical priority over other principles – in complicated (that is, interesting) exercises in applied ethics, important principles will come into conflict and resolution requires a balanced judgment that considers seriously the principles involved and the facts of the case. Yet, a principle is much more than a preference – we feel a serious moral loss when we have to compromise a principle in a particular case. Finally, agreed principles provide not policies but touchstones to be organized into a frame for policy resolution that anticipates and accounts for competing and conflicting principles. The alternative of defining absolute moral rules applicable in all situations seems impossible.

Principles in the absence of "grand unified moral theory." A broad acceptance seems to have emerged among philosophers that the contest among ethical theories is likely to remain inconclusive. While each contending theory has powerful appeal, each is incomplete in some important way, each remains vulnerable to some serious avenue(s) of criticism, and it seems unlikely that any one will defeat the others decisively. Each, also, is inconsistent with the others in important ways, so that a coherent synthesis (the "grand unified moral theory") is unlikely.

The absence of a complete and dominant moral theory (Williams 1985) provides good reason for taking moral principles seriously. As we might expect, some principles are so compelling that they are recognized by many competing moral systems. Agreement might be reached, for example, that real resources should be expended to protect natural environments, among people who would give quite different reasons as to why that should be so. The task of the thoughtful moral agent in the policy arena is, then, to find heuristics – rules for action – that can command broad agreement. Taylor (1989) emphasizes the search for principles capturing and generalizing prior moral intuitions that transcend and precede moral theories – principles that (he argues) routinely go under-valued in standard moral epistemology, but are forced to the front by value pluralism. That way, groups and individuals may accept a surprisingly large body of common principles and thus be able to achieve substantial social agreement about actions, even though their moral theories are incompatible.

Principles in law. As with moral principles, a legal principle is not a complete theory of normative law, but must be interpreted in ways that anticipate and account for competing and conflicting principles. To call a statement a legal principle does not grant it lexical priority over other legal principles. Agreed principles cannot be implemented directly – a principle provides a powerful argument in a particular direction, but does not determine a specific outcome (Cooney 2004) – but must be operationalized in laws, rules, guidelines, etc.

Principles in the policy environment

An ideal model of the relationship between moral principles and policy and management practice would include the following elements. Agreed moral principles:

- emerge from a discourse among citizens in the role of thoughtful moral agents;
- provide moral foundations for public governance and action;
- are organized into a framework that allows resolution of conflicts among principles by considering seriously the principles involved and the facts of the case;
- inform legislation that establishes a framework for resolution of policy issues and implementation of management solutions;
- are translated into clear and applicable principles that guide policy practitioners at the agency level;
- are interpreted and implemented flexibly on a case-by-case basis by policy and management practitioners in the context of genuine dialog with stakeholders.

A challenging environment for principles and facts

Unfortunately, the current times offer a challenging environment for the moral discourse envisioned in the ideal model.

Polarized political environment and value-driven fact-claims. There remains a strong "culture wars" element to political discourse, where strongly worded non-negotiable value statements, rather than genuine value discourse, have become the norm. The goal is not to reach agreement but to win the values showdown.

In this environment, facts are contested as vigorously as values, and it cannot be assumed that participants are motivated by a shared concern for getting the facts right. Just the opposite may occur: a contest of mutually incompatible value-absolutes may exacerbate the temptation to tailor fact-claims to support desired policy outcomes. A values-driven minority may hope to build a majority on a particular issue by persuading others that the facts support their policy position. If the minority's policy goal is no action, then all it may take to build a supportive majority is to persuade enough people that the facts are in legitimate dispute and it is all too confusing for regular folks to figure out.

A current paradigm case is global warming. Small-government conservatives, horrified by the degree of global coordination that would be required to marshal a serious effort to reduce greenhouse gases, have taken to disputing the evidence of warming and to arguing that the crisis has been manufactured by a conspiracy of scientists and bureaucrats determined to impose their worldview on the rest of us. That is, their values drive their view of the facts (Kahan *et al.* 2006), while they accuse those with opposing viewpoints of creating agenda-driven facts. It all adds up to manufacturing uncertainty, with the unwitting help of some climate scientists who have been less than forthright about noise in the temperature data and dissenting opinions among climate scientists.

In situations where it can be claimed that values are settled, fact-claims may have direct normative significance. For example, a strong theme in US constitutional jurisprudence gives normative weight to the intentions of the founders. In light of the on-going "culture wars," it is not surprising that a values-driven contest has emerged over the facts regarding what the founders really believed about the proper relationship between religion and government (Shorto 2010).

Pragmatic, progressive roots of policy processes. Pragmatic policy processes still predominate in public agencies, and are designed to produce fact-based decisions aimed not at saving the world but making us a little bit better-off one step at a time. By "fact-based," I mean only that policy discourse proceeds on a tacit assumption that policy questions can (and where possible should) be resolved mostly by evaluating fact-claims without explicit consideration of values, especially, conflicting values. If fact-claims drive policy, no value matters until it matters. That is, value discourse is submerged and occluded, to the effect that value questions do not arise until value-driven objections to proposed policy are raised, which is hardly the ideal context for fruitful value discourse.

As with value polarization, the tacit agreement to avoid direct appeal to values exacerbates the temptation to tailor fact-claims to support policy positions adopted for value reasons.

Pragmatism has obvious virtues for day-to-day social decisions, but it is ill-equipped for addressing issues concerning the distant future, where values are incompletely developed and poorly articulated. Technologies for meeting objectives (that is, the familiar planning tools) are not useful for defining objectives. We cannot work toward moral consensus via processes designed to submerge moral issues and discourse in pursuit of pragmatic progress. This is pertinent especially for precaution in the "rivet-popper" case, i.e.

threats of regime shift due to overstress of familiar systems in the course of business-as-usual. Issues of conservation, sustainability, and the like are inherently future-oriented. For such issues, it seems there is no escape from the need to address moral issues directly, with special attention to issues best posed as questions of principle rather than mere utilitarian (and therefore fungible) value.

Principled policies to serve the public good. So, there are forces in the current political and policy environment that serve to promote polarization about principles and values rather than consensus-building, and exacerbate the tailoring of fact-claims in support of value-driven policy positions. But there is also considerable frustration with confrontational politics and stalemated policy. There is still room for processes that seek agreement on moral principles that can serve as a frame for policy choice and implementation.

Fact-claims are statements about things, events, and relationships that are at least potentially observable and refutable, which suggests that the long run prospects are not encouraging for value-driven fact-claims. Science has strong defenses against politicization (Chapter 8). The culture of scientific detachment and the political independence of science itself, and the self-policing and self-correcting tendencies built-into the institutions of science sustain a considerable degree of interpersonal reliability in what counts as scientifically plausible and credible. On the other hand, complex systems thinking – which warns us that systems are less predictable and surprises more likely than we might suspect – suggests some fertile ground for disputes about the facts, especially as they concern the future. I never said it would be easy!

Building a framework for precaution

We have established in Part III that there is scope for a PP that addresses squarely the cases that expose the weaknesses of ORM: threats of relatively unlikely but high-damage events, and reluctance in practice to take pre-release screening and testing opportunities seriously. In some of these cases, the decision context is rendered more than ordinarily intractable by complexity, path-dependence, and extreme uncertainty or gross ignorance – conditions that contrast sharply with the stationary and predictable systems assumed in ORM.

Our enquiry has led to a precautionary principle crafted as follows:

Credible scientific evidence of plausible threat of disproportionate and (mostly but not always) asymmetric harm calls for avoidance and remediation measures beyond those recommended by ordinary risk management.

This precautionary principle succeeds if it serves as a principle that guides law and policy, in the sense that it embodies a considerable moral intuition to be consulted along with other pertinent principles and values when the issues it addresses come into play. Now, we begin the task of sketching how this PP might be incorporated into the policy framework and implemented.

Moral foundations for the precautionary principle

First, the society would need to be persuaded to adopt the PP as a normative principle. The PP can be grounded morally in prior moral intuitions that themselves enjoy widespread acceptance. The case for invoking the PP hinges on a scientifically credible threat of disproportionate and asymmetric harm. Moral principles that might support such a PP include the following variations on the general ideas that even when the worst-case outcome is unlikely the amount risked should not be disproportionate to the expected gain, and that exposure to risks should be distributed in roughly the same way as opportunity to gain:

- Do not sell out something unique and potentially very valuable for modest gain.
- Do not take disproportionate risks for modest gain ("don't bet the farm").
- Do not impose big risks on the public for modest private gain.
- Do not impose big risks on the future for modest immediate gain.

These moral precepts may seem simple enough, but they are not just commonsense rationality.

There is genuine disagreement about the rationality of taking big risks for modest gain, in that the expected value theory of decisions under risk may well endorse such risk taking – it all depends on the numbers. To summarize the lesson of Box 10.1, should we take an action with *ex ante* probability of .9999 of gaining $101 and a .0001 chance of losing $1,000,000? EV of this action is positive (about 99 cents). With even a modest risk-aversion factor, the expected utility would be negative. Applying a "do not take disproportionate risks for modest gain" principle, the action would be rejected out of hand – no calculation would be needed. The rationality of ordinary risk management (ORM) could endorse the first or second answers but not the third.

Conservation and preservation issues often pit something unique and potentially very valuable against the prospect of modest gain, but the decisions are seldom no-brainers. While the principle may be respected widely, policy decisions remain contestable due to widely varying judgments about the uniqueness and value of the candidate for preservation – after all, there often is a strong esthetic element in the judgment required.

There is less legitimate controversy concerning the injunctions against imposing big risks on the public for modest private gain, and big risks on the future for modest immediate gain, but there is still ample room for conflicting judgments about the risks and the prospects of gain. And there are strong temptations to socialize the risk and privatize the profit, and to risk the future in service of the present. So, we see these principles violated much too often.

My point is that these moral intuitions are simple and widely accepted in principle, but they are not vacuous. One of them conflicts in some cases with a standard theory of decision under risk; one of them is susceptible to disagreements about esthetic judgments; for all of them, application may be complicated by disagreements about facts and predictions; and all of them take a normative stand in the face of temptations to do otherwise.

One principle among many

A valid frame for resolving policy issues must anticipate and account for competing and conflicting principles and must be operationalized in laws, rules, and guidelines which can then be interpreted and applied to particular cases. The PP is at best one among many principles, values, and commitments that society might take seriously. Calling it a principle does not grant it lexical priority over other principles – in difficult policy cases, important and widely held principles, values, and commitments will come into conflict. Together, a set of agreed principles provides a framework for policy resolution that anticipates and accounts for competing and conflicting principles.

Principles and values that may compete and/or conflict with the PP include:
- utility interpreted as expected value of aggregate welfare – the PP may demand that expected welfare be sacrificed to precaution in cases where there is disproportionate threat of harm;
- progress through innovation – common objections to the PP along these lines range from "the PP stifles science and innovation" to the more

temperate "precautionary regulatory procedures (e.g. those of the US Food and Drug Administration) cost lives by delaying access to new drugs and treatments;"

- individual autonomy, property rights, etc. – widespread implementation of the PP may enhance the power of the regulators relative to individuals and property owners;
- equitable sharing of burdens – precaution to benefit the broader public, and in some cases the future public, may impose undue burdens on particular groups of people unless care is taken to design precautionary institutions to avoid that outcome;
- respect for stakeholders and the ordinary public – unless care is taken to design precautionary institutions otherwise, they may take on the characteristics of high-handed, unaccountable bureaucracies.

A framework for implementing the PP must address these competing principles and values. For example, should precautionary interventions be sensitive in some way to the opportunities foregone due to precaution? Should cost effectiveness be a serious concern in the choice of precautionary remedies? Can precautionary protections be designed to minimize impediments to innovation at the pre-screening and pre-testing stage, while honing in quickly on the genuine threat cases for more intense scrutiny? Can the PP be implemented in ways that respect autonomy and property rights, and ensure an equitable sharing of burdens? Some elements of a framework to implement the PP in the contest of competing and conflicting principles and values are sketched below, for two key kinds of cases: proposed innovations, and threats of regime shift due to overstressing familiar systems in the course of business-as-usual.

Proposed innovations. A framework for precaution in the case of proposed innovations should articulate clear principles and take them seriously in practice. A plausible set of commitments might include the following:

- Commitment to pre-screening and pre-testing proposed innovations in categories that pose above-average *ex ante* risk, and to rapid release of innovations that pose minimal threat. This commitment would minimize impediments to innovation and the regulatory burden on individuals and property owners.
- Commitment to post-release surveillance, to identify and remedy any serious threats that slipped past the pre-screening and pre-testing process.
- Commitment to precautionary exceptions in cases that exceed a threshold of concern, e.g. a scientifically credible threat of disproportionate and asymmetric harm.

- Commitment to PP procedures that encourage learning, to reduce ignorance, narrow the uncertainties, better specify the threat and the possible outcomes and probabilities, and develop and test strategies for avoidance, mitigation, and adaptation.
- Commitment to proportionality and cost-effectiveness in precautionary remedies.
- Commitment to transparent and inclusive public decision processes.
- Commitment to equitable sharing of burdens – especially burdens undertaken to benefit future generations.

Business-as-usual. A framework for addressing BAU issues, which typically involve sustainability, might include the following set of plausible commitments:

- Commitment to weak sustainability, and economic and political arrangements that encourage it ("business-as-usual done right").[2]
- Commitment to precautionary exceptions in cases that exceed a threshold of concern, e.g. a scientifically credible threat of disproportionate and asymmetric harm.
- Commitment to systematic pursuit of early warning of impending regime shift.
- Commitment to PP procedures that encourage learning, to reduce ignorance, narrow the uncertainties, better specify the threat and the possible outcomes and probabilities, and develop and test strategies for avoidance, mitigation, and adaptation.
- Commitment to proportionality and cost effectiveness in precautionary remedies.
- Commitment to transparent and inclusive public decision processes.
- Commitment to respect the autonomy of individuals and property owners, by minimizing unnecessary regulatory burdens.
- Commitment to equitable sharing of burdens – especially burdens undertaken to benefit future generations.

Notice that most of the commitments appropriate for the case of proposed innovations apply also to the BAU case. The exceptions are, for proposed innovations, the commitments to pre-screening, pre-release testing, and post-release surveillance; and for the BAU case, the commitments to systematic pursuit of early warning, and getting the prices right as an everyday policy and management strategy designed to minimize the chances of inadvertently precipitating regime shift. These differences matter a lot in practice – the opportunity for pre-screening and pre-release testing significantly improves the prospects for successful precaution in the case of proposed innovations.

A PP that is both substantive and procedural

As Arcuri (2007) points out, a PP to be taken seriously in policy and management should have procedural as well as substantive elements. The PP defined above has clear substantive elements. It is triggered only by scientifically credible evidence of disproportionate and asymmetric harm, and when triggered it invokes precautionary practices beyond those recommended by ORM. Its procedural elements include decision-making processes and implementation procedures that:

- provide for getting the prices systematically right in BAU cases;
- provide for pre-screening and pre-release testing for proposed innovations;
- encourage early warning in BAU cases and post-release surveillance in the case of proposed innovations;
- implement the "scientifically credible threat" evidence criterion for diagnosis of threats, thereby providing more balance between risks of false positives and false negatives;
- are informed by science and structured to encourage learning about the threat, and development and testing of strategies for avoidance, mitigation, and adaptation;[3]
- are dynamic, sequential, and iterative, as in the case of quarantine and stepwise release for proposed innovations; and adaptation for BAU cases;
- are attentive to proportionality, cost effectiveness and the virtues of affordable remedies;
- are attentive to autonomy, property rights, and the need for policies to reduce or mitigate disproportionate negative impacts on particular individuals and groups;
- are open to public participation and scrutiny.

Notice how closely this bullet list of procedural requirements parallels the earlier lists of principles and commitments. This only underlines Arcuri's point – a serious PP must have procedural provisions to ensure that its substantive commitments are implemented on the ground.

Integrating the PP and ORM substantively and procedurally

A coherent framework for risk management is likely to include roles for both ORM and PP. A strong case can be made for ORM to manage the easy cases, where the outcome set is well specified and we can confidently expect many draws from a stable distribution. After all, the fundamentals of the standard theory of decision making under risk were deduced from analyses of well-specified games of chance. The strongest case for the PP can be made in the context of disproportionate threats. So it is at least likely that a coherent framework for managing the full array of risks will draw upon both ORM and the PP. However, a coherent framework will require us to be quite specific about exactly how ORM and the PP can best be integrated.

ORM for manageable risks, the PP for disproportionate threats

An intuitive first cut at integrating the insights of ORM and the PP into a coherent risk management framework might treat ORM as the default approach to risk, an appropriate stand-alone framework for the relatively simple cases, and a source of insights for even the more difficult cases. But ORM could be overridden by the PP in cases where the risk is extraordinary, or the threat is disproportionate. That is, ORM would provide business-as-usual risk management but subject to a PP constraint to be invoked in specified extraordinary cases. More than ten years ago (Randall 1999, pp. 259–260), I proposed something along these lines for conservation decisions (which I now treat as a particular case of the BAU category).

A society could adopt the practice of deciding these kinds of issues on the basis of [utilitarian considerations such as expected benefits and costs], but subject to some kind of conservation constraint. A safe minimum standard (SMS) of conservation has been suggested by a variety of authors: harvest, habitat destruction, etc. must be restricted in order to leave a sufficient stock of the renewable resource to ensure its survival … The SMS constraint makes most sense when cast transparently as a discrete interruption of business-as-usual.

Formulations like this still make sense, I think, for decision making. However, the discipline of writing this book has made me much more aware of the crucial role of risk assessment. How do we know *ex ante* which risks are manageable with ORM? The "ORM for the ordinary risks, but subject to the PP for extraordinary threats" formulation assumes implicitly that we know already. But, in the absence of risk assessment on a much more systematic scale than ORM practice has delivered to this point, it happens often that we do not know, or at least do not know soon enough – as we have learned, the prospects for effective risk management are so much better before the causal agent is released for general use, or before the impending regime shift has become inevitable, as the case may be.

Jasanoff (2000) has argued that environmental, health, and safety policy in the US took a precautionary turn in the 1960s, when regulatory agencies developed risk assessment procedures and applied them *ex ante* to particular classes of risks. Perhaps so, but surely it depends on the particulars. I find this claim plausible when applied to the Food and Drug Administration, which proceeds systematically through a multi-stage testing protocol before releasing new drugs for general use. But I find it less plausible in the case of environmental risks where rigorous *ex ante* risk assessments are applied not systematically, but in spotty fashion to certain particular categories of substances and practices. As Garrity (2004) emphasizes, the US Environmental Protection Agency routinely agrees to less rigorous *ex ante* risk assessments than it is authorized to require. So, I would characterize ORM in the USA and many other countries as much less than systematic in its effective requirements for *ex ante* risk assessment. ORM in practice is much more focused on remediation, mitigation, and adaptation than it would be if it took a systematic approach to *ex ante* risk assessment.

So, if we take ORM as we find it, and bound its domain by invoking PP for extraordinary risks, we would be operating in perhaps the vast bulk of cases with relatively little *ex ante* intelligence concerning the nature and extent of the risks we face. For novel interventions, too many NI_1 cases would default to NI_2, and risk management would be less about prevention and more about playing catch-up than seems ideal.

ORM, risk assessment, pre-screening, and pre-release testing – proposed innovations. How systematic is ORM risk assessment in the case of a proposed innovation? In practice, it tends to be focused on a few broad categories of threats to which the public is especially sensitive. The public seems very sensitive to potential threats from new drugs and pesticides; and in the case of pesticides, their concern is amplified by the reasonable possibility of involuntary exposure to drift from pesticide applications and pesticide residues in foods. So, we see systematic risk assessment and pre-release testing of new drugs and pesticides, but it is important to understand that the regulatory regime we observe reflects continuing pressures in both directions, i.e. for more stringent regulation and for regulatory relief.

One might expect ORM to have systematized *ex ante* risk assessment of ecological interventions which often have unintended consequences, and new technologies that seem different and in some sense scary. Yet, we typically observe only spotty and hit-or-miss risk assessment.

Introduced exotic species may enter a country in several ways, most commonly by inadvertent introduction via trade and shipping, escape of exotic pets, and purposeful introduction by the private sector (e.g. landscaping and plant nurseries) and public agencies seeking to solve a particular problem (e.g. control a pest by introducing a predator, encourage aquaculture by introducing productive species). While some introductions seem to have been wholly beneficial or benign, and the harmful effects of many others may be balanced roughly by benefits, there is a long catalog of US cases where the damage is unambiguous: e.g. zebra mussels (stowaways in ships' ballast water), kudzu (introduced for stabilizing disturbed land), the Asian carp (introduced for cleaning catfish ponds), melaleuca (introduced for landscaping), and the Burmese python (an escaped exotic pet). A (hypothetical) comprehensive regulatory regime for invasive species would need to address the three quite different avenues of introduction. *Ex ante* risk assessment of purposeful introductions is a hit-or-miss kind of thing, the exotic pet merchants and fanciers have effectively resisted systematic regulation, and regulation to reduce the risks of invasions via of trade and shipping has been mostly *ad hoc*, often after-the-fact, and vigorously contested by the affected industries – witness the struggle, two decades long and still inconclusive, for effective regulation of ships' ballast water following the zebra mussel invasion of the Great Lakes. Meanwhile, invasions continue. For example, the zebra mussel, Asian carp, and Burmese python invasions in the USA are quite recent.

For new and potentially threatening technologies, in the USA the situation is still being contested. Synthetic chemicals are not regulated systematically, despite a history of perhaps infrequent but nevertheless major disasters (e.g. PCBs and MTBE, Chapter 9).

Genetically modified organisms may receive modest pre-release attention, e.g. pre-screening and in some cases certain kinds of pre-release testing, but even this is triggered by regulations addressed to more traditional concerns: if food for human consumption is involved, the FDA offers a voluntary program of risk assessment and pre-release testing; if the GMO has pesticide properties, the EPA performs a risk assessment; and the US Department of Agriculture confers non-regulated status on GMOs that pass a limited review of risk factors. In particular, regulators have been slow to take gene flow and genetic pollution seriously, yet in many parts of the world, including North America, Scotland and Scandinavia, genetic pollution of wild salmon by farm-raised varieties (some of them genetically modified) already is well advanced.

Health concerns have been raised regarding certain kinds of wave processes (e.g. microwaves), electro-magnetic radiation, etc., bringing high-voltage transmission lines, cellular communications towers, and cellphone handsets, among things, under scrutiny. Again, *ex ante* risk assessment is hit or miss.

In all of the above cases, given the rather spotty approach to *ex ante* risk assessment and regulation, it is not surprising that we have experienced particular cases of *ex ante* risk scares and demands for regulation before the intervention takes root, and *ex post* reports of harm leading eventually to regulation, remediation, mitigation, and adaptation. These events and processes come as surprises to entrepreneurs, promoters, and government. Often, they have an *ad hoc* character. The first reports of risk or damage, as the case may be, often come from "unofficial" sources – universities, independent laboratories, NGOs – and it may take a while before enough evidence accumulates to prompt a serious consideration of the concerns raised. Often the evidence itself is contested, legitimately given the inherently critical methodology of science, but perhaps also less legitimately in attempts to manufacture uncertainty, muddy the waters, and delay resolution of the issues (Chapter 8).

Perhaps some of the obvious discomfort of Graham (2004) and Sunstein (2005) with the public's role in generating appeals for precaution springs from the ad hoc and unpredictable nature of this process. Yet, the strategy of encouraging innovation and responding to potential for harm only after credible complaints tends to generate the unpredictable process sketched above. Alarming reports are inherently spotty, and have a speculative flavor at the outset. Innovations readily become entrenched in the economy and environment, and some of them turn bad, which leads mostly to playing catch-up.

Faced with risk, uncertainty, and/or gross ignorance about future consequences of novel interventions, we can stay the course and attend later to harmful outcomes in the cases where they occur, or we can try to get ahead of the game by taking precautions before the potential for harm has been established. There are downsides to both approaches. When things go badly, the costs of damage, clean-up, and remediation can be enormous, as we see in the cases of asbestos and PCBs (to give just two examples), which were widely dispersed throughout the economy and environment before harm was determined. If we prohibited every innovation that introduced a plausible threat of harm, it seems likely that we would bear a substantial cost in terms of beneficial innovations foregone. Cast in these terms, the dilemma is clear – a continuing sequence of occasional disasters on the one hand versus systematic repression of innovation on the other. The choice does not have to be so grim, if we can devise and implement processes that systematize *ex ante* risk assessment for appropriate categories of novel interventions, and quickly identify those cases for which further testing is indicated. Then, precaution would be less intrusive and costly while still providing substantial protection from harm. Yet, the debate continues: might we be better off insisting on systematic *ex ante* risk assessment and pre-release testing, or would that be just another case of over-regulation?

Consider the case of nanotechnology (Box 12.1). It is predicted that nanotechnology will transform many aspects of our lives and economy, and generate huge benefits, many of them from applications yet unimagined. However, it is clear that nanoparticles may exhibit surprising reactivity and in some cases toxicity, and surprising mobility within the human or animal body. Nanoparticles can be molded into specific shapes for particular purposes, and it is clear that shape matters to their properties. Currently, we do not know how nano-products break down and nanoparticles are transported in the environment, but we do know that animal studies have shown their ability to evade some of the body's natural defense systems and accumulate in the brain, cells, blood, and nerves. We do not yet have the knowledge to predict the performance and hazards of particular nanoparticles and products, so we need to learn by experimenting case by case. All of this constitutes, I would claim, a *prima facie* case that nanotechnology presents, along with exciting prospects of benefits, a potential threat to environment, health, and safety. Furthermore, it is reasonable to expect that we will learn in due course that some nanoparticles and products are benign whereas others are hazardous.

We have been down paths like this before. The innovations adopted eagerly for their promised benefits include asbestos (Chapter 5) and PCBs and MTBE (Chapter 9). I was critical of our failure to pre-screen and test MTBE effectively prior to its adoption as an octane enhancer in gasoline (Box 9.3), so one might expect me to take a strong position in support of systematic pre-screening and pre-release testing of nano-products. But our current scientific understanding of nanotechnology does not permit effective pre-screening – we do not yet know enough to sort nanoparticles into more- and less-dangerous categories; basically, we don't know what to look for. We do have the ability to test particular nanoparticles one-by-one for some things, e.g. toxicity and accumulation in sensitive organs of animals, but perhaps not to trace their fate in the environment. Worse, we do not have a reliable inventory of nano-products on the market or under development, there is no reporting process in place, and there is no comprehensive regulatory structure for nano-products – in the US, such regulatory

Box 12.1 An NI₁ example – nanotechnology risk*

Innovation. Nanotechnology patents are being filed at a rapid and accelerating rate. Nanotechnology starts with reducing a substance into tiny particles – a nanometer is a billionth of a meter – that can be engineered into shapes including tubes, rings, shells, wires, beads, cages and plates. These particles and shapes can be incorporated into other materials to add useful properties (e.g. strength and rigidity), and/or serve functional purposes like blocking ultra-violet radiation, protecting against microbial infection, supplementing trace metal particles in food products, and delivering medications more precisely.

Risks. Research suggests that nanoparticles of harmless substances can become exceptionally dangerous: they are more reactive, having a much greater proportion of their atoms on the surface; and they can be transported more readily into the environment and the human body. There is a lot that we do not know: e.g. whether they can enter groundwater when the products that contain them are dumped or broken up. Research on animals suggests that nanoparticles can have surprising toxicity, and can evade some of the body's natural defense systems and accumulate in the brain, cells, blood, and nerves. Their effects depend on the particular shape but, given current knowledge, determining these effects requires case-by-case experiments.

Regulation. Nanotechnology research and development have advanced faster than the capacity of regulators to assess the social and environmental impacts, leaving the risks effectively unregulated. The US National Nanotechnology Initiative is charged with promoting nanotechnology and mitigating its risks and thus, some observers worry, is inherently conflicted. Companies producing nano-products may be liable for damages, but even their insurance carriers are not yet fully able to assess the risks.

US regulatory agencies (e.g. Food and Drug Administration and Environmental Protection Agency) are beginning to pay more attention to nano-products, and it can be argued that existing laws authorize more systematic regulation than is currently implemented. However, some major high-exposure applications such as cosmetics and dietary supplements are essentially unregulated.

Environmental, health, and safety legislation cannot be expected to work until the products of the technology are better understood. Currently we lack even a serious inventory of nano-products on the market – voluntary registries in the US and the UK are estimated to include fewer than ten percent of the existing products. How can we regulate nanotechnology materials while we remain unable to measure their release into the environment? Researchers are optimistic that eventually they will be able to develop a general and systematic understanding of nanoparticles, and predict which will be hazardous before they are ever made. Science, technology, and business could then focus on the materials that are most likely to be beneficial, safe, and profitable.

The risk management challenge. Nanotechnology has the potential to deliver a wide array of benefits, many of them unimagined at this stage. Yet the unknowns, and perhaps even unknown unknowns, of nanotechnology, and the hints of serious potential threats to environment, health, and safety that have emerged from the limited research undertaken thus far, suggest a role for precaution. Can we find ways to protect society against any disproportionate threats of harm, without undue sacrifice of potential benefits from innovation? Should we work purposefully toward a risk management strategy that starts with systematic pre-screening and pre-release testing of nano-products?

* Sources include "A little risky business" *The Economist*, November 22, 2007, Bell, T. 2007. *Understanding risk assessment of nanotechnology* www.nano. gov/Understanding_Risk_Assessment.pdf. and "Nanotechnology regulation: former EPA official highlights shortcomings of current federal oversight" *Science Daily*, July 25, 2008.

authority as exists derives from pre-existing regulations, e.g. of drugs and pesticides, and certain uses already prominent (e.g. cosmetics and dietary supplements) are essentially unregulated. In the case of nanotechnology, it is early in the game but perhaps not early enough – already there is in place a substantial industry and scientific establishment, and they can be expected to oppose effective *ex ante* risk assessment as stifling to innovation. Already, we are playing catch-up, but it is better to get going now than to wait any longer.

The lesson for government, it seems to me, is that the investment in science and technology that provides impetus for major technology shifts like nanotechnology should be accompanied by substantial and systematic research into effects on environment, health, and safety. As soon as the economic prospects for radical new technologies become evident, research should be directed systematically toward building the basic understanding that would allow effective pre-screening of the products that emerge. New nano-products should be reported systematically to appropriate regulatory agencies that would maintain inventories. That way, *ex ante* risk assessment can be systematized and rendered relatively non-intrusive (except in cases where evidence of potential threat is discovered). Ideally, risk management can progress in tandem with the commercialization of the new technology.

ORM and risk assessment – NI$_2$ and BAU cases. In cases of novel interventions gone bad (NI$_2$) and potential regime shift due to overstress of familiar systems in the course of business-as-usual (BAU), *ex ante* risk assessment requires systematic monitoring to detect possible harm. But monitoring of what? We might monitor activities that seem *a priori* risky and activities at alarmingly large scale and those that have been ramped up dramatically. We might monitor environmental, health, and safety systems, either as a matter of course (and given the extent of government involvement in environmental regulation and resource management, we do quite a lot of this already), or because warning signs have been reported, perhaps by "unofficial" sources.

Early warning and adaptive management help control costs of remedy for NI_2 and BAU cases, but require more monitoring than is customary. Ideally, there would be serious investment in monitoring and early-warning systems, which suggests substantial additional costs. But official regulatory monitoring is only the tip of the iceberg – we already do a lot of monitoring if all the research and monitoring in universities, research laboratories, NGOs, etc. (the monitoring that I labeled "unofficial" above) is included. Perhaps there is potential gain from systematizing the data from the various monitoring efforts already underway. In addition, public participation increases monitoring resources (attracting more "unofficial" monitoring effort) and the efficiency of their allocation (Stirling and Scoones 2009).

In NI_2 and BAU cases, too, ORM practice makes less systematic effort at risk assessment than would be ideal.

We can do better than "ORM for manageable risks, the PP for disproportionate threats"

While "ORM for the ordinary risks, but subject to the PP for extraordinary threats" makes sense for decision making, it fails as a coherent risk management strategy because it is insensitive to the crucial role of *ex ante* risk assessment and the rather general inadequacy of risk assessment in ORM practice. In ORM, there is simply too much acceptance of the strategy of plowing ahead with proposed innovations and business-as-usual exploitation of familiar systems, and dealing with any resulting harm after it has been proven beyond reasonable doubt (by which time remedies are often very expensive and disruptive).

Instead, it makes more sense to work toward a risk management framework that integrates ORM and precautionary approaches to risk assessment and systematic learning and re-assessment even as we provide protection, even as we hold precautionary prohibitions in reserve for disproportionate threats.

NOTES

1 A similar list offered by Resnik (1998) served as a springboard for the following discussion.
2 Weak sustainability can be achieved in principle by "getting the prices right"; that is, by internalizing externalities, providing public goods in efficient quantities, and reinvesting the rents earned from resource extraction (Randall 2008). To provide a concrete example, an efficient tax on carbon emissions would contribute to weak sustainability.
3 At least one quasi-judicial body, the World Trade Organization Appellate Body in a case involving European reluctance to permit imports of beef produced with artificial hormones, has ruled that commitment to continuing research and review is a hallmark of good faith in applying the PP (Shaw and Schwartz 2005).

13 Integrated risk management

The integrated risk management that we are striving toward should draw from ordinary risk management (ORM) and the precautionary principle (PP) to develop a coherent framework that incorporates insights from each. Already, we have established the beginning and end points. It should begin with more systematic *ex ante* risk assessment to sort cases into three classes: benign, manageable risks, and disproportionate threats; and the end-points should be tailored to the particular cases: ORM for manageable risks, with more potent precautionary remedies for cases that pose disproportionate threats. Yet work remains in fleshing-out the integrated framework.

The economic, utilitarian foundations of ORM decision theory contribute several key concepts. *Cost-effectiveness* – a given level of protection should be delivered at the lowest feasible cost – is always a relevant consideration. This is not about stinting on quantity and quality of protection, because we have specified a given level of protection; it is about avoiding waste, and it would be wasteful to spend more if exactly the same protection was available at a lower price. *Risk–risk trade-offs* always matter, in principle. If in a given circumstance action entails a risk but so does inaction, and different actions entail different risks, every effort should be made to compare the net risks, apples to apples, and (other things being equal) choose the alternative that entails the least net risk. To put it another way, it always makes sense to think carefully about the risk–risk trade-offs that are entailed in the choice of action. However, the recommended apples-to-apples comparison of net risks can be difficult in complicated situations.

ORM adopts the standard utilitarian decision criteria (Chapter 4): under certainty, benefits and costs should be evaluated and the alternative that generates the greatest positive net present value should be chosen (the *BC criterion*); and under Knightian risk with a budget constraint much greater than the maximum loss from any particular trial, it is the mathematical expectation of benefits and costs that should be compared (the *EV criterion*). This much is unambiguous, but from there it gets messier. In concept, we could substitute expected utility for expected value, to derive the *EU criterion*. The point is that EV differs from EU by accounting for risk aversion, which is appropriate when the outcome set is specified imprecisely and/or it includes the possibility of losses large enough to reduce future prospects. Of course, risk aversion is personal and subjective which, combined with imprecisely specified outcome sets, makes the whole calculation much squishier in practice. Beyond that point – as we move to gross ignorance, unknown unknowns, and threats of disproportionate harm – ORM gets increasingly out of its depth.[1]

The PP literature suggests the concept of proportionality, e.g. remedies should be proportional to the chosen level of protection and the magnitude of possible harm (UNESCO 2005), which suggests a degree of concern with the benefits and the costs of remedies. Yet, PP proponents are typically at pains to dissociate themselves from any commitment to explicit BC, EV, and EU criteria. One way that proportionality differs from EV and related criteria is in the breadth of its concerns – as well as benefits and costs, PP proponents often seek proportionality in disruption of way-of-life and the relative burdens that may be placed upon particular sub-sets of society. Furthermore, most PP proponents consider proportionality to be a matter of judgment rather than explicit calculation, and I have yet to see a PP proponent specify an explicit mathematical factor that should be applied in assessing proportionality, e.g. remedies are acceptable that cost no more than 1, or 3, or 5 times the expected value of damage.

Nevertheless, proportionality is a coherent concept. For one thing, it has coherence and clarity enough to permit a serious discourse among stakeholders as to the extent and cost of remedies for a particular threat that would be considered proportional. It makes sense that what counts as proportional depends on the magnitude of the threat – when the stakes are large and the threat is truly disproportionate, surely drastic remedies would pass a proportionality test.

The approach to PP remedies developed in this book (Chapters 9 and 12) brings to the integrated risk management framework much more than systematic attention to *ex ante* risk assessment. It emphasizes the value of sequential and iterative risk assessment and remedy processes that encourage learning at every step, and address the threat and remedies (regulation, remediation, mitigation, and adaptation) holistically, while matching cases with appropriate remedies.

Integrated risk management – proposed innovations (NI₁)

The paradigm case of quarantine and stepwise release (QSR) is the release decision concerning a "new" organism proposed for purposeful introduction,

perhaps an exotic species or variety, or a GMO. The core idea is an iterative and sequential process beginning with tight confinement and progress-
ing through increasingly less secure steps to learn more and more about
the likely outcomes from general release. The QSR process may start with
screening and testing under laboratory conditions, and proceed through a
stepwise pre-release testing process with monitoring, study, reassessment of
the threat and the remedy, and adjustments in remedy as warranted by emerging evidence at every step – a process that may be iterated many times. As
the process continues toward possible general release, testing should focus
increasingly on remedies for acceptable and manageable risks – remediation,
mitigation, and adaptation – as well as potential harm. Each step ends with
a continue-to-next-step/terminate decision, where termination means prohibiting further release and is implemented only when the evidence suggests
unacceptable risks in the next step. Should evidence of unacceptable risk fail
to arise after all relevant testing steps have been completed, general release
may be undertaken with much more assurance than if we had simply rolled
the dice at the outset. Release would be followed by a program of post-release
surveillance to check for unexpected harmful consequences – possible but
less likely now, because extensive pre-release testing should have revealed
the more likely harmful possibilities (Figure 13.1). Should negative but manageable impacts be determined, post-release research should include remediation, mitigation, and adaptation.

In addition to its obvious applications to proposed release of a new species,
variety, or GMO, I have suggested QSR as a metaphor for a broad class of pre-
release research and testing programs. Yet, further reflection suggests that,
for a more general process, at the end of each step a third option – to proceed directly to release – should be offered (Figure 13.2). The process (called
screening, testing, and surveillance, STS) begins with pre-screening, and one
can imagine proposed innovations where, if no threatening possibilities are
revealed during screening, a decision to release may be appropriate. We might
expect those cases to be concentrated among innovations that rank fairly low
on a scale of increasing novelty, i.e. innovations that tweak the relevant systems only modestly, or in familiar ways so that its past responses to similar
tweaks provide a good guide as to likely outcomes from the proposed innovation. For innovations that seem more novel, the process would proceed to
pre-release testing with three possible outcomes at each step – terminate the
process and prohibit release, continue testing, and general release.

We have specified these processes in terms that are mostly substantive. To
implement them systematically, procedures must be specified to accomplish
the following tasks:

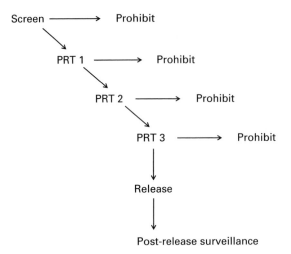

Figure 13.1 Stylized quarantine and stepwise release (QSR) process – assume 3 steps of pre-release testing, PRT

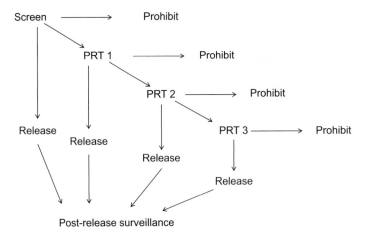

Figure 13.2 Stylized screening, pre-release testing, post-release surveillance (STS) process

1. Laws and/or regulations delegate authority to a specific public entity (which we will call the Agency) that may be created or newly tasked to serve this purpose, and specify the parameters within which it operates.
2. The Agency deals with particular proposed innovations as follows:
   - Developers of the proposed innovation apply to the Agency for some consideration that affects the status and progress of the NI_1 – perhaps a license, certification, some sort of approval, or a letter suggesting that the Agency has no further questions (as in the case of US Food and Drug Administration review of GM-foods).

- Developers submit data regarding the pre-screening and testing they have performed at each stage to the Agency, along with a request to release (R), or continue to the next stage of testing (T). The Agency may demand more data from the developers, and may perhaps produce additional data – ideally, the Agency has the capability to replicate tests submitted and conduct tests on its own initiative.
- The Agency renders a decision at this stage: R, T, or prohibit (P). In deciding, the Agency is guided by the PP evidence criterion (credible scientific evidence). There may be a process that allows the developers to appeal the Agency decision.
- Pre-release testing continues through the specified stages until a decision of R or P is reached.
- If the decision is R, which may imply a judgment that the NI_1 is not risk-free but poses acceptable risks, the Agency specifies any required regulatory restrictions on use, remediation of impacts, and mitigation, and perhaps assists in developing and implementing strategies for adaptation.

3. Agency decision criteria should be attentive to proportionality, cost effectiveness, and the virtues of affordable remedies; and to autonomy, property rights, and the need for policies to reduce or mitigate disproportionate negative impacts on particular individuals and groups.

4. The courts may review this process, and perhaps review Agency decisions, on certain specified grounds (the Agency has failed in its duty, exceeded its authority, etc.). Courts may also deal with issues of responsible party liability for damage and costs of remediation, mitigation, and adaptation.

5. There may be provision for direct citizen access to the process at various stages – for example, release decisions may require prior public hearings or a public comment period.

6. Release should be followed by post-release surveillance, and surveillance should be more intensive if pre-release testing suggests even a small chance of serious harm. The Agency may be capable of conducting a rigorous program of surveillance, or may delegate that responsibility to some standing research organization(s). Independent research organizations and interested citizens may be encouraged to contribute to this effort.[2] Should post-release surveillance indicate a chance that harmful effects are occurring, procedures appropriate for NI_2 cases are initiated.

Once a procedure is in place, questions begin to arise as to whether it achieves the right balance between precaution and innovation. More specifically, the trade-off is among more rigorous pre-release testing (which may discourage and/or delay innovation), more rigorous post-release surveillance to provide early warning of potential harm, and the costs of damage, remediation, mitigation, and adaptation, which may be very large in the relatively few cases where things go very badly. Questions about the right balance apply necessarily to substantive measures and to the procedures for implementing them.

Manski (2009) considers the case of a new drug that may provide hope to those with some serious affliction, who otherwise face grim prospects, and suggests quicker progression through the pre-release testing process to approval followed by more careful follow-up surveillance (e.g. more systematic monitoring) of those who have used the drug. By focusing pre-release tests on patients with serious afflictions, promising remedies reach the target population even as we test and learn about the new drug. The worse the patients' default prospects, and the stronger the targeting (available only to the truly afflicted, with strong safeguard protocols), the more willing a benign regulator would be to allow prescribed use after limited pre-release testing. Yet, safety would be well served, it is argued, by more comprehensive and rigorous follow-up surveillance. It might be conjectured that there are other situations, perhaps many of them, where the general good would be served by some adjustment in the balance between pre-release testing, post-release surveillance, and the potential harm from pre-mature release.

Integrated risk management – NI$_2$ and BAU cases

The distinguishing feature of novel interventions gone bad (NI$_2$) and potential regime shift due to overstress of familiar systems in the course of business-as-usual (BAU) is that the potential for harm is recognized only after the causal factors are embedded into the social, economic, and environmental systems. For this reason, there is always the worry that remedies will be expensive, disruptive, and perhaps incomplete. In contrast to drastic remedies, adaptive management frames remedy as a stepwise process – plan, implement, monitor, adjust plan, etc. (Box 5.3) – designed to increase opportunities for learning, as well as make progress toward reducing the threat. It allows us to learn about remedies "on the job" (so to speak) and to make progress toward remedy relatively cheaply in terms of cost and disruption. But one worries that such remedies may be quite incomplete. Can we really forestall regime shift using adaptive management approaches? Perhaps we can, but only if the warning comes early enough (and in Chapter 9 we learned that early warning is a relative concept – relative to the lead-time required for effective response) and the system is resilient enough.

Adaptive management is also well suited to the "hopeless" cases: those where there is no realistic hope of forestalling regime shift or of restoring the *status quo ante*, and the pragmatic objective is to learn how to survive and perhaps thrive in the new regime. For this assignment, *mitigation and adaptation* loom large among the feasible remedies, and adaptive management is appropriate for on-the-job learning about effective and relatively non-disruptive ways to mitigate the damage and adapt to the changed environment. One of the key tasks in risk management for NI₂ and BAU cases is to delineate the appropriate roles for adaptive management and more drastic remedies.

To implement appropriate remedies systematically, procedures must be specified to accomplish the following tasks:

1. A signal of some kind (an alarm, or an early warning) jumpstarts, or abruptly ramps up, the risk management process.

   - For resources already managed by a standing agency (e.g. forests, fisheries, and public lands in the US and many other countries), the Agency is in place and is likely to be monitoring the situation. While a variety of interested parties also may provide useful information, it is likely to be the Agency that performs an initial risk assessment, sounds the alarm, and initiates the process of remedy.

   - For systems not already managed (e.g. global climate), the alarm is likely to come from a variety of sources – universities, research organizations, NGOs, independent researchers. Governments are likely to get involved, and in the case of a global issue like climate, inter-governmental organizations (e.g. the International Panel on Climate Change) may be established. Effective action requires enforceable international treaties. For problems of national scale, inter-agency organizations are a staple of resource management (including risk management) in the US, and may be empowered to take remedial action in addition to monitoring and research.

   - While awaiting action at the ideal level (global, for climate change), actions – typically less intrusive, more tentative, and in some cases mostly symbolic – may be taken on a smaller scale by cities, states, nations, multinational groupings (e.g. the European Union), and agencies reinterpreting their authority under existing legislation; e.g. US EPA decided in 2010 that it is authorized to regulate carbon emissions.

   - Assume that, eventually, treaties, laws and/or regulations delegate authority to the Agency, and specify the parameters within which it operates.

2. The Agency deals with particular cases as follows:
   - Suppose the alarm is an early warning. Then, adaptive management (AM) is implemented, results are monitored, and in the best case AM proves to be adequate. The Agency orchestrates AM using its regulatory and management authority, but is likely that much of its work involves coordinating the actions of a variety of public and private organizations and individual participants.
   - Suppose more drastic remedies are indicated by the initial risk assessment, or by what is learned from early rounds of AM. Typically, the drivers of threatened regime shift must be curtailed by regulations authorized under laws and/or treaties. The Agency administers this process, promulgating detailed regulations and implementing them. The ultimate goal is to stabilize the system in order to reduce the threat of regime shift, and implement regulatory restrictions, remediation of impacts, mitigation, and perhaps adaptive actions, as appropriate. Of course, there is an adaptive element in the implementation of drastic remedies – they may be adjusted in light of what is learned in the course of implementation.
3. Agency decision criteria should be attentive to proportionality, cost effectiveness, and the virtues of affordable remedies; and to autonomy, property rights, and the need for policies to reduce or mitigate disproportionate negative impacts on particular individuals and groups.
4. Because drastic remedies require major changes in business-as-usual, we might expect a good deal of resistance from impacted parties. Legislatures might intervene to limit Agency authority and/or restrict its scope to act, and plaintiffs may ask the courts to review the process and particular Agency decisions. The Agency, aware that in the end it answers to the public, may implement the remedy tentatively and cautiously, seeking a middle way. Courts may also deal with issues of responsible party liability for damage, and costs of remediation, mitigation, adaptation, etc.
5. There may be provision for direct citizen access to the process at various stages – for example, certain kinds of management decisions may require prior public hearings or a public comment period.
6. Remedies should be followed by continuing surveillance, and monitoring should be more intensive if early results suggest even a small chance of continuing serious harm or disruption from the original problem or from the remedies implemented. The Agency may be capable of conducting a rigorous program of surveillance, or may delegate that responsibility to some standing research organization(s). Independent research organizations and interested citizens may be encouraged to contribute to this

effort (see footnote 2). Should continuing surveillance indicate a chance that continuing harmful effects are occurring, appropriate adjustments in remedies are implemented.

These stylized procedures for all three cases (NI_1, NI_2, and BAU) implement the PP commitment to invoke remedies when faced with credible scientific evidence of plausible disproportionate threat, i.e. before the threat and its causes are firmly established. In effect, this becomes a commitment to act earlier (and, one would expect, more often) than ORM, which suggests that precaution can be costly; but early action also has its cost-reducing effects in many cases. For proposed novel interventions that pose threats above the PP threshold, pre-release testing looms large among the remedies that may be invoked; and for NI_1 cases that can be quarantined, prohibition readily defaults to quarantine and stepwise release which, as we have seen, provides a sequential decision process that allows us to tailor the remedy to the threat as we learn more about both. For novel interventions gone bad and system overstress from business-as-usual, earlier action means rigorous monitoring and early warning.[3] Prohibition or serious restriction of the drivers, and remediation, mitigation, and adaptation are likely remedies should a serious threat be confirmed. For overstress from business-as-usual, earlier action means developing and implementing early warning systems and invoking remedies should the alarm be signaled. Again, the PP impetus to early action is combined with sensitivity to costs and a bias toward remedy processes that provide sequential decision points and encourage learning.

Risk dilemmas are confined to cases where post-release remedies are the only kinds available. That is, we may encounter risk dilemmas in NI_2 and BAU cases but not in NI_1 cases. The stylized procedures for integrated risk management suggested here – which emphasize more systematic screening of proposed novel interventions, and pre-release testing of those that pose non-trivial threats, and systematic monitoring to provide early warning for NI_2 and BAU cases – have the potential to systematically reduce the prevalence of risk dilemmas.

Real-world experience

It is interesting to compare the substance and procedure for integrated risk management sketched above with the practices of real-world agencies that have key roles in risk management. Below, we take a cursory look at four cases involving three specific US agencies – the Food and Drug Administration

(FDA), the Environmental Protection Agency (EPA), and the Department of the Interior (DOI) – and a fifth, fisheries management, where the a multiplicity of agencies are involved and the broad outlines of regulatory practice are similar in much of the world. These cases, together, were selected to represent both novel interventions and overstress from business-as-usual, to demonstrate a range of practice across the ORM–PP spectrum, and because there is some advantage in choosing cases that are familiar to the author. For new drugs and synthetic chemicals, we can speed the discussion by drawing upon earlier chapters.

Drugs – FDA

The FDA regulates drugs, focusing primarily on an approval process for new drugs (proposed innovations). The standard FDA approval procedure, strengthened by 1960s legislation in light of the thalidomide disaster (Box 9.4), follows laboratory and animal testing with three phases of testing with human subjects, each phase involving more subjects and conditions closer to actual clinical practice than its predecessor. Typically the developers of the new drug submit tests they have conducted; the FDA reviews the results, and has the options of requesting more tests, and tests by independent researchers, prior to making its decision. The approval process may take around eight years. If the drug is approved, the FDA does post-market surveillance, analyzing outcomes from use among the general population. If unacceptable risks are documented, FDA approval is withdrawn; but by that stage it often happens that the manufacturer, strongly motivated to minimize liability exposure, already has withdrawn it from the market.

The FDA's systematic pre-release testing, despite apparent wide popular support, has drawn criticism on grounds that innovation is delayed and lives lost unnecessarily. The FDA has been sensitive to this criticism, and has fast-tracked promising drugs for the worst sorts of afflictions. Recent developments regarding thalidomide are illustrative. Thalidomide was prescribed originally for nausea and morning sickness, rather mundane afflictions, and the resulting serious birth defects were obviously unacceptable. However, new applications for much more serious afflictions – where the patients' prospects are grim in the absence of treatment – have been approved, subject to rigorous safeguards to minimize the chance of harm (Box 9.9). Perhaps FDA's response to this situation reveals one of America's few fundamentally precautionary institutions exhibiting some sensitivity to the utilitarian critique.

Pesticides – EPA

All pesticides used in the United States are regulated by federal and state law. International conventions (e.g. the Stockholm Convention on Persistent Organic Pollutants) also impact US regulation of pesticides, including which chemicals can be used in producing food for export. The threats that motivate regulation are to the environment (toxicity to non-target species and persistence are red-flags), and human health which may be impacted during pesticide handling and application, by pesticides in the environment, and by consuming food with pesticide residues.

Here we focus on the federal (EPA) role in regulation of pesticide distribution, sale, and use. If developers (distributors, etc.) of a substance claim that it has pesticidal activity, it is defined by law as a pesticide, which brings certain genetically modified organisms under EPA regulation of pesticides. The EPA's role includes:

- Registration. All pesticides distributed or sold in the United States must be registered by the EPA.
- Testing. Before the EPA may register a pesticide, the applicant must present evidence (including test data) that using the pesticide according to specifications will not generally cause unreasonable adverse effects on the environment, defined as (i) any unreasonable risk to humans or the environment, taking into account the economic, social, and environmental costs and benefits of the use of any pesticide, or (ii) a human dietary risk from residues that result from a use of a pesticide in or on any food.[4]
- Labeling. Pesticides must bear labels instructing proper and acceptable use and disposal of containers and unused contents. The EPA responded to this regulatory responsibility by sponsoring a substantial program of research to design appropriate labels and validate their effectiveness in risk communication.
- Regulation of applicators. The EPA determines which pesticides are for general use and which are restricted to certified applicators, and specifies the training requirements for certification as an applicator.
- Monitoring. The EPA is responsible for monitoring restricted pesticides including some persistent organic pollutants.
- Suspension. The EPA has the authority to suspend or cancel the registration of a pesticide if information shows that continued use would pose unreasonable risks. Such information may be generated by the EPA, but also by independent research organizations and individuals, but the EPA makes the final determination of unreasonable risks.

The substance and procedure of pesticide regulation in the US is broadly consistent with the integrated risk management framework laid out in this chapter for proposed innovations. The elements of a screening, pre-release testing, and post-release surveillance (STS) framework are present, although it is always possible to nit-pick the details as regulatory overkill or laxity.[5] In particular, it might be argued that the suspension process is informed by an information gathering effort that falls well short of systematic post-release surveillance. Proportionality and sensitivity to risk–risk considerations are evident in the definition of unreasonable risk (taking into account the economic, social, and environmental costs and benefits of the use of any pesticide).

Synthetic chemicals – EPA

Despite the enormous cost of remediation of PCBs beginning in the 1970s (Box 9.2), to mention only the most prominent example, the EPA continues to take a relatively hands-off approach to synthetic chemicals. By the 1980s and '90s, MTBE (used as an octane enhancer in gasoline, Box 9.3) and C8 (used in manufacturing Teflon®) were widely dispersed in the environment when it became evident that they were serious environmental threats. A regulatory reluctance to require serious pre-release testing might be defended as pro-innovation, but any harmful effects are discovered belatedly and debated extensively before remedies are invoked. By that time, the substances have become embedded in the business-as-usual economy, with the effect that remedies are expensive, disruptive, and most likely incomplete – the *status quo ante* is no longer attainable and the suite of remedies is tilted toward mitigation and adaptation.

Garrity (2004) argues that US approaches to environmental law often permit precautionary approaches, but in practice they seldom are required or implemented. Existing law provided five specific opportunities for the EPA to require additional safeguards before MTBE became widely used and dispersed throughout the environment. Yet the EPA passed up or soft-pedaled all of these chances.

In contrast to the EPA's fairly strong precautionary stance toward pesticides, its regulatory approach to synthetic chemicals falls far short of the integrated risk management framework. The case of MTBE is illustrative – pre-screening was perfunctory, there was no serious pre-release testing, and post-release surveillance was stimulated at the outset by reports from independent research organizations.

There are signs that the EPA is beginning to take synthetic chemicals more seriously: it has recently placed two classes of chemicals, phthalates, and PBDEs (polybrominated diphenyl ethers) on a "chemicals of concern" list (Grossman 2010). These chemicals are widely used in personal care, household, and industrial applications; there is evidence that they are environmentally persistent and bioaccumulative, and that they disrupt metabolic and endocrine functions. The EPA's action could signal the possibility of further regulatory action focused on these classes of chemicals. For those chemicals already widely used, the EPA's "concern" was triggered by post-release surveillance including bio-monitoring. For new chemicals in these classes, an integrated risk management approach starting with pre-screening and pre-release testing may be appropriate, but it is much too early to know if the EPA will implement such an approach.

Endangered and threatened species – DOI

The core legislative mandate for protection of endangered species is provided by the Endangered Species Act (ESA) of 1966, as subsequently amended, which assigned the preservation of species to the DOI. Species are listed as endangered, in a process involving petition, public notice, public comment, and perhaps judicial review. Considerations of economic impact are not entertained at this stage. A species survival and recovery plan must be developed, designating a critical habitat that must be protected. Negative economic consequences are considered in determining the critical habitat – a process that reverses the "maximize utility subject to a precautionary constraint" rule; here the rule is precaution subject to a constraint that economic sacrifice must be tolerably small. In practice, the DOI looks for compromises that keep commercial and local community interests cooperating, and cases out of court.

A recovery plan and a habitat conservation plan are developed. Because discovery of an endangered species on one's land or in one's community limits future options, controversy and incentive problems (shoot, shovel, and shut-up) abound. Gradually, some of the incentive problems have been resolved – Safe Harbor Agreements protect landowners who have altered their property to protect or attract endangered species from additional restrictions motivated by the success of their efforts; and No Surprises rules protect land owners who have committed to certain conservation efforts from responsibility for unforeseen problems.

Ideally, the endangered species recovers to the point where special protections are no longer necessary, and it is delisted. But there are other causes for delisting: extinction, discovery of new populations, errors in listing, and in one case by amendment of the Act. As of 2009, almost fifty species have been delisted, just fewer than half of them due to recovery.

The listing process for endangered species is often criticized on several grounds, the most frequent being its species rather than ecosystem approach. It is also seen as fostering a crisis approach to species preservation. There is a process for listing species as threatened, which invokes monitoring by DOI and certain protections weaker than those for endangered species; but the "crisis orientation" criticism of the ESA remains – insufficient attention to early warning and intervention leads to expensive and disruptive remedies, and sharp conflict with commercial and local community interests. Twenty-three species (additional to the almost fifty delisted) have been down-listed from "endangered" to "threatened" status.

Several states have enacted endangered species legislation at the state level, and some states are actively protecting species that are endangered at the state level but not nationally.

Serious efforts to preserve endangered species and ecosystems are undertaken in many countries, and the International Union for the Conservation of Nature does good and useful work in guiding conservation efforts around the globe.

The case of North Pacific salmon (Box 9.5) illustrates some of the challenges facing effective preservation of species. Not all north Pacific salmon are endangered or threatened, but several species and varieties are.[6] Salmon are themselves a keystone of a large and complex regional natural system that is pressured by a large and growing human system. Salmon restoration efforts have to this point been expensive and not especially successful, and the toolkit effectively available has been limited by resistance to economic disruption. Perhaps approaches that are more adaptive, and more sensitive to technical and economic feasibility, would be more acceptable and effective.

There is a strong precautionary approach to listing and de-listing of endangered species. Utilitarian concerns are heard-out when determining critical habitat. There are persistent criticisms that the ESA is insufficiently oriented toward early warning, with the effect that it often is invoked at the crisis stage, too late for meaningful compromise and adaptive solutions. Controversy and incentive problems abound, but some incentive issues have been resolved. In practice, the DOI goes slowly, to avoid lawsuits and political harassment on behalf of commercial and local government interests.

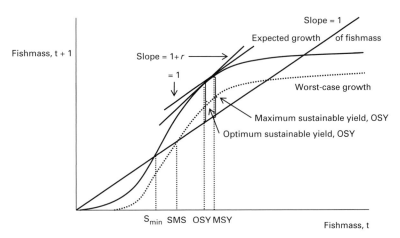

Figure 13.3   Maximum and optimal sustainable yield, and the safe minimum standard of conservation

Fisheries management

The basic principles of fisheries management are rather simple. Building on concepts introduced in Figure 10.1, the maximum sustainable yield of a fishery (MSY) can be identified by the point of tangency of a line of slope =1 and the expected growth curve for fishmass (Fig 13.3). Optimal sustainable yield (OSY) is identified by the point of tangency of a line of slope 1+r and expected growth, where r is the real rate of interest. OSY is a little less than MSY, reflecting the opportunity cost of capital embodied in the fish resource (there is an opportunity cost in waiting until later to harvest fish that could have been harvested now). If life were so simple, fisheries management would be a matter of setting the harvest equal to OSY. Relative to OSY, setting catch levels too high sacrifices future benefits from the fishery, but setting catch levels too low sacrifices current benefits.

Considering that growth of fishmass is stochastic, so that a combination of overfishing and a "bad draw in the growth lottery" might precipitate collapse of the fishery, precaution can be expressed by managing for OSY but in any event maintaining the stock above SMS. This simple concept provides the foundation of fisheries management, and would be adequate for a single species fishery with good stability properties.

Typically, fisheries management poses several additional problems: controlling yield is a challenge when the tools at the regulator's command are better adapted to controlling fishing effort or fish brought to market; commercial fishers are independent operators and their interests may conflict with those of recreational fishers and the regulator; fisheries are seldom single-species (so that incidental catch of non-target species may undermine

efforts to manage *their* stocks); and fisheries often cross jurisdictional boundaries (e.g. state and national) and jurisdiction in the deep oceans is a matter
of international conventions. The details of fisheries management are mostly
about attempts to achieve OSY for commercial fisheries and conservation
objectives for non-commercial species, given these complicating factors.

The institutional details of fisheries management are inherently complex.
For fisheries wholly within US waters, regulators include state, regional, and
federal agencies and organizations. For North American fisheries, bilateral
organizations with representation for Canada or Mexico (as the case may
be) are part of the mix; and for ocean fisheries, multi-national organizations
come into play.

For US domestic fisheries, Regional Fisheries Management Councils (with
representatives of federal agencies and agencies of member states, and persons
appointed by the state governors) are able to monitor fish stocks carefully in
order to nip potential regime shifts in the bud. Scientists are technically able
to achieve early warning, but there is a lot of stakeholder involvement and
the industry can be slow to accept the need for more restrictive catch limits.
Perhaps the Management Councils attempt a kind of rational planning – and
Figure 13.3 and the related discussion suggest a rational planning approach –
but the end result looks more like some sort of adaptive management.

International organizations such as the North-East Atlantic Fisheries
Commission, North Atlantic Salmon Conservation Organization, and the
European Commission attempt to regulate the ocean fisheries; and the
International Council for Exploration of the Seas provides them with scientific advice on the management of 135 separate finfish and shellfish stocks.
Nevertheless, there are inherent limits to the powers of international organizations. There is a paradox in operation: despite the fact that fisheries managers know what to do (or, at least, roughly what to do) to maintain sustainable
fisheries, too many of the worlds' fisheries are in serious decline.

Fisheries managers face three kinds of uncertainties:
• scientific uncertainties in complex and dynamic systems make it difficult
  to predict stock recruitment, the responses of fish stocks to changing fishing effort, and the interactions between fisheries and other aspects of the
  environment;
• management uncertainties over the response of real-world fishing activity
  to different policy and regulatory mechanisms;
• social/economic/political uncertainty about the needs and values of different user groups, and their responses to socio-economic pressures and
  management actions.

A precautionary approach is, in principle, any approach that renders stock collapse and/or significant damage to natural heritage or the supporting environment unlikely. Precautionary instruments may include the standard mechanisms (e.g. regulations, incentives, spatial planning of fishing activity, etc.), up to and including prohibition. Because monitoring often permits warning of potential collapse early enough for effective management response, in many cases precaution can be exercised through adaptive management.

If the managers know at least roughly what to do, what explains the serious decline of many important fisheries? Perhaps one place to start this inquiry is fish mortality: in a mixed fishery managed by regulating allowable catch (actually, landings), the incentives for fishers at the point of catch are inconsistent with the overall objective of sustainable use for the fishery as a whole. The anomalous incentive for fishers to discard species which have reached their catch limit, and to land only the most marketable individuals of species below their limit, results in substantial wastage of fish. Effective precautionary management might begin with monitoring of actual fish mortality rather than landings, and regulating wastage at sea, which is technically feasible with systematic use of vessel monitoring systems.

The standard conceptual framework for fisheries management is classical "maximize utility subject to a precautionary constraint." Precautionary approaches are widely implemented in fisheries management for rather straightforward reasons: most parties recognize that collapse of an important fishery is thoroughly undesirable, and the technical feasibility of early warning often permits adaptive management approaches that are relatively nonintrusive. Nevertheless, due to various technical difficulties and institutional weaknesses, many fisheries (especially international fisheries) are in decline. While the fisheries case is replete with unique details that engage scientists, economists, and managers, it is also illustrates an important case of potential regime shift due to overstress from business-as-usual: the case where everyday management practice is complicated by non-exclusiveness and asymmetric information.

Bottom line

It can be argued that, regardless of whether we think there is enough integrated risk management – and hence enough precaution – in the US, there is more than is generally acknowledged. The cases sketched above illustrate this point.

Proposed innovations (NI₁):

- FDA and new drugs. The approach is consistent with integrated risk management, and involves serious pre-release testing and a degree of post-release surveillance. The public seems to think precaution is appropriate, and that it works, in the case of new drugs; and citizens seem more likely to get exercised about breakdowns in precaution than about excessive precaution. Utilitarian critics argue that excessive precaution sacrifices lives that could be saved by earlier access to new drugs. The FDA has made some concessions to the utilitarian critique, especially in regard to drugs addressed to debilitating afflictions.
- EPA and pesticides. The approach to pesticides is also broadly consistent with integrated risk management. The EPA takes a fairly firm precautionary stance on new pesticides, but is perhaps less aggressive in de-registering widely used pesticides shown to be dangerous.

Overstress from business-as-usual exploitation and encroachment (BAU):

- DOI – endangered species. On paper, the approach to preservation of species deviates from standard integrated risk management, if at all, on the side of precaution. There is a strong precautionary approach to listing and de-listing of endangered species; utilitarian concerns receive their first explicit consideration when determining critical habitat. Some of the incentive problems inherent in preserving endangered species on private land (shoot, shovel, and shut-up) have been resolved gradually by Safe Harbor Agreements and No Surprises rules. In practice, DOI seeks to work with commercial and local community interests, to avoid lawsuits and political harassment.
- Fisheries management. In theory, the standard approach to fisheries management is classical integrated risk management: maximize utility subject to a precautionary constraint; and management is flexible and adaptive, aiming to avoid the sudden prohibitions that come into play when a breach of the conservation constraint is imminent. In practice, the task is more complex due to scientific uncertainty (especially in multi-species fisheries and when ecosystem concerns are involved), and non-exclusiveness and asymmetric information issues.

Novel interventions after the fact (NI₂):

- EPA – synthetic chemicals. In practice, the EPA usually passes-up the opportunities provided in the law for serious pre-screening and pre-release testing. The occasional disasters that follow typically become evident after the chemical is widely used and dispersed in the environment, with the inevitable result that remediation is expensive and incomplete. The EPA has recently placed two classes of synthetic chemicals on a "chemicals of concern" list, which may signal a switch to a more proactive regulatory approach.

Note that the cases sketched above are hardly a random set. I selected four of the five cases with an eye to illustrating integrated risk management in practice. Among the novel intervention cases sketched, synthetic chemicals provide the exception; nevertheless, it is more nearly the norm among NI cases in the US. In this, I will let the noise meter be my witness – if it were not the norm why do we hear so much from PP opponents fretting that systematic application of PP would stifle innovation?

Integrated risk management is clearly the goal in the two BAU cases selected, and it is achieved to some degree. However, this is hardly the norm in the USA for risk management in BAU cases. The largest managers of US public lands are the Forest Service (FS) and the Bureau of Land Management (BLM). Both of these agencies are charged with managing to attain a complicated slate of objectives involving efficient use of natural resources, environmental and ecosystem protection, and prosperity and stability in the communities impacted by public lands. Because public lands dominate the landscape in many western states, Congress and the relevant state governments are keenly interested in how the FS and BLM go about their work, and the various interests involved are quick to express their concerns in public hearings and the courts. Both agencies are attentive to commercial interests, the BLM perhaps more so.

In timber management, the FS is guided by the "maximize utility subject to a precautionary constraint" rule and, because trees are rooted in the soil, experiences fewer difficulties in implementing this approach than do fisheries managers. However, the FS has additional concerns – e.g. managing recreation resources, and ecosystem protection – as well as pressures for inefficient timber harvest to provide employment in impacted communities. The BLM has fairly similar responsibilities but, by reputation, is more attentive to the concerns of ranchers and minerals extractors and corresponding less successful in meeting conservation objectives.

Perhaps the typical BAU case involves mostly private lands. Land, water, and ecosystems come under pressure from growing populations and increasing per capita use of land, yet existing institutions tend to nibble around the edges of the problem – land use controls are implemented mostly at the local level and many states limit local authority, federal protections are in place for wetlands but debate continues about their effectiveness, and various environmental protections from air quality to endangered species may come into play in particular instances. It does not add up to integrated risk management for stresses upon land, water, and ecosystems.

Then, there is the 800-pound gorilla, climate change, the global BAU case that the world has yet to confront seriously.

Summary and conclusions

A substantively and procedurally integrated risk management process seeks to combine the virtues of ORM and PP. The PP takes disproportionate risks seriously.[7] Its evidence criterion is not addressed to the search for empirical laws of science, but to criteria for action under risk, uncertainty, and worse – it is about making the right calls case by case on behalf of the public. The PP approach brings complex systems thinking, more systematic procedures for reconnaissance and learning, and more respect for screening and pre-release testing of novel interventions. The goal is to cast a wider precautionary net, but release the harmless fish with minimal fuss and delay.

ORM brings respect for risk–risk trade-offs, cost effectiveness, and welfare concerns such as might be expressed in the benefit–cost, expected value, and expected utility criteria. It is not true that PP thinking has no respect for these concerns, but rather that it places them in a broader and hence less formulaically decisive context. A big issue in integration is how much weight the final product puts on risk–risk trade-offs, cost effectiveness, and welfare concerns.

The integrated risk management process envisioned here has the following virtues:

- It adopts the PP evidence criterion: credible scientific evidence of plausible threat. This restores a degree of balance to the weight given to null and alternative hypotheses when diagnosing threats in particular cases.
- It adopts complex systems thinking, including alertness to path-dependence and the possibility of surprises, and encourages systematic modeling to identify indicator variables for impending regime shift.
- It calls for more systematic screening of proposed novel interventions, and pre-release testing of those that pose non-trivial threats. The goal is to assign as many cases as warranted to ORM decision criteria and risk management tools as early as possible, and to prohibit the relatively few interventions that warrant it. Integrated risk management:
  - provides for sequential and iterative decision processes that systematically enhance learning while providing protection (QSR and STS);

- addresses credible threats earlier, when solutions are less expensive;
- tests avoidance, mitigation, and adaptation strategies on a limited scale under controlled conditions prior to more general implementation.
- It seeks to incorporate early warning, scope for learning, affordable remedies, and adaptive management (AM) for NI_2 and BAU cases, along with policies to mitigate disproportionate negative impacts.
  - With early warning, AM addresses credible threats earlier, when solutions are less expensive; and tests avoidance, mitigation, and adaptation strategies on a limited scale under controlled conditions prior to more general implementation.
  - When precautionary intervention is not prohibitively urgent, intervention may take multiple forms (avoidance, mitigation and adaptation), and may be implemented in AM processes that may reduce the expense of the precautionary policy.
  - When precautionary intervention is truly urgent and drastic remedies offer the only hope of preventing regime shift, AM may nevertheless play a role in mitigation and adaptation.
  - When intervention comes too late to prevent regime shift, the role of AM in mitigation and adaptation is likely to be crucial.
- It is substantively integrated – it would tilt toward more screening and pre-release testing than ORM usually supports in practice, and would deny ORM's explicit BC, EV, and EU filters on remedies. That is, substantively, it is not just splicing precautionary constraints onto "ORM in the whole."
- It is procedurally integrated – once we have decided how much of the substance of ORM and PP to integrate, then integrating those parts procedurally is the key to implementation in practice.

It can be argued that, regardless of whether we think there is enough integrated risk management – and hence enough precaution – in the USA, there is more than is generally acknowledged. Jasanoff (2000) credits the European Union with a more consistent precautionary stance than the USA in recent years. The implication is that integrated risk management is hardly a radical idea. There is, nevertheless, plenty of room for improvements in its design and implementation.

The cases sketched above are hardly a random set – four of the five cases were selected with an eye to illustrating integrated risk management in practice. Among the novel intervention cases sketched, synthetic chemicals have provided the exception. Nevertheless, this exception is more nearly the norm among NI cases in the US, where the tendency is to charge ahead and deal with damage only after it has become obvious and widespread, and remedies are expensive and incomplete. The case of nanotechnology (Box 12.1) eventually will present an interesting case study – the potential threats are receiving increasing recognition, and there are calls for more active research with a view to systematic STS, once the technical problems of screening for potential damage are resolved. But there is also a burgeoning industry anxious to avoid what it is likely to see as over-regulation.

Integrated risk management is clearly the goal in the two BAU cases selected, and it is achieved to some degree. However, this is hardly the norm in the US for risk management in BAU cases. Perhaps the typical BAU case involves mostly private lands. Land, water, and ecosystems come under pressure from growing populations and increasing per capita use of land, yet existing institutions tend to nibble around the edges of the problem, using institutions designed for other problems (e.g. zoning, air pollution controls, and wetlands protections). It does not add up to integrated risk management for stresses upon land, water, and ecosystems.

Climate change, of course, is the crucial global BAU case, but the world has yet to confront it seriously. The "nibbling around the edges" problem is exacerbated by the difficulties of concerted collective action among nations that are very differently situated in terms of resources and vulnerability to climate change.

So there are models in the USA and elsewhere of effective integrated risk management, despite the efforts of PP opponents to paint the PP as some sort of radical neo-Luddite foolishness. The goal going forward should be to improve the design and practice of integrated risk management, and to institutionalize its application to broad categories of potential threats.

NOTES

1 I recognize that in writing this I am discounting the elaborate decision schemes of, e.g., Gollier and Treich (2003) and Barrieu and Sinclair-Desgagne (2006) that put explicit weight on aversion to risk and/or catastrophe.

2 Stirling and Scoones (2009) argue that citizen participation can be an integral part of an effective surveillance plan. For example, surveillance of the spread of avian flu benefits from public participation – at a minimum, it provides more eyes, and more people knowing what to do and who to tell if they see indications.

3 In this, there is a Catch-22 – if we did not take pre-release testing of this innovation seriously, what reason is there to expect serious post-release monitoring?

4 The Food Quality Protection Act (1996) established a new health-based safety standard for pesticide residues in food, included special provisions for infants and children,

required periodic tolerance re-evaluations, incorporated provisions for endocrine testing, and allowed for enhanced enforcement of pesticide residue standards.

5 Much of the required testing is done on the active ingredient only, not the pesticide as sold and applied, which leads to complaints that there remains a possibility that problems with the pesticide may remain undetected.

6 Salmon issues are complicated by their genetic diversity, and controversy remains about the number of distinct species, and the appropriateness of applying the full force of endangered species legislation to preserve distinct varieties (as opposed to species).

7 ORM does not reject the idea of disproportionate threats; in its standard context of utilitarian rationality, ORM simply cannot deal convincingly with disproportionate threats.

Part V

Conclusion

14   A role for precaution in an integrated risk management framework

Imagine a threat of substantial but uncertain harm. What should we do? If we wait until we are sure about the threat, the best opportunities for effective remedies already may be lost. If we act precipitously to forestall the uncertain harm, we run the risk of wasting resources and foreclosing opportunities for gain, all in pursuit of protection from illusory harm. Recent history provides plenty of examples of the costs of waiting too long to act (e.g. asbestos, Boxes 1.1 and 5.4; PCBs, Box 9.2; and MTBE, Box 9.3) and we risk a similar outcome regarding climate change. The costs and lost opportunities resulting from precipitous action to forestall illusory harm are more speculative but thoroughly plausible. Obviously, both strategies – waiting until we are really sure, and acting before we are sure – have their potential downsides. Proposals for more systematic application of the precautionary principle (PP) come from people who are persuaded more by the arguments against waiting too long. They tend to present the PP as a commonsense defense against unreasonable risks.

Various governments have adopted the precautionary approach or principle,[1] and it has been incorporated into several international agreements (Chapter 2). Even in the USA, which has not made a general commitment to precaution, we see precautionary regulation institutionalized in particular cases (e.g. new pharmaceutical drugs and pesticides), and it can be argued that precaution is expressed via sustainability objectives in, for example, fisheries management (Chapter 13). In various countries, we observe PP applications to environmental threats, threats to public health, and protection of individuals in the contexts of new drugs, clinical trials, etc. Possible applications of the PP to national security and defense against terrorism are discussed in scholarly outlets, as well as polemics.

While the first references to the PP date back to the 1970s, precaution is not a new idea. The US Food and Drug Administration has long taken a precautionary stance toward new pharmaceutical drugs, and the USA was spared the thalidomide disaster of the early 1960s. As realization took hold that there was a fortuitous element to this – but for one skeptical and stubborn FDA scientist holding her ground, the US decision might have gone the other way – the laws directing the FDA were strengthened, institutionalizing a more precautionary stance (Box 9.4). A particular version of the standard argument against excessive precaution – that lives are lost while the FDA works through its testing process prior to approving new drugs – is raised regularly against FDA practice.

I am sure there are PP opponents who are motivated entirely by the sense that the costs and lost opportunities due to precaution are too great relative to the protection it would provide. But it seems that the PP arouses more than ordinary skepticism among its detractors. Critics have moved quickly beyond debate about costs and opportunities foregone to tap into deep veins of conflict about worldview, alleging bureaucratic aggrandizement, stifling of innovation and venturesome spirit, and elevation of irrational fears over the authority of science and professional risk management (Chapter 2).

My objectives for this book are more circumscribed. The working hypothesis is: If precaution can be focused on the cases that present extraordinary risk, and can be implemented iteratively to encourage learning and reassessment and to provide sequential decision points, then precaution would be less intrusive and costly while still providing an additional layer of protection from harm. Accordingly, the objectives are to examine the justification for a PP focused on disproportionate threats, and to sketch a substantive and procedural framework for an integrated risk management that incorporates meaningful precautionary protections while minimizing the opportunities lost to excessive precaution.

Problems with ORM

If there were no problems with the standard approach to risk management (here called ordinary risk management, ORM), there would be little interest in adopting precautionary rules and procedures. However, three problems with ORM are identified.

Utilitarian decision theory (which is foundational for ORM), being modeled on well-specified games of chance, deals effectively with ordinary gambles and risks, but is unconvincing in the case of high-damage but unlikely prospects – consider the St Petersburg paradox (Chapter 5). Chichilnisky (2000) has shown that, given an expected utility approach, the standard assumption of bounded utility (to avoid the St Petersburg paradox) induces an under-appreciation of catastrophic possibilities.

The emerging understanding of complex systems challenges scientific risk analysis as it is usually done, which is reductionist and often linear in logic and assumption. Complex systems theory has alerted us to the surprises that may be in store for us as we manipulate and stress complex systems. It has challenged our tendency to view systems as equilibrating and stochastic processes as stationary, and it has opened our minds to the idea that we can be scientific and rational without committing to a mechanistic and essentially Newtonian worldview. One particular such insight has been emphasized by Weitzman (2009) – complex systems properties tend to generate *ex ante* outcome distributions with greater chances of extreme outcomes than are consistent with normal distributions. This implies that research effort should focus more on the tails of the outcome distribution and less on the central tendency.

ORM practice simply does not call for routine *ex ante* risk assessment. Indeed, it seems that most activities most of the time proceed routinely without any formal *ex ante* assessment of the risks involved. The cases where *ex ante* risk assessment is routine fall in two categories: those for which risk assessment is required by law and/or regulations, and those where organizations (e.g. firms and agencies) have established risk assessment as a routine practice. Beyond those cases, risk assessment occurs on a rather *ad hoc* basis after the alarm has been raised for specific cases and situations.

In summary, ORM does not routinely require *ex ante* risk assessment, it tends to underestimate risk in complex systems, and its decision theory foundations are not convincing when applied to high-damage, low-likelihood prospects. These weaknesses of ORM establish scope for precaution addressed to extraordinary threats.

A coherent PP

Scope for precaution alone is not sufficient to justify a role for the PP in risk management. It is necessary also to address the criticisms of the PP forthrightly, and define a PP that can be taken seriously. The case for taking the PP seriously can be made only for a PP that withstands or circumvents those PP criticisms that are substantive. To develop such a PP, a set of twelve challenges is identified (Box 6.3).

It has been suggested that the problems with many PP formulations are due to, or at least exacerbated by, rather weak connections among the elements of harm, uncertainty, and action. Here, harm is defined as *threat* (i.e. chance of harm), which includes the kinds of uncertainty that are attributes of the real-world system; the uncertainty concept is *evidence*, which addresses the uncertainty attributable to our lack of knowledge; and action is captured by the concept of *remedy*. The general form of a PP that relates these three elements is:

If there is evidence stronger than **E** *that an activity raises a threat more serious than* **T**, *we should invoke a remedy more potent than* **R**.

A PP of this form would focus on the key issues: what sorts of threats might invoke precaution, what sorts of evidence might justify a precautionary intervention, what sorts of remedies might be appropriate, and how might these key elements, **E**, **T**, and **R**, interact? Careful consideration of these questions (Chapters 8–10) suggests a tentative working definition of the precautionary principle, in an ETR framework:

Credible scientific evidence of plausible threat of disproportionate harm calls for avoidance and remediation measures beyond those recommended by ordinary risk management.

Some utilitarian formulations endorse precaution. There are two ways to get such a result: by assuming some form of extreme risk aversion or catastrophe aversion, and by modeling kinks, thresholds, and/or discontinuities in the way the world works; and there are circumstances in which these assumptions are plausible. However, utilitarian precaution is always a circumstantial sort of precaution in that it always depends on the particulars: how much and what kind of risk and/or catastrophe aversion, or kinks, thresholds, and/or discontinuities in the model of how the world works.

PP proponents worry that utilitarian formulations offer only an iffy sort of precaution (Box 10.1). Under any formulation of utilitarian precaution, one can imagine some disproportionate threats that would not trigger precaution. The core question raised by utilitarian precaution is: should we commit to invoking precaution only if it passes a utilitarian filter? Conceding that utilitarian solutions to certain classes of problems (infinite prospects, high damage but unlikely prospects, etc.) are unconvincing, it would make little sense to insist that policies addressed to disproportionate and asymmetric threats must pass a utilitarian test.

By rejecting a utilitarian filter on precaution in cases of disproportionate and perhaps asymmetric threats, this PP does in fact call for remedies stronger than those recommended by ORM.

A framework for integrated risk management

Until Chapter 9, somewhere in the vicinity of Box 9.6, it seemed that the argument was moving steadily toward a justification for an "ORM subject to precautionary constraints" framework for risk management. There is precedent for such a framework in natural resources management, where the notion of managing for economically optimal yield subject to a sustainability constraint (sometimes called a safe minimum standard of conservation, SMS; see Figures 10.1 and 13.3) has a long history (Randall 1999). More recent thinking has exposed some of the limitations of this framework – it is best suited to managing a monoculture (a plantation forest, or a single-species fishery), and it implicitly assumes more regularity and predictability in the underlying systems than ecologists have been able to confirm – and current approaches are more adaptive and less prescriptive than the constrained optimization implied in "optimal yield subject to SMS." Nevertheless, the idea of precautionary constraints continues to have some influence and to deserve it, I would argue. With appropriate amendments to fit particular cases, the above discussion applies to the general class of potential regime shift due to overstressing systems (e.g. by unsustainable harvests or pollution loads) in the course business-as-usual.

What nudged the argument in a different direction was the growing realization that even more fruitful applications of PP may be found in the category of novel interventions. As the outlines of iterative remedies with sequential decision points, to actively encourage learning and reassessment of threat and remedy, came into clearer view (Boxes 7.2, 8.2, 9.1, 9.6, 9.7, 9.8, and 9.14, and Figures 13.1 and 13.2), it became clear that we cannot reliably distinguish *ex ante* the novel intervention cases that pose disproportionate threats. It follows that, while "ORM subject to PP" captures some key elements of a coherent risk management framework for business-as-usual threats, it is literally a non-starter for novel interventions. The systematic learning institutionalized in iterative and sequential remedies argues for a more thoroughly integrated risk management framework with prominent roles for quarantine and sequential release, QSR (Figure 13.1) and screening, pre-release testing, and post-release surveillance, STS (Figure 13.2). The first steps in these processes – screening and perhaps some initial rounds of pre-release testing – enable sorting of cases to isolate those with potential for disproportionate threats for more intensive testing. Compared to ORM, an integrated risk management framework would pre-screen more novel interventions for potential threats but move quickly to release many of them, while providing better protection against the more serious threats. A triage process may be appropriate, assigning cases to one of three groups: approved for unconditional release; cases that present manageable risks, for release subject to a risk management plan; and cases that call for precautionary remedies.

For novel interventions found after release to be potentially harmful and for business-as-usual cases, early warning and adaptive management are the integrated risk management counterparts to pre-screening and pre-release testing. However, to the extent that the causative factors already are embedded in the economy and ecosystem, remedies in those cases are often more difficult, more costly, and less effective.

A substantively and procedurally integrated risk management process seeks to combine the virtues of ORM and PP. The PP takes disproportionate risks seriously, and is open to drastic remedies where justified. Its evidence criterion is not addressed to the search for empirical laws of science, but to criteria for action under risk, uncertainty, and worse – it is about trying to make the right calls case-by-case on behalf of the public. The PP approach brings complex systems thinking, more systematic procedures for reconnaissance and learning, and more respect for screening and pre-release testing of novel interventions. The goal is to cast a wider precautionary net, but release the harmless fish with minimal fuss and delay.

ORM brings respect for risk–risk trade-offs, cost effectiveness, and welfare concerns such as might be expressed in the benefit–cost, expected value, and expected utility criteria. It is not true that PP thinking has no respect for these concerns, but rather that it places them in a broader and hence less formulaically decisive context. A big issue in integration is how much weight the final integrated product puts on risk–risk trade-offs, cost effectiveness, and welfare concerns.

The integrated risk management process envisioned here has several virtues. It adopts the PP evidence criterion: credible scientific evidence of plausible threat. This restores a degree of balance to the weight given to null and alternative hypotheses when diagnosing threats in particular cases. It adopts complex systems thinking, including alertness to path-dependence and the possibility of surprises, and encourages systematic modeling to identify indicator variables for impending regime shift. It calls for more systematic screening of proposed novel interventions – one approach might be to require systematic screening of all novel interventions that fall into categories (e.g., chemicals of concern) that have a history of generating serious threats – and pre-release testing of those that pose non-trivial threats.

For novel interventions, integrated risk management provides for sequential and iterative decision processes that systematically enhance learning while providing protection (QSR and STS); addresses credible threats earlier, when solutions are less expensive; and tests avoidance, mitigation, and adaptation strategies on a limited scale under controlled conditions prior to more general implementation.

For system overstress from business-as-usual, integrated risk management seeks to incorporate early warning, scope for learning, affordable remedies, and adaptive management (AM), along with policies to mitigate disproportionate negative impacts. With early warning, AM addresses credible threats earlier, when solutions are less expensive; and tests avoidance, mitigation, and adaptation strategies on a limited scale under controlled conditions prior to more general implementation. When precautionary intervention is not prohibitively urgent, intervention may take multiple forms (avoidance, mitigation, and adaptation), and may be implemented in AM processes that may reduce the expense of the precautionary policy. When precautionary intervention is truly urgent and drastic remedies offer the only hope of preventing regime shift, AM may nevertheless play a role in mitigation and adaptation. When intervention comes too late to prevent regime shift, the role of AM in mitigation and adaptation is likely to be crucial.

Perhaps there is more integrated risk management, and hence more precaution, in the real world than we think. Jasanoff (2000) credits the European Union with a more consistent precautionary stance than the USA in recent years. Yet, in the USA there are prominent examples of integrated risk management fully articulated with screening, pre-release testing and post-release surveillance: e.g. Food and Drug Administration regulation of new drugs, and Environmental Protection Agency regulation of pesticides (including genetically modified organisms with pesticide properties). In the case of synthetic chemicals, which seems tailor-made for integrated risk management, there is perhaps some movement in that direction. Nanotechnology (Box 12.1) eventually will present an interesting case study – the potential threats are receiving increasing recognition, and there are calls for more active research with a view to systematic STS, once the technical problems of screening for potential damage are resolved. But there is also a burgeoning industry anxious to avoid what it is likely to see as over-regulation.

One implication is that integrated risk management is hardly a radical idea. Another is that, if the FDA procedure for approving new drugs is the paradigm case of integrated risk management in the USA, it remains controversial. The "drug lag" – the charge that FDA procedures cost lives that could have been saved, by delaying the approval of promising new drugs – while it lacks empirical documentation, is a maintained stylized fact in market-oriented academic and think-tank circles. As its treatment of new uses for thalidomide in treating serious afflictions such as leprosy illustrates, the FDA has been willing to adjust its procedures, allowing afflicted persons access to the drug under tightly controlled conditions (Box 9.9). Manski (2009) argues that there are more opportunities to streamline FDA procedures: for example, new drugs for relatively rare but serious diseases could be tested on a substantial fraction of the sufferers, allowing them earlier access to the new treatment. He balances that suggestion with a call for more stringent post-release surveillance.

As the thalidomide example reminds us, utilitarian concerns remain relevant in integrated risk management. Reducing the opportunity costs of precaution (e.g. innovation lag) remains a serious objective, and proportionality[2] and cost effectiveness will always be relevant considerations. For novel innovations in categories that have a history of harmful effects, real progress would be represented by systematic integrated risk management *and* continuing debate as to whether we have the mix of pre-release testing and post-release surveillance right.

For business-as-usual cases, integrated risk management is clearly the goal for regulating fisheries and managing national forests in the US, and it is achieved to some degree. However, this is hardly the norm. Perhaps a more typical case involves the use of lands that are mostly private. Land, water, and ecosystems come under pressure from growing populations and increasing per capita use of land, yet existing institutions tend to nibble around the edges of the problem, using institutions designed for other problems (e.g. zoning, air pollution controls, and wetlands protections). It does not add up to integrated risk management for stresses upon land, water, and ecosystems.

After long study of the precautionary principle, I have arrived at the belief that the goal going forward should be to improve the design and practice of integrated risk management, and to institutionalize its application to broad categories of potential threats.

NOTES

1 Approach and principle have somewhat different interpretations, and it can be argued that the differences have consequences (Peel 2004).
2 The regulatory treatment of new uses for thalidomide demonstrates proportionality in action. Sufferers of serious afflictions were granted accelerated access to a promising new treatment under tightly controlled conditions, whereas such accommodations might not have been made in the case of, say, the common cold.

References

Arcuri, A. 2007. Reconstructing precaution, deconstructing misconceptions. *Ethics and International Affairs* **21**(3):359–379.

Arrow, K. and A. Fisher. 1974. Environmental preservation, uncertainty, and irreversibility, *Quarterly Journal of Economics*, **55**:313–319.

Bailey, R. 1999. Precautionary Tale, *Reason Online*. http://reason.com/9904/fe.rb.precautionary.shtml

Barrieu, P. and B. Sinclair-Desgagné. 2003. The Paradox of Precaution. Cahier 2003–012. Laboratoire d'Econométrie, Ecole Polytechnique, Paris.

  2006. On precautionary policies. *Management Science* **52**(8):1145–1154.

Barro, R. 2009. Rare disasters, asset prices, and welfare costs. *American Economic Review* **99**:253–264.

Berg, P., D. Baltimore, S. Brennen, R. Roblin III, and M. Singer. 1975. Summary statement of the Asilomar Conference on Recombinant DNA molecules. *Proceedings of the National Academy of Sciences* **72**(6):1981–1984.

Bergen Ministerial Declaration on Sustainable Development in the ECE Region. 1990. UN Doc. A/CONF.151/PC/10; 1 *Yearbook on International Environmental Law* **429**, 4312.

Bernoulli, D. 1738 (1954). Exposition of a new theory on the measurement of risk. (tr. L. Sommer) *Econometrica* **22**(1):22–36.

Biggs, R., S. Carpenter and W Brock. 2009. Turning back from the brink: Detecting an impending regime shift in time to avert it. *Proceedings of the National Academy of Sciences* **106**(3, January 20): 826–831.

Bishop, R. 1978. Endangered species and uncertainty: the economics of a safe minimum standard. *American Journal of Agricultural Economics*, **60**(1):10–18.

Brock, W. and S. Carpenter. 2006. Variance as a leading indicator of regime shift in ecosystem services. *Ecology and Society* **11**(2):9.

Brock, W., S. Carpenter, and M. Scheffer. 2008. Regime shifts, environmental signals, uncertainty, and policy choice. In *Complexity Theory for a Sustainable Future* (J. Norberg and G. Cumming, eds.). Columbia University Press.

Bronitt, S. 2008. Balancing security and liberty: critical perspectives on terrorism law reform. *Fresh Perspectives on the 'War on Terror'.* (ed. M. Gani and P. Mathew). Canberra, Australian National University Press. Ch. 5.

Bussiere, M. and M. Fratzscher. 2008. Low probability, high impact: policy making and extreme events. *Journal of Policy Modeling* **30**:111–121.

Byerlee, D. 1971. Option demand and consumer surplus: Comment. *Quarterly Journal of Economics* **85**(3): 523–527.

Canadian Perspective on the Precautionary Approach/Principle – Proposed Guiding Principles. 2001. Ottawa: Government of Canada.

Chichilnisky, G. 2000. An axiomatic approach to choice under uncertainty with catastrophic risks. *Energy and Resource Economics* **22**:221–231.

Ciriacy-Wantrup, S. von (1968), *Resource Conservation: Economics and Policies*, 3rd. edn., Berkeley, CA: University of California, Division of Agricultural Science.

Cooney, R. 2004. *The precautionary principle in biodiversity conservation and natural resource management – an issues paper for policy-makers, researchers, and practitioners.* IUCN Policy and Global Change Series No. 2 www.pprinciple.net/publications/PrecautionaryPrincipleissuespaper.pdf

Cranor, C. 1999. Empirically and institutionally rich legal and moral philosophy. *Midwest Studies in Philosophy* **23**:286–311.

Deblonde, M. and P. Du Jardin. 2005. Deepening a precautionary European policy. *Journal of Agricultural & Environmental Ethics* **18**(4):319–343.

Dickson, B. 1999. The precautionary principle in CITES: a critical assessment. *Natural Resources Journal* **39**(2):211–28.

Dixit, A. and R. Pindyck. 1994. *Investment Under Uncertainty.* Princeton University Press.

Ehrlich, I. and G. Becker. 1972. Market insurance, self-insurance, and self-protection. *Journal of Political Economy* **80**(4):623–648.

Ehrlich P. and A. Ehrlich. 1981. *Extinction: The Causes and Consequences of the Disappearance of Species.* NY: Random House.

European Commission. 2000. *Communication on the Precautionary Principle.* Brussels, February 2. 28pp.

Farmer, M., and A. Randall. 1998. The rationality of a safe minimum standard of conservation, *Land Economics* **74**:287–302.

Farrow, S. 2004. Using risk assessment, benefit-cost analysis, and real options to implement a precautionary principle. *Risk Analysis* **24**(3):727–735.

Fedoroff, N., D. S. Battisti, R. Beachy, P. Cooper, D. Fischhoff, C. Hodges, V. Knauf, D. Lobell, B. Mazur, D. Molden, M. Reynolds, P. Ronald, M. Rosegrant, P. Sanchez, A. Vonshak, and J. Zhu. 2010. Radically rethinking agriculture for the 21st century. *Science* **327**(5967, 12 February):833–834.

Folke, C., S. Carpenter, B. Walker, M. Scheffer, T. Elmqvist, L. Gunderson, and C.S. Holling. 2004. Regime shifts, resilience, and biodiversity in ecosystem management. *Annual Review of Ecology, Evolution, and Systematics* **35**:557–81.

FAO (Food and Agriculture Organization of the United Nations). 2000. *FAO Statement on Biotechnology* www.fao.org/biotech

Foster, K., P. Vecchia and M. Repacholi. 2000. Risk management: science and the precautionary principle. *Science* **288**(5468):979–981.

Freeman, P. and H. Kunreuther. 2003. Managing environmental risk through insurance. *International Yearbook of Environmental and Resource Economics* 2003/2004, 159–189.

Frost, R. 1920. The road not taken. *Mountain Interval.* New York: Holt.

Gardiner. S. 2006. A core precautionary principle. *Journal of Political Philosophy* **14**(1):33–60.

Garrity, T. 2004. MTBE: a precautionary tale. *Harvard Environmental Law Review* **28**: 281–342.

Gollier, C. 2001. Should we beware of the precautionary principle? *Economic Policy* **16**:301–328.

Gollier, C., and N. Treich. 2003. Decision-making under scientific uncertainty: The economics of the precautionary principle. *Journal of Risk and Uncertainty* **27**:77–103.

Gollier, C., B. Jullien and N. Treich. 2000. Scientific progress and irreversibility: An economic interpretation of the precautionary principle, *Journal of Public Economics* **75**:229–253.

Graham, J. 2004. The perils of the precautionary principle: lessons from the American and European experience. The Heritage Foundation. www.heritage.org/Research/Regulation/hl818.cfm

Gray, G. and J. Hammit. 2000. Risk/Risk Trade-offs in Pesticide Regulation: An Exploratory Analysis of the Public Health Effects of a Ban on Organophosphate and Carbamate Pesticides. *Risk Analysis* **20**(5):665–680.

Grossman, E. 2010. What the EPA's 'Chemicals of Concern' plans really mean. *Scientific American* (January 11). www.scientificamerican.com/article.cfm?id=epa-chemicals-of-concern-plans

Guldberg H. 2003. Challenging the precautionary principle. *Spiked Online.* July 1 www.spiked-online.com/articles/00000006DE2F.htm.

Hansen, S., M. von Krauss and J. Tickner. 2008. The precautionary principle and risk-risk tradeoffs *Journal of Risk Research* **11**:423–464.

Harris, J. and S. Holm. 1999. Precautionary principle stifles discovery. *Nature* **400**:398.

    2002. Extending human life span and the precautionary principle. *Journal of Medicine and Philosophy* **27**:355–368.

Henry, C. 1974. Option values in the economics of Irreplaceable assets. *Review of Economic Studies* **41**(Symposium):89–104.

Henry, C. and M. Henry. 2002. *Formalization and Applications of the Precautionary Principle.* Université Catholique de Louvain, Institut de Recherches Economiques et Sociales (IRES) Discussion Paper 2002009.

Holling, C. S. 2001. Understanding the complexity of economic, ecological, and social systems. *Ecosystems* **4**:390–405.

Hubin, D. 1994. The moral justification of benefit/cost analysis. *Economics and Philosophy,* **10**: 169–194.

Hughes, J. 2006. How not to criticize the precautionary principle. *Journal of Medicine and Philosophy* **31**:447–464.

Jablonowski, M. 2005. High-risk decisions when probabilities are unknown (or irrelevant). *Risk Management* **7**:57–61.

    2007. Avoiding risk dilemmas using backcasting. *Risk Management* **9**:118–127.

Jasanoff, S. 2000. Commentary: Between risk assessment and precaution – reassessing the future of GM crops. *Journal of Risk Research* **3**(3):277–282.

Kahan, D., P. Slovic, D. Braman, and J. Gastil. 2006. Fear of democracy: a cultural evaluation of Sunstein on risk. *Harvard Law Review* **119**:1071–1109.

Kahneman, D. and A. Tversky. 1979. Prospect theory: an analysis of decision under risk, *Econometrica* **47**:263–291.

Kahneman, D., J. Knetsch and R. Thaler. 1991. Anomalies: the endowment effect, loss aversion, and status quo bias. *Journal of Economic Perspectives* **5**:193–206.

Kahneman, D., P. Slovic, and A. Tversky 1982. *Judgment under Uncertainty: Heuristics and Biases.* Cambridge: Cambridge University Press.

Kolitch, S. 2006. The environmental and public health impacts of US patent law: making the case for incorporating a precautionary principle. *Environmental Law* **36**:221–256.

Kolstad, C. 1996. Learning and stock effects in environmental regulation: the case of greenhouse gas emissions. *Journal of Environmental Economics and Management* **31**:1–18.

Krutilla, J. 1967. Conservation reconsidered. *American Economic Review* **57**:777–786.

Laughlin, R. 2005. *A Different Universe: Reinventing Physics from the Bottom Down,* Basic Books.

Lindley, D. 2006. *Understanding Uncertainty,* Wiley.

Lofstedt, R., B. Fischhof, and I. Fischhof. 2002. Precautionary principles: general definitions and specific applications to genetically modified organisms. *Journal of Policy Analysis and Management* **21**(3):381–407.

Mandel, G. and J. Gathii. 2006. Cost-benefit analysis versus the precautionary principle: beyond Cass Sunstein's *Laws of Fear. University of Illinois Law Review* **2006**(5):1037–1079.

Manski, C. 2009. Adaptive partial drug approval: a health policy proposal, *The Economists' Voice* **6**(4), Article 9 www.bepress.com/ev/vol6/iss4/art9

Manson, N. 2002. Formulating the precautionary principle. *Environmental Ethics* **24**: 263–274.

  2007. The concept of irreversibility: its use in the sustainable development and precautionary principle literatures. *Electronic Journal of Sustainable Development* **1**(1):1–15.

Margolis, M. and E. Naevdal. 2008. Safe minimum standards in dynamic resource problems: conditions for living on the edge of risk. *Environmental and Resource Economics* **40**:401–423.

Martin, P. 1997. If you don't know how to fix it, please stop breaking it! The precautionary principle and climate change. *Foundations of Science* **2**:263–292.

Matthee, M. and D. Vermersch. 2000. Are the precautionary principle and the international trade of genetically modified organisms reconcilable? *Journal of Agricultural and Environmental Ethics* **12**(1):59–70.

May, R., S. Levin and G. Sugihara. 2008. Complex systems: ecology for bankers, *Nature* **451**:893–895.

Meier, C.E. and A. Randall. 1991. Use value under uncertainty: is there a "correct" measure? *Land Economics* **67**:379–389.

Meinshausen, M. 2006. What does a 2°C target mean for greenhouse gas concentrations? A brief analysis based on multi-gas emission pathways and several climate sensitivity uncertainty estimates. In H. Schellnhuber, W. Cramer, N. Nakicenovic, T. Wigley, and G. Yohe (eds.), *Avoiding Dangerous Climate Change*. Cambridge, UK: Cambridge University Press. 265–79.

Michaels, D. and C. Monforton. 2005. Scientific evidence in the regulatory system: manufacturing uncertainty and the demise of the formal regulatory system. *Journal of Law and Policy* **13**(1):17–41.

Mielke, A. and T. Roubicek. 2003, A rate-independent model for inelastic behavior of shape-memory alloys. *Multiscale Modeling and Simulation* **1**(4):571–597.

More, M. 2005. *The Proactionary Principle* Version 1.2, July 29, www.maxmore.com/proactionary.htm

Murphy, D. 2009. The Precautionary Principle: A Principle to Protect Human Health and the Environment. http://environmentalism.suite101.com/article.cfm/the_precautionary_principle

Naevdal, E. and M. Oppenheimer. 2007. The economics of thermohaline circulation – a problem with multiple thresholds of unknown locations. *Resource and Energy Economics* **29**:262–283.

Narain, U., M. Hanemann and A. Fisher. 2007. The irreversibility effect in environmental decision making. *Environmental and Resource Economics* **38**:391–405.

Noiville, C., F. Bois, P. Hubert, R. Lahidji and A. Grimfeld. 2006. Opinion of the committee for prevention and precaution about the precautionary principle. *Journal of Risk Research* **9**(4):287–296.

O'Neill, B. 2007. Mobile phones are safe but let's panic anyway. *Spiked Online.* www.spiked-online.com/index.php?/site/article/3819/

Parfit, D. 1984. *Reasons and Persons*. Oxford University Press.

  1988. Risk assessment, and imperceptible effects, *Public Affairs Quarterly* **2**(4):75–96.

Parson, E. 2000. Environmental trends and environmental governance in Canada, *Canadian Public Policy* **26**:Supp 2 (August), S123–S143.

Peel, J. 2004. Precaution – a matter of principle, approach, or process? *Melbourne Journal of International Law* **5**(2).

Peterson, D. C. 2006.Precaution: principles and practice in Australian environmental and natural resource management, *Australian Journal of Agricultural and Resource Economics* **50**:469–489.

Peterson, M. 2006. The precautionary principle is incoherent, *Risk Analysis* **26**: 595–601.

2007. Should the precautionary principle guide our actions or our beliefs? *Journal of Medical Ethics* **33**:5–10.

Pindyck, R. 2007. Uncertainty in environmental economics, *Review of Environmental Economics and Policy* **1**:45–65.

Quiggin, J. 2007. Complexity, climate change and the precautionary principle. *Environmental Health, 7* **3**:15–21.

Raffensperger, C. and J. Tichner. 1999. *Protecting Public Health and the Environment: Implementing the Precautionary Principle.* Island Press, Washington, DC.

Randall, A. 1999. Taking benefits and costs seriously. In Folmer H. and Tietenberg, T. (eds.) *The International Yearbook of Environmental and Resource Economics 1999/2000.* Edward Elgar, Cheltenham, UK, and Brookfield, VT, 250–272.

2008. Is Australia on a sustainability path? Interpreting the clues, *Australian Journal of Agricultural and Resource Economics* **52**:77–95.

2009. We already have risk management – Do we really need the precautionary principle? *International Review of Environmental and Resource Economics* **3**(1):39–74.

Ready, R. and R. Bishop. 1991. Endangered species and the safe minimum standard. *American Journal of Agricultural Economics,* **73**(2):309–312.

Resnik, D. 1998 *The Ethics of Science: An Introduction.* Routledge, New York .

Ricci, P., D. Rice, J. Ziagos and L. A. Cox. 2003. Precaution, uncertainty and causation in environmental decisions, *Environment International* **29**:1–19.

Roe, G. and M. Baker. 2007. Why is climate sensitivity so unpredictable? *Science* **318**(5850):629 – 632.

Rosenzweig, P. and A. Kochems. 2005. *Risk Assessment and Risk Management: Necessary Tools for Homeland Security.* Backgrounder 1889, Heritage Foundation, Washington DC. www.heritage.org/research/homelandsecurity/bg1889.cfm

Sandin, P. 1999. Dimensions of the precautionary principle. *Human and Ecology Risk Assessment* **5**:889–907.

SEHN (Science and Environmental Health Network). 2000. *The Precautionary Principle – A Common Sense Way to Protect Public Health and the Environment.* www.mindfully.org/Precaution/Precautionary-Principle-Common-Sense.htm

Shaw, S. and R. Schwartz. 2005. *Trading Precaution: The Precautionary Principle and the WTO.* United Nations University, Institute for Advanced Studies.

Shorto, R. 2010. How Christian were the founders? *New York Times Sunday Magazine,* February 13. p.32.

Sinha, P., C. Kriegner, W. Schew, S. Kaczmar, M. Traister and D. Wilson. 2008. Regulatory policy governing cadmium-telluride photovoltaics: A case study contrasting life cycle management with the precautionary principle. *Energy Policy* **36**(1):381–387.

SIRC (Social Issues Research Center). Undated. *Beware the Precautionary Principle.* www.sirc.org/articles/beware.html

Slovic, P. 2000. *The Perception of Risk.* London: Earthscan.

Stirling, A. and I. Scoones. 2009. From risk assessment to knowledge mapping: science, precaution and participation in disease ecology. *Ecology and Society* **14**(2): 14. www.ecologyandsociety.org/vol14/iss2/art14/

Sunstein, C. 2005. *Laws of Fear: Beyond the Precautionary Principle*, Cambridge: Cambridge University Press.

2006. Irreversible and catastrophic. *Cornell Law Review* **91**:841.

2008. Precautions and nature. *Daedalus* **137**(2):49–58.

Taylor, C. R. 1989. *Sources of the Self: the Making of Modern Identity*. Cambridge, MA: Harvard University Press.

Thomas, M. and A. Randall. 2000. Intentional introductions of nonindigenous species: a principal-agent model and protocol for revocable decisions, *Ecological Economics* **34**:333–345.

Turvey, C. G. and E. M. Mojduszka. 2005. The precautionary principle and the law of unintended consequences. *Food Policy* **30**:22, 145–161.

UNESCO. 2005. *The Precautionary Principle*. World Commission on the Ethics of Scientific Knowledge and Technology. Paris.

Viscusi W. K. 1985. Environmental policy choice with an uncertain chance of irreversibility. *Journal of Environmental Economics and Management* **12**(1):28–44.

Weisbrod, B. 1964. Collective-consumption services of individual-consumption goods, *Quarterly Journal of Economics* **78**(3):471–477.

Weitzman, M. L. 2009. On modeling and interpreting the economics of catastrophic climate change. *Review of Economics and Statistics* **91**(1):1–19.

Wexler, L. 2006. Limiting the precautionary principle: weapons regulation in the face of scientific uncertainty. *UCDavis Law Review* **39**:459–475.

Wiener, J. and M. Rogers. 2002. Comparing precaution in the United States and Europe, *Journal of Risk Research* **5**(4):317–349.

Wiener, J. and J. Stern. 2006. Precaution against terrorism. *Journal of Risk Research* **9**:393–447.

Williams, B. 1985. *Ethics and the Limits of Philosophy*, Harvard University Press, Cambridge, MA.

Willis, R. 2001. Lighting the leap in the dark. www.forumforthefuture.org/greenfutures/articles/60288

Wingspread Statement on the Precautionary Principle. 1998. www.gdrc.org/u-gov/precaution-3.html.

Index

adaptation, 3, 49, 96, 100, 107, 140, 144–145, 149, 154–155, 157, 159–160, 162–164, 169, 184, 190–191, 206–207, 209, 211, 218–219, 221–225, 228, 237, 249

adaptive management, 75, 158–160, 162–164, 167, 169–170, 172, 183, 187, 189–190, 215, 222–224, 232–233, 237, 248–249

American Trucking Associations, 126, 133

asbestos, 3–4, 7–8, 17, 79, 106, 117, 126, 138, 142, 161, 185, 211–212, 243

AT&T Wireless, 126–127, 132–133

availability heuristic, 90, 128

benefit–cost analysis, 13, 25, 46–50, 56–57, 60, 110, 173, 186

benefit–cost test, 47–48

Berra, Y., 55

biodiversity, 148–149

biotechnology, 4, 7, 170

Bohr, N., 55

burden of proof, 9, 11, 13, 16, 24, 88, 93, 95

Bureau of Land Management, 235

business-as-usual, 8, 15, 41, 45, 91, 106–107, 115, 133, 135–136, 139, 141–142, 156–157, 162, 164, 179, 206, 208, 215, 224–226, 228, 233–234

Byerlee D., 57

C8, 129, 168, 228

cancer, 4, 11–13, 21–22, 79, 139

Cartagena Protocol on Biosafety, 9

Cellular Telephone, 126–127, 133

Clean Air Act, 12

Clean Water Act, 12

climate change, 3–4, 6, 37, 112, 130, 137, 139–140, 156, 158, 160, 171, 180, 223, 236, 238, 243

complex adaptive systems, 65–67

complex systems, 5, 26, 35, 37, 56, 60, 64–67, 69–70, 73–79, 83, 104–105, 110, 120, 150, 157, 163, 168, 170, 182, 186, 188, 202, 236, 245, 248

complexity theory, 35, 73, 80

Convention on Biodiversity, 13

cost effectiveness, 101, 168, 205–207, 217, 221, 224, 236, 248, 250

coupled human and natural systems, 68

damage dilemma, 161

Daubert, 125–126, 131, 133

DDT, 20

Department of the Interior, 226, 229–230, 234

discounting, 47, 238

Dupuit, J., 46

early warning, 7–8, 70, 106, 132, 143, 157–158, 162–164, 169, 172, 183–184, 187, 189–190, 206–207, 215, 222–225, 230, 232–233, 237, 248–249

Ehrlich, P. and A., 40, 52

emergence, 64–67, 69, 73

endangered species, 9, 156, 175, 229–230, 234–235, 239

Endangered Species Act, 229–230

endocrine disruptors, 21, 229, 239

entropy, 57–59, 71–72

Environmental Protection Agency, 43, 53, 79, 95, 126, 133, 138, 142, 170, 209–210, 213–214, 223, 226–229, 234, 249

ETR framework, 108–109, 173, 185–186, 246

evidentiary standards, 88, 91, 95–96, 100, 126, 189

expected utility, 39–40, 49, 51–52, 56, 61, 76, 86, 92, 168, 171, 173, 175, 177–178, 181, 203, 218, 236, 244, 248

expected value, 5–6, 32, 36, 39–40, 49–50, 60–61, 92, 104, 110–111, 130, 146, 151, 161, 168, 171, 173, 181–182, 203–204, 217–218, 236–237, 248

false balance, 131

familiarity bias, 127

fat tail, 77